DITTRICH

L.I.F.E. METHOD I.

A Book for Understanding Your Life
— A Guide to Increasing
Your Mental Vibrations

L.I.F.E. METHOD I.
A Book for Understanding Your Life
— A Guide to Increasing Your Mental Vibrations

1. edition

Responsible publisher:	Magya Klímavédelmi Kft.
	7630 Pécs, Hegedűs János u. 8.
Author:	Dr. Ernő Dittrich
E-mail:	justdobetterworld@gmail.com
Professional proofreaders:	Judit Pap *psychologist-kinesiologist*
Proofreader:	Robert James Robson
Translator:	Edina Hajnal
Cover design:	Attila Márok // www.weiser.hu
Design & layout:	Zoltán Novreczky // www.hangtars.hu

https://justdobetterworldeng.blogspot.com/

https://www.justdobetterworld.com

https://www.youtube.com/@justdobetterworld

© 2024 Dr. Ernő Dittrich – All rights reserved!

ISBN: 978-615-82554-1-7

„Be the change you want to see in the world."

MAHATMA GANDHI

This book is independent from any political or religious organizations or from any ideological or other groups. The spirit of this book considers every living entity as equal; this way, it is obviously unnecessary to belong to any group. The only and selfless aim of this book is to get Humankind out of its climate change crisis. This principle itself makes it obligatory for the book not to belong to any economic or other interest groups, which would otherwise prevent the book from being objective and useful.

About The Author

Content

WHAT ARE YOUR CHANCES OF HAPPINESS WITHOUT AWARENESS? 9

CHAPTER 1: SPIRITUAL VIBRATION LEVELS 17
1.1. The wisdom of your body is obscured
by your thinking 15
1.2. Quantifiable Happiness – or Soul Vibration Levels 22
    Shame and Guilt (values 20 and 30)........................... 27
    Apathy and Sorrow(values 50 and 75) 29
    Fear (value 100) 31
    Desire (value 125) 33
    Anger (value 150) 36
    Pride (value 175) 39
    Courage (valued at 200)... 45
    Impartiality (value 250) 47
    Willingness (value 310) 50
    Acceptance (value 350) 54
    Reasonableness (value 400)..................................... 58
    Love (value 500) 61
    Joy and Peace (values 550 and 600) 63
    Enlightenment (value 700–1000) 67
1.3. The group dynamics of psychic vibration levels,
or how do energy vampires work? 70
1.4. Which level of mental vibration is right? –
Reality & Psychic Vibration Levels 74
1.5. Signs of low and high mental vibration levels 88
1.6. Our daily activities and mental vibration levels............... 92

CHAPTER 2: VIBRATION LEVELS OF THE MIND...101
2.1. States of consciousness and brain waves 101
2.2. Melatonin or cortisol? 104

CHAPTER 3: VIBRATION LEVELS OF THE BODY AND THE RELATIONSHIP OF BODY-SOUL-MIND VIBRATIONS...113

CHAPTER 4: EGO AND VIBRATION LEVELS..........117
4.1. Levels of awakening..117
4.2. What the ego really is and the 3 main types of ego 119
4.3. Some features of your ego 135

CHAPTER 5: THE MAIN TOOLS OF THE DESTROYER-EGO..151
5.1. False self-image 151
5.2. Comfort zone 154
5.3. Compensation..156
5.4. Addictions 160
    5.4.1. Addiction basics 160
    5.4.2. Intergenerational addictions 167
    5.4.3. A sure-fire recipe for quitting addictions 172
5.5. Games 177
5.6. Rationalizing mind 182

CHAPTER 6: THE L.I.F.E. METHOD 187
6.1. The Ego Streams, or the Three Basic Rules of the L.I.F.E. Method 187
6.2. Optimize your vibrations! 192
6.3. Methods of the L.I.F.E. method and their grouping......194
6.4. Method of application of the tools of the L.I.F.E. method.. 197
6.5. Always have a helper!... 197
6.6. The Law of Delay: The Virtues of Perseverance, Tenacity, and Patience ... 207
6.7. A few more tips to get you started 212

CHAPTER 7: TOOLS FOR YOUR HAPPINESS (BASELINE) 217

The First Step to your happiness (soul):
Gratitude 217

The Second Step to your happiness (mind):
Affirmations – how to learn to think positively 222

The Third Step to your happiness (body):
Meals and vibration levels 229

The Fourth Step to your happiness (soul):
Live your time differently – 'Me' time 232

The Fifth Step to your Happiness:
What is good and what is bad? How to get better?
– The daily scale method 237

The Sixth Step to your happiness (body):
Symmetry and "posture-cure" 245

The Seventh Step to your happiness (soul):
Step into the light! (Ventilation) 249

The Eighth Step to your happiness (mind):
Order and System – Avoiding Extremes 254

The Ninth Step to your happiness (body):
Boost your melatonin production! 257

The Tenth Step to your happiness (soul):
Love languages 259

The 11th Step to your happiness (mind):
Reduce stress I. – boundaries 264

The 12th Step to your happiness (body):
Reduce stress II. – two basic breathing exercises 269

The 13th Step to your happiness (soul):
Letting go of negative emotions—the balloon
and cloud method 271

The 14th Step to your happiness (mind):
Neutralizing your fears 275

The 15th Step to your happiness (test):
Sports 283

The 16th Step to your happiness (soul):
Don't color or gray out reality! 285

The 17th Step to your happiness (mind):
Reduce stress III. – The method of the door left behind combined with the method of balance 290

The 18th Step to your happiness (body):
More smiles 295

The 19th Step to your happiness (soul):
Best-case method 297

The 20th Step to your happiness (mind):
Affirmations upgrade - Kaleidoscope videos 300

The 21st Step to your happiness (body):
Water 303

AFTERWORD 311

ACKNOWLEDGEMENTS 314

REFERENCES (AND SUGGESTED READINGS) 315

ANNEXES 317

Annex 1: Estimation of Spiritual level and self-awareness (with table) 317

Annex 2: Emotions related to mental vibration levels... 319

Annex 3: Energy centers (chakras), or the body as an energy system 323

Annex 4: Curiosities about vibrations 337

What are your chances of happiness without awareness?

Are you happy now? If you're not really, it's for a reason. Let's please take a look at what should have happened differently in your Life so far—in other words, what main reasons have led you here. That's why I'm going to list the most important happiness factors for you:

I. When you were a fetus, your mother and father would have been able to 'tune in' to you with great love. They would have planned and waited for your arrival and considered your conception the greatest fortune in their lives.
II. You would have been born in a place on Earth where the living conditions were suitable for a 'Life Worthy of Human'.
III. When you were a child, you would have received a lot of selfless love from everyone in your family, especially your parents.
IV. During your childhood and adolescence, you would have received a lot of selfless attention from your environment.
V. Your parents would have been addiction-free, self-loving, and accepting People, and they would have instilled these good patterns in you.
VI. Your parents would not have divorced and would have passed along happy, peaceful, harmonious family and relationship patterns to you.

VII. By the end of your adolescence, your parents would have done everything they could to develop your mind, soul, and body at the right level.

Those who have received the above seven points up until the time they became young adults will surely live happily, regardless of how much money they have, where they work, or what tasks they do in the world. But let's see what the chances are.

According to a survey conducted in the United States, 52% of children born there are unexpected. Today, many psychological studies confirm that the child feels its mother's state of mind perfectly at the fetal age. The same was true of me. I know this because I was able to relive it using a special technique. Our emotional memory contains our entire Life so far, and it becomes perceptible above a certain level of spiritual vibration. But let's not jump too far ahead. The point is that if the child is not expected by their parents, or even if the mother feels that the fetus carried under her heart is a burden, that child already feels shame and guilt in their mother's belly. They do not yet know that they are a separate being. They still feel that they are one with their mother, and so if they are a problem for their mother, then they are a flawed part of her. The main problem is that those who come into the world in this way feel some inner emptiness throughout their lives, even if they have received everything from their parents on other important issues. This is confirmed by the Life paths of many children who are immediately adopted at birth. But what are the chances that you came to Earth as an expected child? Since I'm not aware of a global survey, let's take the American results as a basis. However, conditions are much worse in many parts of the world, where women are vulnerable to men's sexual desires and the economic situation does not allow for contraception. So, in my opinion the world average must be much worse. My estimate is that there's a 30% chance that one's parents were wholeheartedly waiting for them to arrive.

The 'Life Worthy of a Human' formulated in Section II is currently unavailable to approx. 3 billion People on Earth. (Author's note: *I will deliberately capitalize the words Man, Life, and Nature in this book, paying homage to these three wonderful entities.*) After all, so many People live in such a way that they don't even know whether they will have something to eat or get healthy drinking water tomorrow, or whether they will remain homeless in the evening or live in some terrible shack in miserable conditions. These people live at a level of extreme poverty where the chance of escape is minimal. What is the probability that you will not be born in such a place? At the time of writing these lines, there are 8 billion People on Earth, so the chance is 5 billion/8 billion, or 62.5%.

For the sake of simplification, I will also discuss the issue of selfless attention and love in childhood formulated in points III and IV. A child needs an incredible amount of unselfish attention and unselfish love. The ideal is for a child to receive these—while they are awake—from at least one adult (*Dittrich, 2021; Redfield, 2005*). Let's look a little deeper and think about the chances of this happening. Today's adults are already about 80% incapable of selfless attention and selfless love. If we add to this how many parents have enough time to pay attention to their children regularly and unselfishly, the chances are further reduced. If all this is taken into account, my optimistic estimate is that 10% of children receive an adequate amount of selfless love and attention.

To simplify our estimation, I am also looking at the topic of parental addictions and relationship patterns in points V and VI. It should be clear to anyone why these are important to the soul of a child or a young person. It's important to emphasize that a lack of these factors should not be underestimated, because they have a great impact on our later Life. For example, if a child grows up with separated parents, they lose faith in the existence of full spiritual intimacy, so they are less likely to be able to live in harmony. But for the experience of unity, average people need a true companion. Today, approximately 60% of marriages and life partnerships in my country end in divorce. Thus, optimistically, there is a 40% probability that a child will receive the related needs. This is also a highly optimistic estimate because in many families, the absence of divorce does not necessarily imply harmonious relationship patterns.

Among those mentioned in point VII, most parents in today's Western world focus on the development of the body and the acquisition of knowledge, so we have the best chances in this area. At the same time, spirituality is a neglected topic in many families. Many parents prefer to devote most of their resources to selfish purposes and devote little attention to their children in this area, so the child's spiritual development is usually incomplete as well. Nevertheless, I estimate a 70% probability of it happening here, admitting that my estimate is highly optimistic.

Now let's see how likely you are to start your life as a happy young adult. This requires the combined realization of the chances presented above, which is very simple to calculate. Its value is: $0.3*0.625*0.1*0.4*0.7= 0.00525$, or a 0.525% combined probability. This means that about one young adult in 200 People is truly happy without the need for any kind of spiritual or thoughtful self-improvement. They are the lucky ones who are instinctively balanced, have no inner emptiness in them, and whatever they touch turns to gold. They are the ones who amaze us, because to the rational mind they seem to be the favorites of Fortune. Yes: they really are lucky, but not because whatever they do always works out well; this is "just" a consequence of their past! They instinctively use their intuition well and because they do not have a Life-destroying level of spiritual vibration (or only a few of them do), they make the right decisions. So, they're lucky because that's their past.

You can understand why so few People get what they want. At the same time, you can see why it seems so unfair to many that these rare people are given what we cannot have. After all, they are smoothly happy without any self-improvement.

But what about the others? Unfortunately, without spiritual self-improvement and spiritual self-healing, they only have a chance for happiness for a short time. But the good news is that there are incredibly many great ways to heal our past traumas without damaging our future. If you're that lucky 1 in 200, I'm glad you're holding this book in your hands, because with this method I hope you will help others even more effectively. Your main job is to help others raise their spiritual vibration. However, if you are within the other 199, then I am happy you are holding this book because I can give you the method that has already helped me, as well as those who have asked for my help and listened to me so far.

Never before have there been so many Humans on the planet Earth, and never before has there been so much knowledge in the average rational sense. If we look at the Western, "developed" part of the world, the standard of living and public security has never been higher. Yet there has never been as many lonely, unhappy and spiritually insecure People as there are today.

I am convinced that we are on the verge of a huge global change. This is definitely going to happen! If we continue our Life in the same way as we have been, there will be a global transition. For many, it will be a terrible change, which could take the form of drastically escalating climate change or the outbreak of another world war. However, if more and more of us wake up and realize that our current thinking patterns are faulty, this change could also happen with a peaceful and harmonious transition (*Dittrich, 2021*). I work toward the realization of this latter vision every day. If you do something in your own Life to raise your spiritual vibration level, you will not only do yourself good, but you will also give the world the most you can. This idea is supported in more detail in later parts of this book.

Those who stubbornly remain in the prison of their ego will face enormous suffering, through which they will either learn the lessons or continue to suffer. Most of the time, they don't understand why this is happening to them and why they deserve all the bad things Life has given them. They are convinced that Life is being unfair with them.

At the same time, another path can be chosen—the path of spiritual development. Since you're holding this book in your hands right now, there's a good chance you've chosen this path. From this line on, it's all about you. The selfless purpose of every sentence is to lead your Life into a happy, peaceful future! For this to be successful, we need to work together, so please take two important pieces of advice right here at the beginning of our journey together.

My first request is that you do not "devour" this book in a short time! When I became interested in spiritual literature in my early 30s, I made a big mistake: I began to consume dozens of books by speed-reading. I went for quantity. I wanted to get as much information as possible in the shortest possible time. I was convinced that, in this way, I would reach my goals more effectively, but that's not how spiritual growth works! Knowledge is not enough here! **Gaining information about certain spiritual issues will not change your Life! Acquiring knowledge is only the first and easiest step.** Spiritual growth requires experience and inner change. Knowledge must be built into our everyday thinking system, our actions, and our emotional world. Only in this way can effective change take place. For this reason, I ask you to proceed slowly with this book. Where there's nothing new for you, of course you can keep up the pace. However, where you find lines that affect your soul, stop reading, mature your thoughts, memorize those lines and make them a part of your life. If you can't contemplate a new thought at least four or five times within two days, it will be lost from your memory forever. To prevent this from happening, the best method is self-observation. If you come across an idea that is valuable to you, observe yourself from that aspect over the next one or two days. This self-observation will deepen your self-awareness, while at the same time it will connect the new thought with your personality. This way, it will become integrated into your daily life. Already this one rule will bring a significant increase in happiness levels in your Life by the time you reach the end of this book.

My second request is that you never punish yourself! Spiritual development is not a linearly ascending process. There are always missteps! However, if you're on the right track, the recession will never be as deep as it was before. These are indicators for you from which you will see how much you have developed. If you punish yourself, you will push yourself even deeper! In the next chapter, you will learn that self-flagellation leads to a spiritual vibration of Guilt, which is a very deep and self-destructive state. By accepting the inconsistency of your development, you create an action of high spiritual vibration (Acceptance) and get out of the spiritual hole more easily and in a shorter time.

Armed with these two pieces of good advice, please take a deep breath and start making your Life better! How? Take it step by step; you will know everything in its own time! But in order for your conscious self to understand what is happening to you, I will first teach you the system of spiritual vibrations, the knowledge of which will in itself trigger significant changes in your Life! If you have read and remember the annex on spiritual vibration levels in my book *FutEARTH- A Solution to Climate Change and World Peace*, namely the Six Programs of Change (*Dittrich, 2021*), then you can skip chapters 1.1.-1.3. Of course, if you don't remember it, it is worth re-reading here because I'll discuss this issue from a slightly different angle and in more detail.

CHAPTER 1

Spiritual vibration levels

1.1. The wisdom of your body is obscured by your thinking

For decades, I've wondered how a dog weaned from its mother early on and growing up alone knows exactly which grass to chew when it has an upset stomach. Or how does it know which puddle to drink from and which not, even if the contaminants in it are odorless? How does the carp in the lake know that the octopus-flavored bait is good for them, while it has never tasted octopus in its life, and why does it like corn when it doesn't grow underwater? The answer was given to me by the science of kinesiology.

It was incredibly interesting when I started reading about it. I wholeheartedly recommend Dr. David R. Hawkins' book titled *Power vs. Force*. This book confirms the scientific foundations of the chapters on the levels of spiritual vibration.

The science of kinesiology started from the observation that the body neither makes mistakes nor is able to lie. This may seem strange or unbelievable at first, but it really is true. Thousands of studies were conducted in the 70s and 80s at the dawn of kinesiology, and they were able to confirm this assumption with 99.9% certainty. Among other things, lie detectors are based on this knowledge.

Kinesiological measurement was performed using the so-called body response method. In this method, the body's response can only mean 'yes' or 'no'. The disadvantage of the method is therefore that we can only get answers from the wisdom of our body to questions that it can either say 'yes' or 'no' to (*D. R. Hawkins, 2004*).

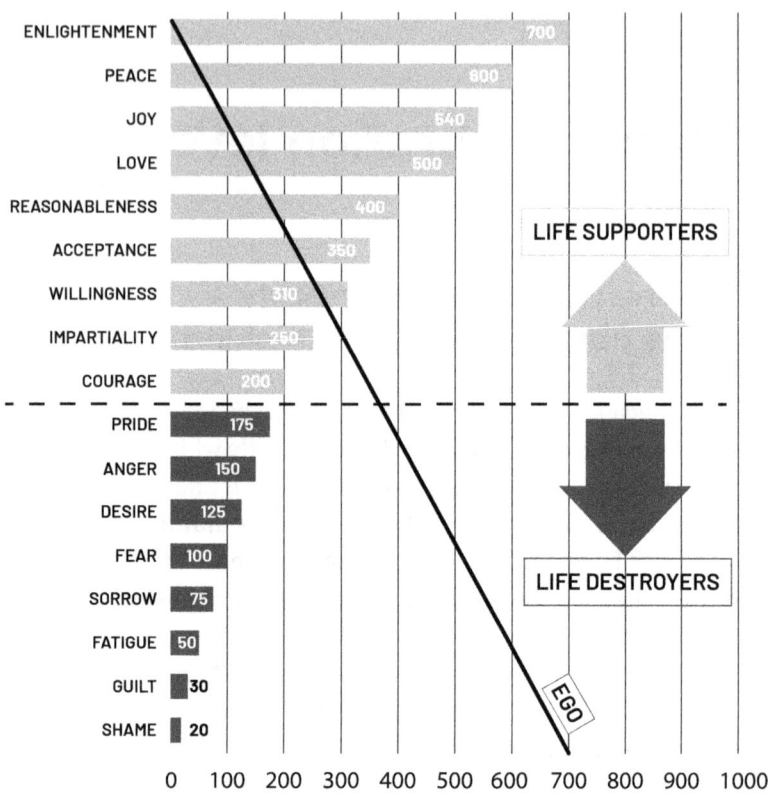

1. figure: Spiritual vibration levels and their relationship to the ego (Dittrich, 2021)

In one experiment, there were five sealed envelopes with one pill each. Four of these were toxic, and the fifth was a vitamin C pill. To make sure that the experiment was completely reliable, despite the fact that the experimental subjects could not open the sealed envelopes, each one was filled with tablets of the same size, weight, shape and color. The subjects were asked to select the envelope containing the good pill. Of course, their guesses were according to statistical norms. That is, 20% of the participants hit the good pill and 80% hit the poison. In a second test group, the response of their bodies was examined by kinesiology specialists. Based on this, more than 99% of the subjects chose the right pill—a result that was impossible with rational thinking. Just as the dog is not wrong about which of the many grasses they can eat, the Person body is not wrong in such a case. Kinesiology is now a proven and accepted science that is widely used in the world. For example, certain kinesiology methods are an integral part of the training programs of elite athletes. If it works for them, why not use it to change your Life?

Dogs and fish differ from Humans in that their rational thinking does not mask the instinctive feelings and implications of their bodies. The dog and the fish sense what is good for them and what is not, and they rarely make a mistake. (Author's note: *Once during one of my lectures, a Person was indignant at what I was saying. He said it was nonsense because his cat and others on his street had been poisoned with rat poison. Why didn't the cat sense the trouble beforehand? My answer was it is no coincidence that the accuracy is not 100%, but is nonetheless more than 99% accurate.*

So, there are some counterexamples. Unfortunately, his case is also logical from the point of view of kinesiology. The number-one law of the universe is the law of free will. If a cat senses that the poisoned food is not good for them, but they still taste it out of wishful thinking, they will unfortunately meet their death. How many times do we do things against our gut that we feel we shouldn't do? This is a certain number of events—between 0-1%—where an animal acts differently than it should. Cats are curious and playful creatures. That particular rat poison was probably presented to them in such a way that their curiosity was stronger than their intuition.)

Humans' rational thinking causes them to lose communication with their body. They are not able to pay enough attention to their body's signals. Yet rationality very often fails, in which case an animal is much wiser than a Human. It's strange to think about, isn't it? It may even be unacceptable to our human arrogance at first. After all, we were educated to believe that the ability to think lifted us out of the animal world. This is true, but in exchange for knowledge, we have lost the wonderful ability that the world of intuition gives us. By the time the guidelines of this book are incorporated into your Life, you will be able to use this "tool" to support your happiness! However, it is important to point out that rationality is a very good thing! The problem with it in our current world is that we want to use it for everything.

For example, if you want to create a new type of software that would bring a better quality of Life to thousands of People, you would program it on the basis of rationality to make it work well. At the same time, how many Life situations have you had where it was very difficult to force your rational thinking on yourself, and this caused great internal tensions in you? Or when, despite your rational knowledge, you were completely puzzled about what was right? Your body (and soul) would know the right answer! The internal tension stems from the fact that you have suppressed the signals of your body and soul in yourself. Since I began paying attention to these, my Life has become much easier—not only because my inner tensions have been relieved and I live a more peaceful, happier Life, but also because my decisions, which may seem irrational or even stupid at first, almost always prove to be correct. For example, one morning a few days ago I had a feeling that I should leave for a meeting in a remote city 15 minutes earlier than the timetable planning software said I should. I didn't understand what the earlier departure would accomplish, but I listened to my gut and set off. After about an hour on the highway an accident occurred, causing much congestion. Regardless, I arrived at the meeting on time. If I had made a rational decision, I would have been late. However, when I listened to my intuition, the accident had not even happened yet. This could not be explained with rational logic. The world of intuition is already scientifically proven, many aspects of which have been supported, for example, at the HeartMath Institute in California. Among other things, my next book will explain exactly how this works. I hope you will honor me with your attention then too.

So, the problem is not with rationality, as this is what we owe our technical and scientific progress to; the problem is the loss of the correct proportions. In Western society we believe in the Holy Grail of rationality, even though this actually results in partial blindness. This will not be the case in the society of the future. We will handle everything in its place, including rationality and the world of intuition. For this to happen, we need to change and rediscover our inner powers at the individual level.

Thank you for being on this journey with me!

I have some good news! It's true that you can't (yet) use your brain to access your body's deep, subconscious signals, but a good kinesiologist can. With a simple body-response method, you can view your body responses to any question. What is it used for? A lot of things, because your body is much, much wiser than you are (sorry!) and your body never lies (sorry again!). You, on the other hand, even if you don't intentionally lie to others, you are unconsciously unsure of yourself so you may also be lying to others. Let everyone decide that for themselves.

We often lie to ourselves because it's easier to believe someone else's truth than to look inside ourselves. But we also often lie to ourselves out of a desire to please others. It's very rare for a Person to be able to be completely honest with themselves. Our body, on the other hand, knows exactly what is being suppressed in it.

So, what is a kinesiologist good for? For deeper self-knowledge, and for opening and dissolving psychological wounds. A good kinesiologist knows so much more than a good psychologist because they always work from the truth. In a traditional "talking" psychotherapy, the patient often twists and beautifies things in a way that is more favorable from their own point of view. For example, there may be factors behind your problems that you don't even dare to admit to yourself, let alone to your therapist. Conversely, the kinesiologist cannot be lied to because they work from the always-honest body response. This is very important for the reliability and measurability of the method.

But the most effective approach is to go to a professional who is both a psychologist and a kinesiologist, since some kinesiologists do not have the appropriate spiritual sensitivity or professional knowledge to heal the soul. I will elaborate on this question later in this book.

But what is the purpose? First, to quantify the current level of happiness of each Person, and this will open a door for you to measure your own spiritual development.

1.2. Quantifiable Happiness – or Soul Vibration Levels

This chapter presents a very important set of basic concepts. Whoever understands and learns this will have their view of People and the functioning of Person society change significantly. The broader perspective that will be gained in this way is important for reaching new milestones on your path to happiness. At the same time, it provides a decisive basis for you to better understand the other People around you and become more accepting. The development of our acceptance increases our happiness in itself, as there will be less tension in our Lives, and our Person relationships will improve.

The basics of the system to be presented now are explained by Dr. David R. Hawkins, who summarized them in his book *Power vs. Force*. Perhaps it is not an exaggeration to claim that his work is among the best in the literature about the

Person Soul, so I sincerely recommend it to all my readers.

It is scientifically proven (*D. R. Hawkins, 2004*) that the Person Soul has a certain level of vibration. The soul is a special type of energy that affects surrounding Humans and also reflects the quality of our own inner state of mind. Different vibration levels of the soul can be linked to different defined levels, which are illustrated in **Figure 1.**

Of the 17 feeling systems presented here, you have probably already felt many. However, the average value of all your feelings gives you the current vibration level of your soul, which is characterized by one of the main feelings listed above. Therefore, the value of your vibration level depends mainly on where your soul spends the most time among the 17 spiritual emotions presented above on an average day. Every thought, feeling, and conversation has a psychic vibration value, so the average of your daily existence determines the level of spiritual vibration you live in. It's important to state the fact, right here at the beginning, that the higher the level of spiritual vibration you rise to, the happier, more balanced and more peaceful you will be. This book puts it all in your hands! Please stay with me and take charge of your destiny! The good thing about the system I'm going to present is that you don't have to believe in it—it works even if you don't. You just need to take and follow the advice that I give you.

Obviously, we all have a fluctuating state of mind, which is why we're sometimes more enthusiastic and happier, and sometimes we sink into a lower spiritual state. From the level of Shame to the level of Pride, People emit negative spiritual energies that make a person destructive of Life, that is: they have a negative effect on the Humans and all other living beings around them. Every day, they make decisions and actions that have a Life-destroying effect. Characteristic of the levels from Courage to Enlightenment, the Person soul emits Life-supporting energies, with a positive overall effect on its environment (*Dittrich, 2021*). Determining your mental vibration level with the body-response method takes approximately three minutes if you can give a good kinesiologist this much time. To do this, you need to show them **Figure 1** in this book and ask them to measure the vibration level of your soul accordingly. It's important to take **Diagram 1** with you because there are multiple scales in use, so in this way you can make it clear to your body and the kinesiologist what you're looking for.

I am sure you have experienced that in the environment of a spiritually mature Person, you feel more peaceful, cheerful, and energetic. At the same time, there is a good chance that you have noticed that with a complaining, self-pitying Person, your energy decreases rapidly. The latter people are called energy vampires. This is because the energies of Person Souls interact with each other and always strive for balance. Therefore, when two or more Humans are close to each other, they affect each other's spiritual energy levels even if they are not communicating. For example, if you stand in the crowd on the subway and don't focus on anyone, this will still happen to you.

When a Person on a very high spiritual level gives a lecture, the audience in the room is usually captivated by the positive mood being radiated without them being aware of it. A Person like the lecturer can be at such a high spiritual level that they can even counterbalance the negative spiritual energies of more than 10,000 people. Think of Buddha, Jesus, or Mother Teresa and the impact they had on the people around them. Based on my interpretation, Buddha and Jesus were enlightened People, but I don't want to offend anyone's faith! Religious explanation and kinesiology do not oppose each other, but rather are complementary and make the other more understandable.

If we look at our Life from the point of view of this system, we get the answer to why it is so important to deal with the development of our soul. With this—in addition to our own happiness—we also affect the happiness of others without even being aware of it. The most important stage of spiritual development is when we move from the level of Pride to the level of Courage because at that point we go from being Life Destroyers to becoming Life Boosters. This is the step you can take to have a supportive effect on your environment and thus begin to make your Person relationships more qualitative, peaceful and harmonious. At the same time, instead of attracting self-destructive actions and negative events, positive, self-building processes begin to predominate in your Life. If you want to have a happier Life, a more peaceful family or more devoted friends around you, you need to raise the vibration level of your own soul. It's the most you can do for yourself, your loved ones, and the world! That is why the great sages say that happiness comes from inside you and is not the result of external influences. If you change the vibration level of your soul in a positive direction, it will be more peaceful, harmonious and loving, and your soul will not attract so many bad things either. It's worth it, isn't it? I can tell you from experience that the answer is "YES".

A few years ago, I unconsciously lived with Life-destroying psychic vibrations. Now I live my Life on the high level of spiritual vibration of Life Affirmation. I am telling you this because if I was able to succeed, you will too if you work openly and persistently for it! This book was written from this one selfless motivation: so that I could help others with my experiences of success.

The effects on your life of having increased levels of psychic vibration are almost unbelievable. Quality changes have occurred in every area of my Life. If I had to describe my Life seven years ago in one word, I would choose the word "suffering". If I had to describe my Life today, the word "miracle" would be the most appropriate.

It is important to know that at each level of spiritual vibration, you see the world differently, and your view of the truth is different. If you understand this, you can be much more empathetic to People, as it becomes more understandable how others can think and opine about things so differently from you.

In my Life, reviving and reliving the healed negative emotions has brought me even closer to understanding People. How many People on Earth could have repressed so much suffering and, as a result, unconsciously played their increasingly crazy games?! Your soul is vibrating at a low vibration level, even though it is conscious about it, which shouldn't be the case! Childhood traumas, divorce or loss of parents, loss of attention due to the appearance of a sibling, parents who trample their children's souls into the mud, deprivation, exploitation, harassment, intimidation: these and similar deep psychological wounds burden the multitudes of Humans. This gives us the realization that we cannot judge anyone because we never know for what reason that other Person is the way they are. Perhaps an even more interesting and exciting thought is to realize that if I had been in that other Person's Life, I would probably be behaving like them now. That's what Christ's words meant when he said 'forgive those who have sinned against us'. They do what they do unconsciously, as a result of the repression of their damaged soul. If I strike back, I only deepen that Human's wound. However, if I forgive them, I will help them heal their soul. Obviously, it is not possible to live according to Christ's words below a certain level of spiritual vibration. Most People have such a psychological burden on their shoulders that they do not have the strength to deal with others, and instead respond to the slightest attack with great resistance and suddenness. The world of systematic forgiveness begins to emerge above the Life-supporting spiritual level of 200. But in order for you to delve deeper into the possibilities of this exciting system, I ask you to get to know the individual spiritual vibration levels with me.

Shame and Guilt (values 20 and 30)

On the levels of Shame and Guilt, we live in the deepest, blackest, darkest feelings that a Person can experience. There, we are so close to the level of death that we consider our own value to be zero. Most often, at this level an individual sincerely desires death. Those who commit suicide sink into and are more permanently trapped here before they perform their final act. My knowledge of my father's suicide confirms this. At this level of psychological vibration, the feeling of self-worthlessness unfortunately triggers despicable, hateful reactions to the world. Through this miserable feeling toward Life, we see the world as evil and imagine the future very darkly. From this level of vibration, the evil of Humanity is so infinite and incurable that Humanity deserves its extinction. It is no coincidence that in the past, invaders tried to trample their opponents into the mud by shaming the People, and this is still not uncommon today. Shame and guilt were some of the effective tools of dictatorial regimes in the past and, unfortunately, are still used today.

Shame and guilt often appear in families as well. Many parents try to control their children in this way, without even considering the devastation they are doing to their souls, undermining the foundations of the child's happy future. Of course, the parent does this unconsciously, as they are also struggling with their spiritual dragons and since they are unhealed, they pass along their burden to their child, who continues to carry it. When a parent embarrasses or shames their child in front of others, they are literally tramping that child's soul into the mud.

A Person who lives at the level of Guilt and Shame is often excluded by society. But if we look deep into the process, the individual excludes themselves by perceiving themselves as someone who is completely worthless and their environment as being evil and dark. The feeling of reproach and humiliation often permeates the spiritual Life of a Person. Such a Person is highly impressionable and can be made to do almost anything. Humans at a higher (but still Life-destroying) vibration usually get their Person peers to do the dirty work, whatever it is. Thus, many of these People are in a state of fantasy. The greater the power in the hands of such a Person, the more devastating their impact will be on their environment. After all, such a Person wants to destroy everything they see as evil. With great probability, Napoleon, Hitler and Stalin could have lived at this level of spiritual vibration. Their low level of mental vibration was coupled with exceptionally high intellectual and low emotional intelligence. That's how they were able to make such a huge negative impact on the world.

Please observe yourself for a few days. Think about how many times and for how long you feel shame or guilt. How many thoughts and feelings do you have related to this level of spiritual vibration, either towards yourself or towards the world? Until you have carefully observed this in yourself, please do not proceed further. You will find a table in Annex 1. Write down the approximate number of hours or minutes your soul, body or mind spends here on an average day. Observe yourself carefully! After all, emotional or thought patterns that have long been ingrained in us are so commonplace that we don't even realize how harmful they are to our Life! The more you discover in yourself, the more effectively you will be able to change. The first step in choosing is always recognition.

It's important not to confuse shame with shyness! Shyness is an emotion with a high level of psychological vibration, which is about sharing one's intimacy only with those who have already deserved it. And don't confuse repentance with guilt. Someone who is aware of their errors and tries to make them right is a repentant Person. This is a sign of the spiritual vibrational level of Courage—when we begin to face our true selves.

Apathy and Sorrow (values 50 and 75)

The measure of the vibration level of Apathy is 50, while Sorrow is 75. These are already much higher than the levels of Guilt and Shame described in the previous section. As surprising as it may seem, being sad or apathetic is a far less negative level of spiritual vibration than the levels of Shame and Guilt. I was on these levels for a long time and of course I don't wish it on anyone, but there is a way out for those who are there.

However, looking at the world from the point of view of Shame and Guilt, Apathy is already a serious step ahead. It is Apathy and then Sorrow that provide a way out of the deepest levels of the soul. That's why it's not right to criticize an apathetic Person! They may have just leveled up, but since you're judging them through your own filter (which is naturally faulty), you can't even imagine that it could be an improvement over a lower state. After all, the person may have jumped from the level of Guilt to the level of Apathy. This is a huge development, but by criticizing their apathy, we can push them back to lower levels of vibration. You have to let them rest a little at this level, then suddenly there will be an inspiring force that will pull them out of it. Then you will have to help them, but not with criticism! Of course, it is also possible to fall from a higher level of spiritual vibration to this level. In such cases, we must allow ourselves to dwell on the level of Sorrow.

It can also happen that the pain of grief torments us so much that it pushes us to the level of Apathy, where our soul rests before it begins to develop again. Both levels should be allowed enough time! Those who walk away from this and suppress their sadness will often slide backwards in their Lives. But if the level of Apathy or Sorrow is too persistent, it's time to seek outside help. This level of mental resonance is so deep that it is difficult to get out of it without external help.

A Person who lives at the level of Apathy is no longer interested in anything, and nothing matters to them anymore. They feel that this world can no longer give them anything of value. At this level, there is complete hopelessness, but at least the feelings of Shame and Guilt no longer torment the soul. Here, too, the feeling of a death wish often arises, but the desire for external help also arises—we just may not have the strength to pursue it. That's why it's good for family or good friends to lend a helping hand. Since our futures are mostly permeated by despair and hopelessness when we're in this state, we're very pessimistic and we see the future of the world as dark. The positive things flowing towards us are welcomed with resignation—often with apathetic indifference. Because of the negative attitude that permeates every nook and cranny of our souls, we are condemned by our environment, which is naturally able to push us away from helping intentions.

The level of Sorrow is already an improvement over the level of Apathy, although it is still a very deep level of spiritual vibration. Some kind of psychological activity already appears here, as we have active emotions, even if they are very painful. At the level of Apathy, we no longer feel pain, or if we do, we don't care. At the level of Sorrow, there is a desire for spiritual pain to go away. This will help us rise to a higher level of spiritual vibration. Of course, this will be healthy and lasting if we let the sadness, grief, or any other cause pass through us, live through it and do not run away from it. This heals rather than obscures the spiritual problem. At the level of Sorrow, the darkness of our vision is still very intense. We are mentally stagnant and tend to be trapped in the depths of self-pity. We see our life as tragic and we respond contemptuously to the helpful intentions of our environment: *"They don't know what I'm going through..."*. This is the state in which we lick our spiritual wounds, but this is what will heal them if we do it for long enough!

Please observe yourself again for a few days. Think about how many times and for how long you feel apathy and sorrow. Watch how many thoughts and feelings you have related to this level of mental vibration, whether towards yourself or towards the world. Until you have thoroughly studied this in yourself, do not proceed further. Please find the table in Appendix 1. Write down the total number of hours your soul, body, or mind spends here on an average day. Observe yourself carefully! After all, emotional or thought patterns that have long been ingrained in us are so commonplace that we don't even realize how harmful they are to our Life. The more you discover in yourself, the more effectively you will be able to change. The first step in choosing is always recognition.

Weakness, aimlessness, and depression are related to the psychological vibration level of the Apathy. At the same time, do not confuse it with impartiality or neutrality, which are signs of Life-supporting spiritual vibration levels. The level of spiritual vibration of Sorrow includes grief and deep spiritual pain. At the same time, similar feelings arising from compassion represent a high level of psychological vibration.

Fear (value 100)

We have all been afraid, which is the natural reaction of our souls. This in itself is healthy and appropriate. The fact that we are sometimes afraid does not put the vibration level of our soul at this level, since all our feelings must be considered as a barrier. Our soul is at the level of Fear when most of our thoughts are imbued with fear. I, too, was at this level for a long time, and I do not wish this on anyone. This state of mind vibrates at a value of 100, which clearly shows that it is above the level of Sorrow discussed in the previous section.

A Person at the level of Fear is usually not afraid of a single thing, but is prone to fear overall. For them, the whole world is a scary place and they very rarely feel safe. Of course, all such Humans have priority fear topics. Because of this, this Person is an anxious type. If you are in company or in any place where you do not feel safe, you will be withdrawn. But sometimes the opposite is true, and where you can, you may enthusiastically introduce the cause of your fears to your environment. The vision of such People is strongly pessimistic toward both their own Life and the future of Humanity. They are the ones who wore masks even on deserted streets during the coronavirus outbreak, or who envision the immediate collapse of the world due to alarming climate news. Often, the fear of venereal diseases or pregnancy is so ingrained that they stay away from sex, or even if they don't, they can never be liberated. These people feel threatened in almost every situation. Their ego is constantly scanning the future to see where they are being attacked. Because of this, their souls are in a constant state of readiness and rarely dare to be liberated. The consequence of this is that they get out of their comfort zone very quickly, get angry easily, and often do things that they later regret. They tend to consume mind-altering substances (alcohol, drugs), as this is the only way they can experience the state of liberation. These Humans imagine God or Fate as a punishing force that is very strict with them and others for all sins. This exacerbates their fear. If they can possibly exercise power over someone, they become criminals themselves. Because of these characteristics, such People unconsciously emit a lot of Life-destroying energy, but not as much as those at a lower level of spiritual vibration.

Moving from the levels of Shame, Guilt, Sorrow or Apathy discussed so far is a major step forward. Above this level, the psychological activity of the individual is already much higher. Of course, we can also descend from a higher level of vibration to this level, from which it is very difficult to climb back up. I advise these People to dare to ask for external help! Most People are ashamed to tell others about their fears. In fact, people who live at the level of Fear are often afraid to talk about their fears. Unfortunately, fear-mongering has been and still is a serious weapon of both political power and some churches throughout history. For centuries, the Christian church kept People in fear of the possibility of going to hell. Man was pushed to the vibration level of Fear in order to influence and control him. Unfortunately, there are still political and other power forces or religious sects that use fear as a serious tool. These systems cannot survive permanently, as the basic instinct is that Humans want to live abundantly. This level of vibration is very far from happiness and lacks respect for Life too.

Desire (value 125)

The value of the spiritual vibration level of Desire is 125. As I have already mentioned, vibration levels below 200 are Life- and self-destructive, so this vibration level is still very negative, having a degrading effect on both the person radiating it and their environment. It is true that a Person whose soul vibrates steadily at this level reaches a higher level than the aforementioned vibration levels. If we examine the levels of spiritual vibration from Shame to Fear and look at the level of Desire from there, then some more effective spiritual activity finally appears here. Since this vibration level is no longer so low, hope becomes stronger and our soul begins to desire good. Thus, this vibration level can also function as a springboard towards higher vibration levels. Desire gives us the strength to pursue our goals. At the same time, the level of Desire as seen from higher vibration levels is very negative. This level is a world rampant with addictions. I can also say that those who are permanently at this level of spiritual vibration all suffer from addictions. The basic feeling of addictions is craving (*Gábor Máté, 2010*) and we are so accustomed to the hormonal effervescence caused by craving that it is no longer actually important to achieve the goal—just to maintain the craving. This pathological state of mind causes many addicts not to realize that their addiction is a problem and that they should quit. At this level of spiritual vibration, we are so attached to the feeling of craving that we feel that without it our Life would become more empty, dreary, boring. For example, porn addicts love to crave the sexual goals they see in the movies, but if they can finally experience them in reality, the experience isn't as good as they imagined. In real life, the extra "taste" of craving is removed, and often the orgasm doesn't happen. Although the porn industry is a good example of this, it can also be said that one of the main engines of the current economic system and social functioning is craving. Through commercials and other media, exciting products and services are a carrot being dangled in front of People to make them crave. It is this social setup that causes an incredible proportion of the People in the world to live at this level of vibration. It's very easy to find goals for our cravings, and since we have a strong tendency to do so at this level of spiritual vibration, the social system achieves its goal and "excites" us for consumption. Porn and sex addiction are typically more common in men, but there are addictions that are not widely considered as such that affect women as well, including shopping, binge reading and binge watching. The characteristic of addictive forms is that our own addiction is "normal" because our egos make us believe that it's okay. The dependences of others, on the other hand, are considered reprehensible. However, addiction is addiction, with the same psychological root and the same negative psychological vibration level. Such a Person is not to be criticized or condemned, but to be helped to reach a higher level of spiritual vibration. By condemning them, we only keep them at that level because criticism makes them suffer yet another disappointment and escape into their addiction.

Anyone who remains at this level of mental vibration and nevertheless gives up their addiction (e.g., due to its perceived harmful effects) will instinctively choose other addictions instead. I know several People who quit smoking overnight, but have been addicted to other things ever since.

Living on the vibrational level of Desire, a Person's concept of Life revolves around disappointments. This is quite logical, because if there were no disappointments in their life, they would sooner or later reach their goal and then there would be nothing to yearn for. I myself "stayed" at this level of mental resonance for many, many years, and I also experienced a lot of disappointment. I always started to achieve my goals with renewed force, and then when they collapsed, I would start all over again. I couldn't understand why great goals were always preceded by something "unlucky". If I had reached my destination in one area of my life, other areas collapsed. Thus, it was always possible to yearn for unfulfilled goals.

This disappointing perception of Life is very often accompanied by a denial of the existence of God. These People believe that if God existed, then the world would not be like this. After all, they do not realize that they are the cause of many of their own delusions. They believe that Life is conspiring against them, or they were born under an unfortunate star. Obviously, the beginning of the way out of this situation can be the realization that we are the cause of all the trouble that happens to us.

These People undertake their unattainable goals with tremendous force, at the end of which failure and disappointment arrive. Their conscious mind desires the goal in vain; their subconscious is looking for failure because they need disappointment on the spiritual plane. They choose large goals because they tend to be maximalists. This makes this energy system at this level a Life destroyer that the soul radiates to its environment and to itself. The other main cause is well perceived by the harmful effects of addictions on their environment and on the individual.

Please observe yourself again for a few days. Think about how many times and for how long you feel fear or longing. Look at how many thoughts and feelings you have connected to these levels of spiritual vibration, either towards yourself or towards the world. Until you have carefully observed this in yourself, do not proceed further.

In **Appendix 1**, please find a table. Write down the total number of hours your soul, body, or mind spends here on an average day. It's important to keep a close eye on yourself. After all, emotional or thought patterns that have long been ingrained in us are so commonplace that we don't even realize how harmful they are to our Life! Often our ego idealizes why it is good. Recently, I explained to an unhappy Man that his perfectionism was too much of a burden for him and made him unhappy. His response was that he loved being a perfectionist. The ego trap is subtle, but the more you discover these feelings and thoughts in yourself, the more effectively you will be able to change. The first step to change is always recognizing what you can see behind your ego. The level of psychological vibration of Fear is associated with worry.

However, do not confuse this with caution or prudence, which are signs of Life-supporting spiritual vibration levels. The spiritual vibratory level of Desire includes craving and the setting of perfectionist goals. At the same time, purposefulness and determination are signs of higher levels of spiritual vibration.

Anger (value 150)

Looking at the levels presented so far, there is already a serious level of activity here. At this level, although the individual is negative toward their environment and themselves, they already strongly express their self-defense, so dynamic energies emerge. One of the main characteristics of a Person at the level of Anger is that they always blame others and express this with very harsh criticism. Instinctively, they are always looking for opposition. Most of the time they don't even notice it. They are convinced of their truth, but they do not perceive that they unconsciously always see a truth as logical that is opposed to others. Such a

Person condemns everyone in their environment who does not see the world as they see it and does not react to things as they expect. Empathic skills at this level are very low. We have all been angry before, so we must know this feeling well. Those who live at this level of vibration feel this way for most of their lives. A good example of this vibration level is Grouchy Smurf, although it is clearly shown in that cartoon in a more solid and lovable way. In real life, it works much more destructively. The main feeling is hatred and hostility that permeates the soul. A Person at this level of vibration is always looking for a target for his anger. They are often involved in tough arguments, fights, and other aggressive scenes. They're a constant troublemaker at nightclubs. These People almost always sue someone and lose the case so that they can hate the judge afterwards. This does not end the chain of hatred. At this level of psychological vibration are most climate activists who try to influence the world with force, quarreling and harsh words in order to force it to finally change. Of course, they are also right on a certain level, as we have to somehow get the world out of this bad situation.

For the Person at this vibration level, the essence is the feeling of anger itself, even if it communicates its opposite outwardly most of the time. The individual instinctively seeks opposition in every situation. He is convinced that the world is full of bad things and evil, most of which is at his expense. If he is a believer, he experiences at this level of vibration indicate that God is a vengeful being who will punish all evil deeds. Such People are accustomed to standing at the head of a group and fight against other groups with fire and iron.

If you live at a lower vibration level than this, Anger can be the next stage of development. This is the first level where we dare to stand up for ourselves. People who live at lower vibration levels are eating their insides: they very rarely stand up for their own interests. They usually humble themselves, withdraw, and adapt. However, at this vibration level, there is opposition whereby the individual stands up for themselves.

At the same time, if we sink here from a higher vibration level, there are serious dangers of permanently sticking here. Obviously, it is possible to descend here for a short time to go up to a higher level of spiritual vibration with renewed force. Looking at it this way, we also need to "blur" ourselves out in order to move up. Suppression cannot be a solution at all, as it keeps us at this level permanently or pushes us deeper. If you are stuck here for a long time, it is recommended to seek the help of a professional. If you feel opposed to the world, in most cases you will find that the real reason not in external factors, but within yourself.

Most of the time, we project our inner dissatisfaction with ourselves—our anger towards ourselves—onto the world. It is much easier to blame others or to be angry at others than to look at ourselves and put things in order. If you were at this level for a long time and came out of it, you'll understand what I mean. If you recognize yourself in this writing and feel that you are living at this vibration level, then you may be reading these lines to move towards higher, happier vibration levels. Anger destroys and burns us from the inside out, so it's a permanent source of serious mental and physical illnesses. That's why it's very important to evolve and take things to the next level. Anger is one of the basic feelings we can have at any time, as it is one of the basic feelings we are born with. Anger, shame, hatred, disgust, fright, despair, joy, love and curiosity are core emotions (as drawn from Paul Ekman's book *Revealed Emotions*) that we learn from others, not in relation to others. A Person is an open material and energy system, so they constantly need the supply and flow of both. Energy is above matter, however inversely we think of it in our current materialistic views. If there is no energy, there is no embodiment, no material reaction, no activation energy. Anger is one of the final activation energies that we unconsciously or consciously touch in order to have the strength to oppose or stand up for ourselves. This is one of the reasons so many of us get stuck at the level of Anger.

Crouched in anger, a Person most often does not "dare" to move on from this level because they fear that their Life will become empty and boring if they let go of the exciting feeling of constant opposition and the extra energy produced by anger. You don't have to worry about that! At a higher vibration level, Life is happier and not more boring, and there is much more spirit. The Person living with anger is also afraid that if they are not angry with others, they will have to look at themselves and—at least for the time being—won't dare to do so. They are afraid of what they will find in themselves. Thus, hatred flowing outward is an effective way to escape from ourselves.
However, what you will find inside yourself will be the key to your happiness, so you have to be brave enough to look there!

Pride (value 175)

The emotional world of a Person who lives at the vibration level of Pride is set up in such a way that he instinctively tries to separate himself from other Humans. He or she always sets up situations so that they appear to be different—more different than the criticized or the target person or target group used for reference. The main direction of emotion is downsizing. We try to make ourselves look better by minimizing others. This world of emotions is associated with pride and arrogance. A person living at this level of vibration, if they're intelligent enough, usually masks their infinite selfishness well. After all, it is in their selfish interest not to be seen as selfish. Thus, it is common to find them to be a kind and superficially attentive Person despite their Life-Destroying vibration level. You can only see behind the armor created out of self-interest by getting to know the individual more deeply. This is why many relationships fail: a partner who seems so pleasant at the beginning is otherwise unsuitable for altruism, which is the basis for intimate relationships.

Since today's world is constantly telling us to be selfish and to take care of ourselves, most People live at this level of vibration. Since this is a Life-destroying level of mental vibration, the indirect consequence is that unprecedented environmental degradation and ominous climate change projections are coming to light. I wrote about this and the solution to climate change in my previous book (*Dittrich, 2021*). Due to the "blessed" activity of the Internet and the media, most young people live at this level of vibration. This is due to the disintegration of real communities in younger generations, the disappearance of the actual community, and the rate of breakups being above 80%. Everyone cares about only themselves and expects others to engage with them. Thus, it is quite improbable to build real and deep human relationships. Of course, it's always the other party that's causing the relationship to run aground. At this level of vibration, the individual does not notice the fact that the more selfish they become, the more they move away from real and quality Person relationships and, incidentally, the more they destroy the natural resources of the Earth. After all, the selfish Person is absorbing everything he desires! They don't have enough self-control, and they don't need it. At this level of spiritual vibration, the essence is to experience every experience, to achieve every desired goal, to possess every material good— everything that can be achieved.

A Person living on the vibrational level of Pride can do everything only for self-interest. Their only motivation is to achieve their own goals. They cannot love unselfishly; they love someone because they expect something in return. Moreover, such People are convinced that there is no such thing as altruism, because the altruistic Person also appears to be that way only because they are aware that they will benefit from their altruism. Such People are accustomed to identifying with the saying "they look after their own first". When I lived at this level of vibration,

I was also convinced of this and didn't understand those who talked about real altruism. I thought I was right, and that they were just idealizing and beautifying the concept of altruism. The real situation is that a Person living at the vibration level of Pride and who has not been at a higher vibration level cannot believe that a real lack of selfishness can exist, since they have never experienced it before. In this way, you cannot be condemned for your limited vision. It's like someone has been looking at the sky from the depths of a narrow abyss all their life and we want to explain to them what a sunrise looks like.

At this level of vibration, there are many People who are successful in their work, the material world or the political world. This success deceives many; it's hard to imagine that these People radiate Life-destroying energies both to themselves and to their environment. Well, I did. The root of Life-destructive energies lies in the Person's inability to put social, ecological or other public interests before themselves, and their selfishness causes them to forget the real goals of their lives. They can only identify with things if these are in line with their personal goals. Therefore, it's obvious that they will adopt and embrace those views and ideas that can support their self-interest. They always believe in what strengthens their self-interest and self-image, and constantly want to convince their environment of this. This is how we behave about anything that is built into the ego.

As a result, our consciousness is incredibly narrowed without us noticing it. Moreover, in most cases, we know and believe ourselves with full awareness how much smarter, more beautiful, or better we are than others. Such People fully believe that they deserve to reach their goals. They do their best to achieve them, often even being willing to bypass the rules. Their conception of Life is a forum for demanding their own benefits, which means that they are demanding of themselves in every way.

By the way, they hide this well as long as they are making good progress towards their goals. Until then, their behavior is polite and calm on the surface. However, if the achievement of their goals becomes questionable, they actually become demanding. They show the whites of their teeth, so to speak.

The most common aspect of these People is atheism or indifference to God. After all, the image of God radiates altruism and is also taught by all the major world religions. However, this is not compatible with the selfish personality and its goals. Most of these People believe that religious principles are not for them. They feel that they're above making such "nonsense" binding on their own Life. Of course, it's not that they don't keep any of the ten commandments; only if you cross a line or two will you justify to yourself why it's an exception and why it's right. The ego, by strengthening itself, is above the rules and even aids in the individual not having any remorse at this level of vibration. The ego explains away the problem and stifles the remorse.

I lived at this level of vibration for a long time. I was convinced of my rightness and I didn't even realize what a Life-destroying way I was living. My narrow-mindedness was incredibly distorted, yet I thought the opposite of myself. I thought I was on the right path, but now I know that selfishness is very far from the right path if we are looking for true happiness. At this level of vibration, we are blinded by professional, financial or other successes. Our egos make us believe that what we do is the right thing to do, as this allows us to consider ourselves to be greater than others and to earn the appreciation of others. The way out of this vibration level is to be able to look behind our ego and see through the mirage of it. Very few are able to do this, so most People are stuck at this vibration level. However, the truly successful and happy People have all gone beyond this and reached a higher level.

If we look at this vibration level from a higher one, we see a narrow-minded, selfish and narrow Person. If we descend back here from a higher level of vibration, the soul will rest here for a short time, temporarily dealing only with itself. For as long as we struggle with our spiritual muddles, we have no power for selflessness. Our field of vision narrows, and we become selfish precisely because the fight against inner spiritual problems consumes too much spiritual energy.

However, if we move up from this level, we can only get to a Life-supporting vibration level. Thus, this is the last vibration level above which real value creation, success and happiness await us. This is enough motivation to step out of the world of self-deception and into a more real-life, valuable vibratory level.

If we look at the vibration level of Pride from the level of Anger (or lower), this is a serious development and progress, because here the individual already uses a much more sophisticated system of self-expression. Fear of others or opposition to others is no longer the driving force of the ego— "only" separation from others. It is no longer so aggressive, heartless and environmentally destructive. It is no coincidence that this level is the highest among the Life-destroying levels.

At the same time, it is the most difficult level to swing out of and move up from, because there our egos make us believe that everything is fine, as we are different from those we compare ourselves to. We feel that we're better, more beautiful, more reasoned. Our subconscious relates to individuals against whom we can feel this superiority. When we meet individuals who are clearly better than us, we usually try to get close to them and make ourselves even better by flaunting our acquaintance with them. Our other strategy is to look for an excuse for why we don't want to be so good. Since this vibration is a self-deceptive mirage, many People are so deceived that they don't want to go higher than this level. The encampment of the unconscious losers is therefore this group, who meanwhile imagine themselves to be winners, while the real winners experience themselves consciously.

It's also important to know that a Person who lives at the vibration level of Pride is always lonely inside. Selfishness sets you apart on a deep spiritual level because the individual does not believe in the power of unity. The Person who lives at this level of vibration is actually afraid inside. The root of this fear is the fear of oneness with others—of dependence on others. We don't want to depend on anyone because we're afraid of getting hurt. We don't dare to love anyone as much as they love us because we're afraid of being abused by them. Our ego is constantly on standby, watching to what extent everyone reciprocates what we give, and at the slightest sign that the other is not acting according to expectation, we withdraw into our separate, selfish world. From this point of view, it's clear that Pride is a self-defense armor that we have built up because of our childhood or other grievances.

By now, you have gained practice observing your own thoughts, emotions, and actions. This is a very important skill that is essential for spiritual development. Now I will ask you to observe yourself again for a few days. Think about how many times and for how long you feel Anger or Pride. Notice whether you have thoughts and feelings connected to these levels of spiritual vibration, either towards yourself or towards the world. Until you have carefully observed this in yourself, do not proceed further. Please find the table in Appendix 1. Write down the total number of hours your soul, body, or mind spends at these levels on an average day. Please be honest with yourself. Do not embellish reality, because you are only delaying and making it difficult to achieve your happiness! The following pages will tell you exactly why this is the case.

Anger, hatred, and indignation are associated with the level of psychological vibration of opposition. At the same time, do not confuse it with objective self-defense, which is a sign of Life-supporting psychic vibration. The latter is characterized by unemotional self-control. The psychological resonance of Pride includes egoism, selfishness, snobbishness, prudishness, hedonism. This should not be confused with standing up for our interests based on objective facts.

Courage (valued at 200)

The level of Courage is where the soul is raised to a Life-Supporting vibration. Here, although the subconscious self-destruction does not cease, self-building becomes stronger. Thus, the soul—and with it the individual— begins to move towards a change that leads to a happier future. Following this, a significant qualitative change occurs in a Human's Life when they move from Pride to Courage. This happens gradually, of course, because solving the problems of the past takes a lot of time.

Recently, a student told me about a teacher who dared to openly admit in front of his class that he didn't understand the kind of mathematical solution invented by the three smartest students; he taught it in a simpler way. Surprisingly, students still look up to this teacher and like him. This is no coincidence, as this gesture shows that he lives on the level of the spiritual vibration of Courage. He admitted to his own disciples that he was less intelligent than they were. At the same time, he has authority and popularity, because this is how a Life-supporting vibration level affects the People in its circle, among other things.

It is at this level of spiritual vibration (compared to the Life Destroying vibration levels discussed so far) that the individual honestly looks at themselves for the first time. This is the most important change compared to the vibration levels discussed so far: the Person already dares to look into the mirror; they are starting to see their own mistakes and weaknesses realistically. They even venture to open up the repressed fears and pain stored in their subconscious mind. Therefore, Courage is the first Life-supporting vibration level, as it is here that we begin to have a realistic self-knowledge and a realistic worldview. It is important to remember that all People at a Life-destroying psychic vibration level are convinced that they have good self-knowledge. It is only at higher levels of spiritual vibration that we begin to doubt this. Here we begin to walk on the path where we no longer run away from ourselves, but rather accept ourselves as we are. Here too we begin to present ourselves to the world with all our bad and good qualities, and in the face of our deep pain we begin to get rid of those spiritual dragons that have attracted so much evil into our lives. It is tremendous that at this level of vibration, the individual finally takes full responsibility for their actions and does not always excuse themselves by blaming others. Compared to losers, this is also one of the basic characteristics of successful People. At this level of vibration, the unfortunate Person can become successful, the unsuccessful can become successful, the selfish Person begins to open up to altruism, and we begin to dare to give love without expecting reciprocity. Of course, at this vibration level these are not yet routine, but they already appear in our Life and begin to have a positive effect. As a result of all this, the soul overcomes some of its spiritual dragons and the soul turns in a freer, happier direction. Here, too, we sometimes have spiritual energy left over for things that build our souls, and we will increasingly have a need to listen to others unselfishly. At this time, we begin to step out of the suffering world of daily life support and struggle and take actions in the direction of our real Life tasks. Of course, I'm not talking about mean whether you can buy a better car, although it's a fact that success can also manifest itself in our material Life starting to become stable. For me, until reaching this mental vibration level, my financial situation had always been very volatile.

Of course, if a Person has recently passed to this level from a lower level of spiritual vibration through their spiritual development, they are only at the gate of happiness. In order to enter and stay there permanently, you have to work hard at the difficulties that confront you in facing yourself. Getting rid of your inner fears and pains is very hard work and usually takes a lot of time. Thus, at this level of vibration, People who want to develop tend to stay for quite a long time.

Anyone who falls back to here from a higher level of spiritual vibration descends here precisely because their soul needs to gather courage to struggle with new—probably subconscious—psychological problems in order to jump above the level of vibration they were on before their fall.

The main emotion of a Person at the level of Courage is affirmation, which encourages and strengthens them to behave in this way with others. The main purpose of such a Person is to be able to achieve their goals. They put their development at the service of achieving these skills. If they succeed in this, they will jump to a higher level of spiritual vibration for an understandable reason. Such a Person actively strives to achieve their desires, but does so without also harming, negatively representing, exploiting or deceiving others. Among other things, this is where it is fundamentally different from the Person who lives in a vibration level of Pride or even lower. If the individual is a believer, then at this level of vibration they see God as a forgiving being, from whom love flows to those who sometimes make mistakes and sometimes are weak. Therefore, these People can no longer be influenced by demagogues or the intimidating tactics of churches and sects.

Impartiality (value 250)

If we move up in our spiritual development, we reach a level of Impartiality at 250. At this level, the individual has already entered the gates of abundance and things are stabilizing in their Life. The main motive of their Life will be to experience positive events. People living at this level of vibration usually reach their success without too much trouble, and more importantly, there is no harm to others or excessive self-assertion. People who live on a level of Pride are often successful, but exploiting, belittling or otherwise undermining others is always part of their own success. But at this level of vibration, it doesn't even come up anymore.

From lower vibration levels, we used to admire these Humans and wonder how they did it. In the past, I didn't understand how someone could get ahead from one step to the next with so little struggle and torture. At lower levels of vibration, Life is about everyday struggles, but at this level of vibration the positive and peaceful experience of Life begins to be powerful. At this level, the struggle is important, but the tension caused by problems is already minor.

The level of Impartiality is the first of the vibration levels where we are already relatively satisfied with our Life and ourselves, without any self-assessment. After all, the same thing happens at the spiritual vibratory level of Pride, but through self-deception. This is a very big word, because so far we have not discussed any vibration level where this would have been true. When I arrived at this level, suddenly my view about the world and the future as well as my attitude towards People changed, and I started to feel a very deep and reassuring peace and harmony inside. Before, this kind of spiritual security was completely unfamiliar to me. My vision also shifted from pessimistic to optimistic. I wish everyone could live at least on this level! If that were the case, then there would surely be world peace, and the pollution of the environment would fall to a very low level.

If they are a theist, a Person who lives on the vibration level of Impartiality experiences God as a being who gave him their unique abilities in order to use them for the benefit of others. At this level of vibration, I realized that I was born a teacher and that this is the ability that I was privileged to receive from Life. Since I know this with absolute certainty, I have been teaching my classes at the university with even greater empathy and conscientiousness, and this has inspired me to write this and my previous book.

At this level of vibration, the main development process of our soul is recovery. Here we part with our spiritual dragons—the addictions that have pulled us down so far. This process is not yet complete however, as there is still room for improvement, but many habits, games and addictions that pull us towards a lower vibration level (more on these later) will be permanently removed from our lives. This causes a level of uptake that suddenly releases a lot of energy in us. Up to this level, we were constantly struggling with our internal problems, which consciously or unconsciously took a lot of our energy, and we were also struggling with the consequences of our instinctive bad decisions. Here, our liberated soul suddenly becomes lighter and strives towards the main directions according to our Life task. At last, the energies are devoted to life-supporting and selfless actions. Writing this book is also Life-supporting and selfless, but it is very pleasing because all this positive energy wants to break out of me and make the world a better place.

The great breakthrough at this level is even reflected in the fact that it is here that complete trust becomes an integral part of Life. A CEO at the level of Pride doesn't trust any of their employees and wants to keep them under control. A leader at the level of Impartiality believes in the success of self-dependence and thus achieves greater success. After all, the basis for managing a high level of teamwork is to trust the decisions of one's teammates. Of course, this success is not measured in profit, but in the social usefulness of the team or in the spiritual and professional development of its members. In this vibratory Human relationship, one is not jealous and can fully trust the decisions of their partner. It's important to point out that you just leave something to your partner or completely trust their decisions, it's far from the same. At this level of vibration, the individual begins to trust in the goodness of Humans and in a positive future. This is also a novelty, because neither strong confidence in the future nor a belief in Human goodness were characteristic of the vibration levels discussed so far.

Those who look at such a Person from a lower vibration level often see them as naive or idealistic, since they consider it impossible from their vibration level that such optimism can be objective and grounded. But it can! It's a wonderful level of mental vibration. Unfortunately, most of the people living today will never get there in their lifetime. Why? The answer is quite simple. It's because most People spend their Life not within their spiritual selves, but with externalities. Pursuing money, a career, or a better outward appearance isn't a bad thing, but it certainly doesn't lead to happiness. Impartiality is really the spiritual vibration level of a Person who has entered the island of happiness. Since being at this level for many years, I know how good this is, and I really, really want you to experience this if you have not been here permanently, because beyond your own happiness, this is the most you can do for the future of the Earth!

Willingness (value 310)

I am very glad that you have come this far with me in reading the chapter on the vibration levels of the soul. The level of spiritual vibration that follows in this article and those that follow it are all real scenes of happiness. At these levels, there will only be differences in the way of living and stability of happiness. The vibration level of Willingness is operating at an energy level of 310, so we are well above the limit of 200. At the time of writing this book, it has been less than four years since I passed this level and my life has reached an even better quality of Life. A Person at the vibration level of Willingness mainly deviates from the vibration levels discussed so far in that they are fundamentally optimistic. Such a Person is already very difficult to dislodge from their positive perspective. Here it becomes instinctive to look at the glass as being half full, and if something bad happens, we usually draw a positive conclusion from it. A Person here carries within them a "good time," which means that regardless of the events of the outside world, there is a basic optimism about their Life. Of course, this does not mean that one cannot be moody or nervous at this level of vibration, but it does mean that it happens rarely and only for a short time.

At this level, the individual has already expressed an intention to develop further in the spiritual world. Here, we already want to consciously break with our inner spiritual processes that cause all kinds of negative vibrations. It becomes clear to us that the abundance comes from within and is almost completely independent of external influences. Here we understand what the spiritual leaders who keep telling us this are talking about. Almost all my Life, I have been eating up accolades from other People because I have tried to bury the self-doubt and lack of self-acceptance suppressed in my soul. Unfortunately, this was not successful. Although a lot of appreciation embedded in the ego can bring a sense of complacency, this unfortunately does not bring happiness because it is based on self-deception. Inwardly, we do not accept ourselves; we only believe that we are valuable through the feedback of others. When my soul changed internally, that is, self-acceptance and self-love developed, my external worldview immediately turned into a positive one, as external reinforcements were no longer needed. Thus, this is a real solution on the way to happiness. This book is all about how you can bring about this inner change! There is nothing more you can do than incorporate into your life what this book has to offer you. I have already made this journey and poured all my selfless energy into this book so that you can do the same with much less energy and time investment. After all, with a map in our hands, it is much easier to reach your destination.

At this level of vibration, our vision is hopeful and optimistic. Here, it is always the search for solutions and trust in Life (or God, in the case of believers) that characterizes an individual's vision of the future. Given that the individual is a believer in God, at this level of vibration he experiences God as an inspiring being who motivates him to use his talents to change the world in a positive way.

If someone comes here from a higher level of vibration, the intention to do so will give them the strength to rise to a higher level again. In my internal work at this vibrational level, I was working on resolving such deep psychological repressions and problems whose presence I had no idea about before. This is how spiritual development works: when we reveal a layer and solve the spiritual problems that arise from it, new layers appear that were hidden until then. Of course, this is true at all levels of spiritual development. However, the experience of finding more and more solutions after 18 years of conscious spiritual development is overwhelming. This shows the infinite diversity of the Human soul; the more you experience, the more doors will open for you. You don't have to work all your life to achieve happiness, but spiritual growth is a lifelong task.

When someone comes here from a lower vibration, they experience a new dimension of self-reception that brings an inner balance to their Life. At this level, a person feels and understands why inner peace is the basis of happiness—not the pursuit of positive experiences. Balance is what matters here, not constant experience-seeking.

When a spiritual leader writes or talks about how it's not good, for example, to fall madly in love or consciously run away from all evil and instead devour only good experiences, most People will not understand this. In fact, their reaction can be hostile because everyone wants to fall madly in love, and everyone wants to have only good experiences. But at this level of vibration, a Person understands this message. Here the soul finds a balance that results in a wonderful inner peace. If the soul gets out of this balance, either positively or negatively, the soul wants to get back to this level. This is like the difference between turbulent and smooth water flow. The lower the level of mental vibration a Person lives at, the more volatile and turbulent their spiritual processes can be. At the lower vibration levels, there are high emotional extremes; positive waves are followed by deep negative waves. But here at the Willingness vibration level, the soul more and more often resembles smooth water that can easily fluctuate due to external influences. However, the surface is quickly tamed into mirror-smooth water, because the soul is already instinctively gravitating to this state. To a Person at a lower level of spiritual vibration, this may seem boring or monotonous. They do not see peace and harmony in this, but rather uneventfulness. They need to love passionately and then suffer deeply. They need active water. This is natural, because it is precisely these sufferings that will carry them forward in their spiritual development. Their soul resembles mirror-smooth water only for short periods of time—only when they are so mentally tired that they do not have the strength to change. However, this is the psychological vibration level of Apathy, which is not Life-supportive and therefore not happy.

One of the biggest mistakes of today's Western society is that, above all, we try to distance ourselves from the negative things and almost devour all the good things that Life can give. Meanwhile, we forget about our spiritual development, and the result is often that suffering comes into our Life very intensely and very persistently. Why? Because after a sustained positive wave, an even more sustained negative wave will come. The soul is also an energy system, so the basic laws of physics work here as well, but I would like to write about this in my next book.

By now, you have gained practice observing your own thoughts, feelings, and actions. This is a very important skill that is essential for spiritual development. Now I ask you to observe yourself again for a few days. Think about how many times and for how long you feel opposition or pride. Notice how many thoughts and feelings you have connected to these levels of spiritual vibration, either towards yourself or towards the world. Don't go any further until you've mapped this out for yourself. You can find a table in Annex 1. Write down the total number of hours your soul, body, or mind spends at these levels on an average day. Be honest with yourself. Do not embellish reality, because you would only be delaying and making it difficult to achieve your happiness! The following pages will tell you exactly why this is the case.

Anger, hatred, and indignation are associated with the level of psychological vibration of Opposition. At the same time, do not confuse the above with the objective self-defense mechanism, which is a sign of a Life-supporting psychic vibration level. The latter is characterized by unemotional self-control. The psychological resonance of Pride includes egoism, selfishness, snobbishness, prudishness, hedonism. It should not be confused with standing up for your interests based on objective facts.

Courage should not be confused with recklessness. Blindness is a symptom of Life-destroying vibration levels. The reckless Person may seem brave for many reasons (they are cornered and therefore fight back or ignore the possible consequences, etc.). A Person at the level of Courage is thus not necessarily known by the extent to which they dare to stand up to their enemies. On the contrary, someone who is at the level of Courage dares to admit their weaknesses and mistakes in front of others.

Acceptance (value 350)

The spiritual vibration of Acceptance is a truly wonderful and happy world. I have come so far from the levels of Shame and Guilt in 18 years, experiencing several strong waves of relapse. This book is written to make this journey a lot shorter for you! This means that you don't have to make unnecessary deviations on your way to development; you can follow a beaten path.

The vibration level of Acceptance exerts its effects at a value of 350. This is far within the Life Supporting range. Since the increase in vibration levels is not linear (but logarithmic), this is such a high level of mental vibration that it can neutralize the negative energy of up to 10,000 Life-destroying People. That's why if you sit in on a lecture where a Person at the vibration level of Acceptance performs, you are so captivated by the lecture that you almost don't notice the time passing, and strangely enough the inner tension and irritation you brought with you into the lecture hall slowly dissipate. This is how seriously the interaction of mental vibration levels works.

It is at this level of vibration that the individual first comes to accept themselves as they are. This is not due to self-suggestion or resignation. By self-suggestion, I mean a conversation where we explain to ourselves that we are good as we are. By resignation, I mean when an individual feels unable to change and therefore becomes uninterested in himself. At this level of vibration, self-acceptance is an honest feeling from within. It's not that we become conceited, because we actually see our positive and negative qualities realistically. Rather, here we already love our positive values, but at the same time we accept our negative characteristics. I have been running away from myself almost all my life. Having made it here is a miracle; I never thought it was possible. Self-acceptance brings inner peace and harmony. It was as if my soul had finally come home. Here we begin to find our true selves, and at this level we are already living according to our Life task. Of course, accepting our negative qualities internally does not mean that we do not want to be better or change them. Here, too, we want to improve our self-esteem, but we no longer tear ourselves up for the evil that lives in us. Here, the internal frustrations are gone.

Self-acceptance brings acceptance of our environment. If our vibration level changes inside, then our vision also changes. We will be tolerant of the People around us and accept the world as it is. Of course, this doesn't mean that we don't want to improve our environment. Rather, it means that the energies released from the absence of unnecessary resistance can actually be used to change the world positively. Many people ask me, "How do you have the energy for this book with so much to do?" The answer is simple: the energies I used to devote to struggling with myself and the world have all been released. I used to suffer from a lack of spirit almost all the time. These days I feel it about once or twice a year, for a few hours at most. At lower levels of spiritual vibration, an incredible amount of spiritual strength is burned by our inner struggles. However, at this vibration level, harmony is the philosophy of life that permeates our way of life, so these internal struggles are eliminated.

At this level of spiritual vibration, in addition to acceptance, the main emotion is forgiveness. We forgive ourselves for the sins and bad deeds of our life so far, and we do our best to make them right in the future. It is at this level of vibration that we truly realize how much we have done wrong in our Lifetime so far. At the vibration level of Pride (or any other Life-destroying level), we don't even notice how much harm we do, or if we do, our ego idealizes the correctness of our actions. We destroy our environment unconsciously, all the while being convinced of our personal truth. At the vibratory level of Acceptance, we are already able to feel and see with full honesty how many bad things we have done and are doing. Here, we fully accept the consequences of our actions and do everything we can to make amends.

Forgiveness also works externally, of course. We may not be really angry at those who sin against us in the first place, but if we are, it will last only a short time, because we understand exactly what deep spiritual dragons the other is fighting, and therefore they do what they do unconsciously. We even help them If the individual allows it, but unfortunately in the case of the one who sins against us, they exist at the spiritual vibratory level of resistance, so they do not accept the helping hand, and most of the time they are not even able to understand the situation. They imagine behind-the-scenes intentions because they cannot believe that unselfish help can come from an "enemy". This is incomprehensible to them. In any case, it is at this level that Jesus' words first gain real meaning: "as we forgive those who sin against us." At the level of Acceptance, our soul begins to become transcendent. Here, the narrow-mindedness of rationality and the boundaries of rationality are already clearly outlined. As an engineer, researcher and university lecturer, I have great respect for rationality. But today, I can see for sure that the world of rationality is a very narrow one. Even if we can't describe something with mathematical-physical relationships, it can still exist. In fact, by transforming this line of thinking, we know only a very, very small fraction of the existing things so well that we can describe them with mathematical-physical correlations. Think of Love or its counterpart: fear. Surprised? Hatred is not the opposite of Love, however strange this may seem at first. Every Person knows that these exist, yet they cannot be grasped rationally.

If one is a believer in God, then at this level of vibration they see God as a righteous being who forgives our sins and supports us in making amends for them. Life support is reflected here in the fact that we actively work every day to make up for every bad thing we have done in our lives so far. Since our inner tensions are replaced by harmony, we have the free capacity and the spirit to act. If 20% of Humans reached this level of vibration, there would be world peace and environmental pollution would be reduced to such an extent that the destruction of Nature would stop and our planet would begin to regenerate globally. Since I've been down this road, I know it's possible! You too can embark on this journey.

By now, you are beginning to have practice in qualifying your thoughts, feelings, and actions from the point of view of spiritual vibrations. This is a very important self-awareness exercise. Now I ask you to observe yourself again for a few days. Think about how many times and for how long you feel emotions, actions or thoughts related to the vibration levels of Courage, Impartiality, Willingness or Acceptance. Until you have carefully observed this in yourself, do not proceed further. You can find a table in **Annex 1.** Write down the total number of hours your soul, body, or mind spends at these levels on an average day. Be honest with yourself. Do not embellish reality, because you are only delaying and making it difficult to achieve your happiness! It's no coincidence that complete honesty with oneself begins at the level of spiritual vibration of Courage, so you are raising your spiritual vibration by being honest with yourself!

Reasonableness (value 400)

I have a close friend who has lived at this vibration for a long time. I've always admired him for it. This vibration level is characterized by a value of 400 and indicates a very high Life-supporting level. Einstein and Newton also lived on this vibration level. If this level is paired with a high IQ, it will bring very high scientific performance. My good friend also pursues what he does on a serious level, even if not at the quality of the aforementioned scientist celebrities. The highest level of our profession belongs to this vibration level. However, this is not the level of a workaholic Human, as the latter feeds on deep Life-destroying energies.

It is at this level of the soul that a Person enters the world of actual objectivity. But it is important to emphasize that this statement is true only within the range of traditional sensory perception and logical relationships. Many people imagine that they live at this level of vibration, even though about one in a million People gets here. This is because most People are convinced of their own objectivity, even though 99.99% of People are far from objective. The individual's perception is distorted by their narrowed vision and emotions at lower vibration levels. In most cases, this happens unconsciously. At these levels of vibration, Humans are more rationalizers than rationalists. This means that an emotional or experiential decision has long been made at the subconscious level, which the individual subsequently supports with rational thoughts. Meanwhile, on the surface, they think they have made that decision rationally. This is also used in professionally prepared advertisements that affect our emotions. In most cases, these advertisements are more effective the lower the vibration level of the target audience. For example, I was always proud to distance myself as much as possible from advertisements so they would not affect me—which was completely false "objectivity" at the time. After all, I distanced myself from them precisely because they affected me very strongly, and this bothered me. This example shows us how we rationalize things, which we then think of as objective in total hubris and are convinced of our rightness. The level of Courage is where we begin to dare to see through this tendency.

At the vibration level of Reasonableness, the individual is able to evaluate and analyze the information received by their perception completely objectively, regardless of their emotions. They are able to do this because they can distance themselves from the problems, worries and everything else that is not related to the given perception. Thus, at this vibration level, the consequences of the individual are free from distorting effects. According to the individual's view, the law of cause and effect influences and directs the evolution of the Universe. This often makes such a Person insensitive. Since we are at a high Life-supportive level, they use their free energy and the fruit of their conclusions to improve their environment, so this is not true. Einstein was also infinitely an idealist and humanist. He used his incredible energies to steer Humankind in the right direction. When I was younger I read a collection of his writings from outside the science of physics (*Gerner–Nagy–Szécsi, 2008*). He radiated the idealism and the desire to turn the developmental tendencies of Humanity in a better direction. If Humanity had listened to him more, we would not have been here for such a long time. But at that time, the world was held captive by wars and overheated nationalism. With all that negative energy, Einstein didn't stand a chance. In today's world, these negative energies have been reduced and global communication systems are helping to give space to good thoughts, so the opportunities to make the world better today are much better than they were then. It would be nice if Einstein could be here with us right now! In any case, the global awakening has begun and since you are holding this book in your hands, you are one of those who are awakening.

The main emotion at this level is understanding. Since we can turn this vibration away from our own problems and viewpoints, we are able to fully understand others. Therefore, the keyword is "understanding". After all, if we objectively look at our internal problems—or at least some of them—it opens a door to change. That is one of the aims of this book: to help you take a higher and more objective view of yourself and bring this knowledge into your Life. Similarly, it follows that People living at this level of vibration are also able to explore processes in the world that seem incomprehensible to others. Most Nobel Prize-winning researchers, inventors, famous thinkers and philosophers live at this vibration level. The Concept of Life of such People is the significance they feel that they have been given their abilities to give the right direction to society with significant results and examples. If the Person living at this level of vibration is a believer in God, then they imagine God as an infinitely wise being who directs the fate of the world with correct and objective decisions.

For a long time, I was of the opinion that there is no perfect objectivity, since every Person understands this world through their own distorted filter. Today, I know that perfect objectivity exists, but very few Humans have the opportunity to experience it. People at this level of spiritual vibration are so fortunate that they can experience it on an everyday level, but they can only experience it in those areas in which they acquire appropriate skills, knowledge and insight.

Love (value 500)

At this level of vibration, a Person understands that their unselfish Love permeates everything and is the supreme force of the Universe. The law of cause and effect, which is strengthened on the spiritual vibratory level of reason, is permeated by the all-pervading power of love. This understanding takes place in the individual in such a way that they feel the presence of love or the desire for love everywhere and in everything with full experience. Here, the individual no longer needs a partner or companion in order to experience Love, as they feel this feeling towards all living things. Whoever reaches this level can feel the "Love radiation" of the entire Universe. You don't need to receive Love feedback from some individuals in order to feel like you are lovable. For example, Mother Teresa lived at this vibration level. Such People radiate a level of Love that transcends their environment, and wonderful feelings are also induced in those near them. The whole person is imbued with the harmony that you instinctively feel when you get close to them. Increasingly, they feel a sense of oneness with all living things. Because of this, such a Person cannot harm even a fly. They respect and love all living things infinitely. When I reached this level of mental vibration, my heart expanded tremendously and a constant pleasant tingling tension appeared in my chest. My love really extended to all living and non-living things, and thus the law of cause and effect became in itself a "dry" system of reality. After all, the poles of Love and the desire for Love are integrated into the law of cause and effect, thus making a more colorful and broader view of the Universe non-general.

This is really the level of the uppermost spiritual leaders. The value of the vibration level is 500. Very few get there in their lifetime. I know a lady who I am convinced lives at this level of vibration. From the hospital, she takes in children born with severe disabilities who are abandoned by their parents immediately after their birth. These children are on the verge of death because the pain of their abandonment alone is enough not to mention their disabilities for which doctors use the term "incurable". She raises self-sufficient, happy adults from these tiny, near-death babies with the power of selfless Love. She heals them with the power of Love, while according to the current state of medical knowledge, this is impossible. She is infinitely peaceful, harmonious, patient and unselfish. In the past, I didn't understand how someone could be like this and how she gets so much spiritual energy. After all, she raises 10–12 children at the same time alone, only with donations, at the age of 65. Today, I can feel the emotional world of her existence, as well as the fact that she gains so much energy. The more selfless Love we radiate to the world, the more energy it radiates back to us.

Although the average Person is still far from this, when they will be at this level in the distant future, Humankind will live in complete world peace and in perfect harmony with Nature. There will be no selfishness, aggression or environmental destruction.

At this level of vibration, the main emotion is devotion, which the individual feels towards the nature of Life (or God, the Almighty, etc. according to their religion). The individual is infinitely benevolent and tries to reveal this wherever they can find understanding ears. At this vibration level, the famous words of Jesus are understood: "If someone throws a stone at you, throw bread back". Here, a Person sees perfectly that if he hurts someone else, then he actually has the biggest problem with himself and his desire for Love causes all the problems. Instead of confrontation, the only solution is Love, with which the poor sufferer can be turned in the direction of healing. At this level of spiritual vibration, fear completely ceases to exist in the soul of the individual. With the end of fear, we enter the world of the room-ego, about which I will write in detail later in this book.

If they are a believer in God, a person living at this level of vibration experiences God as an infinitely compassionate being.

The spiritual vibration level of such a Person is already so high that they alone can counterbalance the negative spiritual vibration level of hundreds of thousands of People. This is why we like to be in the environment of such People, because we are then also more elevated and more harmonious. This is also why such People quickly gather followers who take their fame far if they are open to it. Although modesty is an essential typical feature at this level, I am convinced that many Humans in society live at this level of vibration in seclusion, without being aware of the power they radiate and with which they drastically slow down the destruction of the Earth. They do this by healing Humanity, raising the average level of spiritual vibration, thereby indirectly doing a lot for the Earth. Of course, many of these people do all this selflessly and unconsciously, as they are not aware of the scientific discoveries of kinesiology described here.

Joy and Peace (values 550 and 600)

I will describe the vibration levels of Joy (value 540) and Peace (value 600) in this single subchapter. Obviously, we have all felt these feelings before, and all People with realistic values like to be in this state of mind. However, there are also levels of peace and joy. It often happens that we feel peaceful when we shake our feet, though a simple online test reveals that we are actually slightly irritated. This is because our brain compares us to ourselves. When we feel peaceful or joyful, we feel this way in comparison to our usual irritation, but most of us don't even know what total inner peace is because we've never been there. This should be imagined in the same way as the vibration level of Love discussed in the previous section. Obviously, most Humans have felt pure Love, but very few people have felt a comprehensive and completely unselfish Love for all that exists, especially constantly, like those who live on the spiritual vibratory level of Love.

The proportion of those living in the vibratory levels of Joy and Peace is even lower than those living on the vibratory level of Love. The higher the vibration level we are discussing, the fewer Humans we are talking about. Those who live on these two levels of vibration are one single individual out of tens of millions of Humans. I regularly listen to Gunagriha's lectures on the Internet, and I was connected to Gyöngyi Spitzer (Soma Mamagésa) with a pure heart. I consider them my masters. I am convinced that they live at least at this level of spiritual vibration. Humans living on the vibrational level of Joy experience a sense of wholeness in oneself, which means they love themselves fully. This should not be confused with arrogance. At the same time, the inner spiritual attitude emanates here as well. After all, such a Person lives the Life at its fullest. When I reach this state of spiritual vibration, the present moment is perfect as it is. I feel infinite gratitude for the infinite Love that comes with humility and altruism. The overflow of these emotions raises you to a state of inner joy that is independent of the state of the external environment. It is a state of inner serenity, which, from its point of view, there is no sense in trying to separate good and evil. Everything is fine in the Universe as it happens.

The vibration level of Peace is a leap even compared to this, as there the individual experiences the miracle of the perfection of Life outside and inside. Humans living at these vibrational levels are able to neutralize the negative energy of hundreds of thousands of Humans living at Life-destroying vibrational levels. If such a Person lives in a city, its citizens are more peaceful without realizing that it's because such a person lives nearby. There will be fewer accidents and fewer crimes in that city.

A Person who lives on the vibrational level of Joy is imbued with a sense of serenity. There is always a smile on the face of such spiritual leaders, which is not a learned armor like with many ordinary individuals, but is actually a projection of the constant joy that lives in them. If such a person looks into your eyes, you will feel a high level of peace and harmony, your spine will tingle, and then you will be under the influence of that moment for hours.

Living on the vibrational level of Peace, a Person lives in a feeling of bliss. He experiences himself and the world as blessed, and in this spiritual security, the strong foundation of his soul is the immense peace. This is why there is no more nervousness, no more stress, no more fear or other forms of psychological pain at these levels. In terms of their perception of Life, these People are characterized by infinite benevolence and experiencing the fullness of Life. If there are believers in God at this vibration level, then a Person living at the vibration level of Joy experiences a feeling of unity with God, while a Person living at the level of Peace perceives God as existing in everything. The individual will merge into the divine will; these two can no longer be separated. These People are already transcending ordinary religious practice, living in a world of pure spirituality, which is the basis and root of every religion. They no longer study religion, but often transform it. At the same time, they live in seclusion in many cases, because their] consciousness of God does not allow traditional everyday life. They put everything they do at the service of Life, and so they do a lot to save Humanity and Life on Earth. However, they are infinitely modest, so in most cases we don't even know about their ability. Many of the People living on the vibrational level of Peace were canonized in the past and were the founders of new religious tendencies.

Perception at this level is like seeing the world in slow motion in some incredibly illuminated context where everything that happens makes sense. Consciousness no longer tries to form a concept for everything here. Here, the mind is always silent, the perceiver becomes one with the perceived, which means that there is no significance to being absent. At this vibration level, it already makes sense and "everything being connected with everything" is part of daily perception. The Individual lives in the state of perfect presence that meditation practitioners are constantly looking for and sometimes find for minutes or hours.

These levels of vibration are also a world of miracles. People living at this level of vibration are already able to do things that ordinary Human beings cannot rationally comprehend. Therefore, some experience miracles, while skeptics are constantly looking for a rational explanation to prove that the miracle they see is the result of fraud or quackery. However, at this level, there are already outstanding personalities among spiritual leaders, and there are also true spiritual healers who can heal even with the laying on of hands. They can mobilize high-level spiritual energies that are beyond the laws of physics as we know them today.

It is also common for people who have had near-death experiences to jump to this high level when they return to the living. Most people are skeptical of them too, because one of the cornerstones of Human narrowness is that we do not believe in what we have not yet experienced. We are told that it does not exist, hence our often-felt instinctive inner resistance to the revelations of such Humans. During my life I used to say that certain things were impossible; I have since learned that this is one of our greatest follies. Of course, in most People this is also unconscious and instinctive, as they see their own experiences as an inner anchor and feel that if they let this go, their uncertainty will only increase. The reality is that it will be the other way around. When I temporarily enter this state of Peace, the joy, love, gratitude and humility in me are transformed into a thoughtless silence that just watches and has no resistance to the present moment. Inner silence is nothing but infinite order. The culmination of this state is the complete cessation of the ego, which dissolves in a state of infinite silence, order and peace. When this arrives and becomes stable, there is a chance for a breakthrough in enlightenment, which can only be broken by external influence, since there is no independent desire or will to control anything here. This is exactly the state you need to reach the gate of expansion.

Enlightenment (value 700–1000)

We have reached the highest stage of Human existence: the spiritual vibration of Enlightenment, which is between 700 and 1000.

At this level of vibration, everything becomes perfect. Consciousness sees Life and the world that surrounds it as a shining miracle. In fact, there is no ego, no mind, no soul, and no body here anymore. The Universe is bathed in the light of consciousness. The soul at this level is perfectly pure, so it fades away; the consciousness does not attach a thought, an emotion, or a sign to anything. The individual lives in a sense of pure being, but the individual is no longer separate, as this loses its meaning in the egoic state. You just exist as part of a perfect system called Life, in which you are one. It's such an uplifting and perfect feeling that it's very hard to find a word for it. Peace, joy, selfless Love and the harmony of humility almost overflows and rises into something completely new. I was only here for a short time while this book was being written, and I do not know if I will have the infinite honor of experiencing it again in my life. When I temporarily crossed the gate of Enlightenment, suddenly a lot of people started to gather around me without me asking them to do so. The light of consciousness draws upon the subconscious of Humans. That's why the enlightened have many followers.

An incredibly rare state, only one in hundreds of millions or even billions of Humans are permanently at this level. At this level of vibration, existence itself becomes the meaning of Life. Existence itself is the goal, although this is not an accurate sentence either, because in fact there really are no goals. Realization itself is perfect as it is. Here, you no longer need anything that ordinary People desire because existence itself is also perfect as it is. The perception of time is lost, but time has no meaning here. From this point of view, everything that has happened in the Universe so far and everything that will happen is perfect. Good and bad are meaningless concepts, as this distinction can only be understood from the point of view of the ego. The world is perfect.

People who live on the vibratory level of Enlightenment are constantly in this world of feeling. Nothing can "drag" them out of there. Here, the self is already part of the great unity. It is no coincidence that Jesus did not resist being crucified. Those living at lower vibration levels can get into a state of Enlightenment for minutes, usually when everything around them is perfect and they can get into a properly deepened meditative state. Meditators are looking for this or researching it throughout their lives, often without results. On the other hand, even the crucifixion of a Person living at this level of vibration cannot pull him out of this state. This is the huge difference between being enlightened and experiencing it for a short time. There is such a "distance" between an ordinary Person and an enlightened one that ordinary consciousness is almost incapable of comprehending it. Humans who have lived permanently at this level of vibration in the past have had a tremendous impact on the world. The spiritual vibration level of such a Person can compensate for the Life-Destroying vibration level of millions of People. At this level of vibration, miracles become commonplace, as here the soul is at an energy level that enables the individual to do things that seem logically impossible. When I experienced this state, I was a possessor of unearthly energies—energies that the ordinary rational mind cannot even imagine. Lacking practice and having no instructions from anyone, I could not control these energies, so they did incredible and random things to my body. But this experience was good for me to feel; whoever can control these energies can control matter, space and time. It is no coincidence that there are descriptions of masters who existed without food or water for months, or who could just put their hands inside a granite block. It was at this level of vibration that the founders of the great world religions and the world-changing sages such as Jesus, Buddha, Krishna, Lao Tzu and for a short time Mohammed lived in the past. They are the ones whose words will endure as long as the world exists and will affect Humanity. They are the ones about whom many miracles are recorded. Huge world religions were built on their words, although it is true that those living at a lower level of spiritual vibration distorted and destroyed these revelations with their interpretations and additions. Therefore, the church can never remain as pure as the root from which it developed. The complete purity of the churches could only be preserved if they were constantly led by a spiritual leader who lived at the spiritual vibratory level of revival. Unfortunately, this has not yet been given to Humanity. While it is true that the enlightened usually only exist, they do not proclaim themselves. They do not want to be at the heads of organizations. At most, People naturally start to follow them. If we look at it from this point of view, there will be no need for churches in the distant future. The church can be the "crutch" of the transitional development period; if it can preserve it, it can regain its purity.

Now that you can see the evolutionary stages of spiritual vibration levels, it has become clear which path our evolution will take. Today, I know that the purpose of Human evolution is to develop our spiritual consciousness by raising the level of spiritual vibration. It is the only way to lead Humanity into a world of global peace and harmony with Nature. Otherwise, we will be extinct; it is only a matter of time. At the same time, it is the only path that leads to increased personal happiness. As we live more consciously from generation to generation, the average person will gradually rise to higher levels of spiritual vibration and more and more enlightened People will appear on Earth. Meanwhile, the average spiritual vibration of Humanity is elevating to a higher level and environmental pollution will decrease, world peace and the average happiness of the individual will increase. If you think about it, a part of this process has been taking place from prehistoric times to the present. I wrote about this in detail in my previous book, which is about climate change and the human soul (*Dittrich, 2021*). As I confirmed in my book, the higher the spiritual vibration, the smaller the ecological footprint of a Human, but they do so from an inner impulse. In addition, their impact on others is becoming more loving and peaceful, with every action it takes to move our society towards world peace. I invite you to join with the People who are on this path whenever the opportunity arises. And you're holding the method in your hands.

In order to provide a quick overview of the mental vibration levels, I have prepared a table for you in Annex 2. This lists the emotions and synonyms belonging to each spiritual vibration level. If you are uncertain about the emotional vibration level of a feeling or action, you will be able to identify it quickly based on the table. Thus, this chart will help you quickly and objectively incorporate a system of spiritual vibrations into your Life.

1.3. The group dynamics of psychic vibration levels, or how do energy vampires work?

A spiritual vibration level is a special type of vibration that can be perceived outside the body. As it moves away from the body its strength decreases, but how far it moves depends on the individual and the other Humans around them. This system of vibrations works like any other energy system in the Universe: it strives for balance. Think about it: sooner or later a fire will go out, the wind will calm down, and all the water will flow towards the sea. Each of these is a Natural manifestation of the striving for equilibrium. To understand how the soul's vibrational energy system works, first we should take a look at simple example. Imagine that there are only two of you in in a square—no one else. Your mental vibration level is 270, while that of your friend is 30. You talk in the square. What will be the consequence? The spiritual vibration levels of you two Humans unconsciously and+ uncontrollably affect each other, and the energy system thus formed strives for balance. That is, at the beginning of the conversation, your spiritual energy level begins to fall while theirs begins to rise. If the relationship function were linear, your mental vibration level would decrease to (270 + 30) / 2 = 150, while theirs would increase to this level. (The relational function is actually logarithmic, but I don't want to scare anyone). Thus, let's just say that the equilibrium is set at approximately 150 (in reality it is much higher than this). This is not done consciously; it's a naturally operating circumstance in the event that neither of the two People influences it. They only feel the following: the person who starts with a mental vibration level of 30, who is tormented by guilt and barely lives, more and more enthusiastically enters the conversation and comes away feeling more energetic. After all, their spiritual energy level begins to rise in response to your influence. Your spiritual energy level, on the other hand, starts to decrease, and when your level drops below 200, you first become more restless and then distant, since you are already on the spiritual vibration level of Pride. Then, when you reach the level of psychological vibration of Anger at the same time (equilibrium situation of 150), a quarrel between the two parties erupts and both of you leave the square. Your friend will fall back to the spiritual vibration of Guilt, and there will be even greater guilt for causing a quarrel. He blames himself and hates himself for it. Thus, he sinks even deeper into his present state and realizes how bad this world is. Thus, his negative image of the world also gains reinforcement.

You, stepping out of the quarrel, are at first baffled by the situation: how could you quarrel so stupidly when you are basically a very peaceful Human? And you don't understand why you felt like you were drained of your Life force. Slowly, your peace of mind returns, and you vow that the next time you meet this Person you will try to ask them to forgive your behavior and try to clarify the problem with them. After all, you are at the spiritual vibratory level of Impartiality, which is already the level of a sufficiently realistic perception of Life.

Now you know how energy vampires work. They are not consciously draining your energy; it is a consequence of their low level of spiritual vibration. Because they feel better around a Person with a higher level of spiritual vibration, they like to meet those kinds of People. Conversely, those with low energy levels prefer to avoid them.

Imagine that the spiritual energy of all People affects those around them in this way, whether or not they're talking. For example, if two People start arguing on a noisy bus, and even though you don't understand what they're talking about or even know they're arguing, you start to feel tense. Your spiritual vibration level will begin to sink towards the vibration level of Anger.

Of course, there are more positive examples. It has happened to me several times that talking to someone made me feel more enthusiastic and balanced. It has also happened that every student in my lectures was captivated by what I had to say, and they almost didn't notice the passage of time. I once meditated with a Zen master and had the deepest meditation experience of my life, which is no coincidence, since his high spiritual vibration raised me to a level where I have rarely ever been. Therein lies the power of group meditation and community. Therefore, these can be elements of your spiritual development!

So, whether you are talking to the People around you or not, they are affecting your spiritual vibration and you are affecting theirs. The exciting thing is that people with extremely high and extremely low levels of psychic vibration can compensate for the psychic energy levels of many, many individuals. That is why Jesus, Buddha and Mother Teresa could positively affect so many People, and why Hitler and Stalin negatively affected masses of People. People at an extreme level of deep or high spiritual vibration can affect the spiritual energy of hundreds of thousands or millions of People. This is due to the logarithmic function relationship. For example, if you reach an approximate mental vibration level of 350, then you can neutralize the negative energy of approximately 10,000 individuals at the spiritual vibration level of Pride. That's why the example just now with your friend alone in the square was oversimplified; the equilibrium value would not actually be 150.

Now comes the most interesting part of it all: raising your spiritual vibration is the most you can do for your own happiness, for the protection of the climate, and for the peace and happiness of the world. This was the subject of my previous book, which presents the solution system of climate change and world peace based on mental vibration levels (*Dittrich, 2021*). However, this present book focuses exclusively on your personal spiritual development, although it feels good for all People to know that raising their own spiritual vibration is a serious benefit to the whole world. If you have a high level of mental vibration and live in an apartment block, the other residents won't know why they feel more peaceful when you get home. They may think it's because of the warmth of being home, while it's your spiritual energies from two floors down that are causing it. Thus, if your spiritual vibration level is high, wherever you go you will raise the average spiritual vibration level everywhere, and in doing so you will help your fellow Humans in a way that they're not even aware of. It's the same with your family; you will come home and bring peace and harmony with you. It's incredible what a wonderful impact this will have on your life and the lives of your loved ones. And you will do it all selflessly. Your family members don't need to know it's true—it will just happen every day. This is true self-improvement, which affects your environment like waves of pebbles thrown into smooth water. Everyone is connected to everyone! You can be the one to help steer the world in the right direction!

1.4. Which level of mental vibration is right? – Reality & Psychic Vibration Levels

How many times have you met a Person who told you his truth, his worldview, and you stood in front of them baffled because you thought something like, "How can they think they're right?!" Or you saw someone on TV and didn't understand how they could announce their strange opinion with such arrogance. Because you see things completely differently, you think differently and you are convinced that you are right.

For example, a selfish Person living on the spiritual vibratory level of Pride is baffled when someone is unselfish for no reason. For them, there is no such thing as complete altruism. They are convinced that everything is controlled by selfishness. If they do experience altruism, they look for some hypocritical underlying reason because they want to prove to themselves that their worldview is correct. If they can't find one, they believe the giver is simply too naive or stupid. I know this because I have experienced this level of spiritual vibration and have seen things the same way. Until I discovered that perfect altruism existed, I considered its existence impossible.

Most People cannot feel enough of the truth of others because they only live on one level of spiritual vibration all their lives, so the perspective of others is incomprehensible to them. However, if we understand and accept this system, we can be much more empathetic with others. You can understand why others, for example, are hostile in a situation that you accept completely peacefully. Or why someone you know feels guilty about something that is completely natural to you. I had the "good fortune" of experiencing everything from the deepest levels of spiritual vibration to the medium-high levels, and I could also experience very high levels of spiritual vibration for a short time. It was only afterwards that I became acquainted with the system of spiritual vibration levels, so I can say with certainty that the system is true and works. It is scientifically proven, so I don't really have to prove it here (*David R. Hawkins, 2004*).

If 100 different people go into a snow-white room one after the other, where there is only one table and a chair, soothing gentle music, a stable pleasant temperature, and there is a red rose on the table, all 100 People will perceive something different from this one-size-fits-all experience. The 100 People will come out of the room with 100 truths. There are many components and reasons for this, but let's see what the main ones are (*Beau Lotto, 2017*):

1. Everyone perceives only one field of view, as we do not see in 360°. Thus, the order and durability of the resulting image depends on who stands where in the room in what order and how they rotate their head. That is, everyone's perception of the room will be different, they will observe something else, some things less, and in a different order.
2. Everyone will pay different attention to their different senses. Someone will be more captivated by the beauty of the flower than, say, the sounds they hear or the smells they smell.
3. Everyone has a different "sharpness" to their individual senses. For example, a synesthete can distinguish many more shades of color than the average person and can see them more clearly. But every Person's heat sensation, visual acuity, auditory

acuity, and sense of smell are also different.
4. Each Person's brain processes less than 1% of the information delivered by their perception over a period of time, because that is "only" what they are capable of. The "gaps" between the information created in this way are filled on the basis of memories, and the unprocessed part of the sensed information is lost. Based on our memories, our brain associates unique information with what we see. Since everyone has different memories, the picture you think you see is never completely objective!
5. People still filter incoming information through their emotional "filter", which distorts the image judged to be seen. Emotions, conclusions, and thoughts are attached to the image, and the combination of these comprise the "something" we call reality.

The result is that everyone handles the reality differently, even in the simplest things. **No two People feel exactly the same truth.** How do psychic vibrations come into play here? Basically, our prevailing level of psychological vibration determines what emotions we associate with the information brought in by our perception and what conclusions we draw for ourselves from our resulting reality. That is, my answer to the question in the title is **that all People are right, no matter what level of spiritual vibration they live on.** This explains why Buddhists respect the other person's opinion even when it's directly opposite to their own. They know that every Person has a different truth. Now you know it too! That is, the arguments arising from outrageous statements are completely meaningless! How many times in my life have I made the mistake of getting involved in meaningless arguments?

Of course, this doesn't mean that you don't have to argue and try to convince the other person of your view. It is possible to open their eyes, or for them to open yours. A constructive discussion can even be useful. The problem comes when we get emotionally involved in a debate because we are convinced of our rightness and don't understand how the other person can't comprehend or think differently about this obvious thing, but it's just realistic that it is their truth. You don't have to understand them! This should be respected. If you can't convince them with rational arguments in a short time, you must give up, saying "this is my truth and that is your truth" and not get involved in the meaningless continuation with emotions. If you do, there will be serious contradictions and more angry arguments—maybe even aggression or something else that you will later regret deep in your soul. Please think about how many times in your life you've been in an awkward situation because you put emotion into an unnecessary argument without being able to convince the other party.

Understanding just this one thing and making it a part of our lives greatly enhances inner peace, improves the quality of social life a lot, and drastically reduces the number of family and relationship quarrels, so it's worth incorporating into your life!

To better understand and deepen the matter, let's look at how it works within the system of spiritual vibratory levels. By the way, you can use the next section to further deepen your self-knowledge. **Thus, our image of the world is always formed as a reflected image of our spiritual world arising from our level of spiritual vibration.** This is the case even if the problems that cause the level of mental vibration are repressed, so the person is not aware of them. Let's look at how the known or suppressed inner spiritual world is projected into our worldview at each level of spiritual vibration. But I'm also inviting you to play a little game with the help of the lines below! I will briefly introduce you to how People living at each vibration level see the world and what their image of God is, as well as the realities of these Humans. In order to effectively deepen your self-knowledge through the

lines below, I ask you to observe the innermost feelings that the lines generate in you at each level of spiritual vibration. You may have one of three types of feelings:
1. Wow, that must be really bad for someone who lives like that. I'm sorry for them. I'm lucky I don't feel that way.
2. Yes, that's realistic. That's how I feel about the world.
3. That's going too far. That feeling of Life is difficult to process or incomprehensible to me.

Write the above number that represents your impression next to that vibration level. I ask you to please be honest with yourself and not to listen to your rational thinking, but to your feelings about the sentences you read at each spiritual vibration level. If you take the test thinking rationally, you will get a false image of yourself! It's important to know that there are no wrong answers—whatever you feel is right! Don't let your rational thinking overwrite the correctness of your senses. If you want to make your life better, you have to be honest with yourself!

When you're ready, let's get started! Feel free to read what I've written about each vibration level in a row, and as you read each one, observe how the stories generate feelings in you. Classify your feelings according to the three groups above and write the number next to each of the levels below.

For a Person who lives at the level of spiritual vibration of **Shame**, the world is a morose, unpleasant place, where God is a being who despises Humankind for his frailty and the many evils that live in him. The Person who lives at this level of spiritual resonance actually has deep shame within themselves. Because of their shame in front of other Humans, they find themselves unacceptable. They feel miserable, defective, flawed (remember, they may not be aware of this because they were so repressed in their childhood). For them, the world is a miserable, unpleasant place. Here, Humans are fundamentally bad and incapable of love.

A Person who lives on the spiritual vibration level of **Guilt** feels guilty because they blame themselves for things that are unacceptable to them, yet they have done them. Such a Person sees themselves as fundamentally bad or unfit. According to their worldview, the world is a dark, evil, sinful place where Humans are fundamentally bad. The world is full of falling into sin, which is repulsive and unacceptable. Thus, a Person who lives on the spiritual vibration level of Guilt sees Humans and the world as evil. Here, Love is a superficial false glaze that does not actually exist. Their image of God is a hateful being who avenges Humans and all the evil that lies within us.

A Person who lives at the level of **Apathy** condemns themselves because they are weak; they feel powerless to do anything or change anything. It is a natural consequence that they experience the world and the future as hopeless. A Person at the level of Apathy sees God as condemning. In this world, Humans are malicious and judgmental. Love is only available to the rare and few privileged, lucky People.

At the level of spiritual vibration of **Sorrow**, the individual lives in the depths of spiritual pain. They are not yet able to process or digest their psychological pain caused by grief or other reasons. Their soul is dominated by this feeling; it permeates them. Thus, the world is a tragic place where they are not understood by most Humans or even by God. People in this world don't listen to each other and we can't count on them for help. The chance for Love exists in the fog of hopelessness.

The vibratory level of **Fear** is dominated by inner fear in our soul. In fact, we are afraid of ourselves, which can be caused by many different effects. For example, we are afraid of not being lovable enough or not being able to meet expectations properly. But in general, the feeling of fear is more complicatedly linked to many of the qualities of ourselves (whether knowingly or repressed). Consequently, the world is a place with many threats lurking around us. Worry, fear of others, constant readiness to unexpected external attacks and anxiety are all symptoms of this level of mental vibration. At the vibratory level of Fear, God is a punishing being who punishes us for all our mistakes. People are fundamentally malevolent. Love can only be imagined within a narrow circle, such as a family. Unfortunately, Love goes hand in hand with worry.

At the spiritual vibratory level of **Desire**, a Person expects things from themselves that are actually unattainable or difficult to achieve, but most of the time this is not apparent to them. Because of this, longing permeates their soul and they fall into its trap. This generates a reality in which the world is full of hard-to-reach things that require a lot of struggle. The meaning of Life is struggle itself. Disappointments arising from achieved and unachieved things are also characteristic; these revive new desires. In this world, everything has to be fought for, often meaninglessly. The spiritual vibratory level of Desire generates a worldview in which the world is full of injustices. God is a being who stingily distributes happiness to other Humans and makes it very difficult for the Person on this level to get a little happiness. People are basically inattentive to each other; everyone only cares about their own matters. Competition between People comes at the expense of each other. Love exists, but only a very few are able to achieve it on a lasting basis. We usually love People who don't reciprocate. The desire for Love is dominant, and the chance of its lasting survival is small.

A Person who lives at the spiritual vibration level of **Anger** is actually angry with themselves, but in most cases they refuse to admit it, so they are always looking for enemy images in the world. This is Grouchy from The Smurfs. This state of mind shapes the perception of the world into an opposing place, filled with people, views, organizations, and events directed against the Person, and God will avenge their "folly." In this worldview, many of the People think differently than the Person at this level, and this creates resistance and resentment in them. We only love those whose truths can be paralleled with ours, so we usually try to belong to certain groups, despising or hating everyone who does not agree with us. In this reality, there is little chance of respecting otherness—groups or individuals who are different from the Person. It's also typical at this level of mental vibration that we are only able to accept perfect things because we are always able to see the imperfect parts as problems and objects of criticism.

At the vibration level of **Pride**, a person hides their inner problems from themselves by feeling detachment, superiority, and deviation from others. This pride develops in them because they hide their unacknowledged weaknesses from themselves and the world. It's in today's Western world where we can see this type of People the most, especially among those who seem to be successful. They are characterized by the maximum strengthening of the ego. Therefore, for them, the world is a selfish place where everyone acts only in their own interests. Selfishness is the fundamental force that moves the world. There is no altruism at this level of vibration, and it's even more inconceivable to think altruistically. For, as these People "know", "everyone looks after their own". In this situation, a Person experiences God as an indifferent being. Thus, it's no coincidence that most atheists live in this spiritual vibration. (Of course, this does not mean that those who are atheists live unconditionally on the spiritual vibration level of Pride!) At this level of spiritual vibration, Humans are selfish and can excel in competing against each other with the help of strength, knowledge and ingenuity. At this level of spiritual vibration, we only love those who reciprocate.

A Person who lives on the level of **Courage** already dares to face their own weaknesses and their own mistakes. Although they don't fully accept them yet, they see more and more of them and dare to accept them first to themselves and then more and more to the world. They are already facing the fact that they are wrong, faulty or guilty in certain things, and they are stepping onto the path to happiness. Thus, it is understandable that the world is a place for them to realize their spiritual development and to work hard, sweating blood for their prosperity. A Person who lives on the level of Courage sees God as a permissive being who is willing to overlook our frailty and whatever evil lives within us. At this level of spiritual vibration, Love is an important part of the evolution of the world, but Humans are cautious in expressing Love.

A Person who lives at the spiritual vibration level of **Impartiality** does not yet accept their own weaknesses and mistakes, but is already able to look at them without contempt, self-pity, or self-loathing. Thus, understandably, for them, the world is a satisfying place where they can realize their basic desires, but Life is still difficult and full of struggles. In their eyes, God is a being who gave them abilities so that they could use them for their own happiness and for the betterment of the world. At this level of spiritual vibration, People are more benevolent than malevolent. The existence of unselfish Love is already credible here, but only a very few are able to experience it.

An individual living at the level of spiritual vibration of **Willingness** begins to believe that it is possible to accept the evil that lives within them, and they already dare to believe that their past mistakes can be forgiven. As a result, the world becomes a hopeful place for them, where the vision is relatively optimistic. At this level of vibration, God is an inspiring being who motivates us to make this world better. At this level of spiritual vibration, the largest proportion of Humans is fundamentally well-intentioned. Love is an important tool for making the world a better place.

The Person living at the level of **Acceptance** accepts the bad traits living in them and forgives themselves for their past "sins" as well. There's a good chance they've already healed most of their psychological wounds. Self-acceptance radiates, so the world is a harmonious place to live. For a Person at the level of

Acceptance, God is an extremely compassionate, accepting being. People are good and want Love. Evil in People is also acceptable because it is a lack of Love.

From the point of view of **Reason**, the world and Humankind are both a significant miracle, accompanied by an infinitely wise image of God. Everything is governed by the law of cause and effect. People's Love for each other permeates society. God gave us our abilities to use for the betterment of the world. Here, selfish interests are completely neglected. The superior ideals of society and of Life govern the individual. On the vibratory level of **Love**, a person not only accepts themselves as they are, but even loves themselves. They feel that they are lovable, so they see goodness and benevolence in every Human Being. According to them, Love is the supreme force pervading Life, in whose existence they not only believe, but can feel in reality. At the vibrational level of Love, the Person sees goodness and benevolence in all Humans, but at the same time they see and experience God as the being who loves everyone unconditionally. All Humans, indeed all living and non-living, things are worthy of Love.

At the **vibratory level of Joy**, there is an almost constant inner cheerfulness and serenity in the soul. For these People, the world is a place where everything exists in its own entirety. Their joy is independent of the negative events taking place around them. This is not indifference, as the level of compassion is already very high here. For a Person who lives on the vibrational level of joy, God is the One in everyone, imbued with all and everything. Humankind is a part of God and thus a creator being. Love is the unshakable foundation of joy that is behind everything.

At the spiritual vibration level of **Peace**, a very deep, inner and almost unwavering inner peace reigns in our souls. Humans living at this level of spiritual vibration are now very, very rare. For them, the whole Universe and everything living in it is perfect as it is. The main pervasive feeling is the inner order that feeds on silence. God is the Universe itself, imbued with its existence. Everything is as it is.

At the level of **Enlightenment**, our very existence is perfection. The ego ceases to exist here, and consciousness unites with the Universe as one great luminous source. So here, the individual and the Universe have become one. Our worldview is not a reflection of our soul as in other levels of spiritual vibration, because here these two things can no longer be separated. At the level of Enlightenment, our mere existence merges with the Universe and God.

Now that you've finished the test, let's evaluate it and then draw exciting conclusions together. Please see where all the 1s, 2s and 3s are. There are many variations and they are all correct! The only way to have a wrong solution is to be dishonest with your feelings. By the way, if you are wondering how to be honest with your feelings, this is a sign that you are actually running away from yourself. You don't know how to do it because you don't do it. You don't do it because at some point in the past, you broke away from your true self through repression of your emotions, and you've been "practicing" it ever since.

If you answered honestly, then where you see a value of 1, your soul is not there. This either means that you've never been there or that you've been there but you've already solved it. Where you see a value of 2 is the most characteristic of you at the moment. Where you see a value of 3, your soul is not there, but you can still reach these levels during your spiritual development. This book will also help you to raise your spiritual vibration and thus become happier!

And never say never: I have experienced things in my spiritual development that I used to be convinced were impossible or non-existent.

If you only have a value of 2 in one place, you are a Person with a stable spirit. Your worldview and self-image are stable.

Where there is a 2, your soul is almost always at that level of spiritual vibration. That's super rare. If you are such a Person, decide how happy you are and how comfortable you feel in your skin. If it's good, then all is well. You will probably stay at that vibration all your life, and that's okay. But then this book wasn't really written for you. After all, the main goal of this book is to raise your spiritual vibration and thus help you become happier! If you are not really happy, your development is guided by the next higher level of spiritual vibration. Please re-read the detailed description of that psychic vibration level and think about it.

If you have written '2' in more places, your soul is more insecure the more places you have marked that way. But this is not a problem! There is no wrong answer. It just means that your soul is either evolving or not really finding its place, or you may be in the middle of a big change process. By the way, this is the most common case, as our souls often flutter, unable to stay in one place.

The location of the numbers also helps with self-assessment. If there are 1s first, then 2s, then 3s, this is the most common case. The 2s mark the contiguous band where your soul resides. However, there may be 2s followed by 1s and then 2s again. If this is the case, you still need to heal the causes of the vibration levels characteristic of the lower 2. As the first step in your spiritual development, you should focus on this. For example, at one time, even though I had 2s at the levels of Willingness, Acceptance, and Reasonableness, I still had 2s at the levels of Shame, Guilt, and Fear. So, in these areas, I still hadn't attained the perfect renaissance at the time; I still hadn't fully dealt with the spiritual dragons of my past pains. Even if the feelings associated with the 2s are weak, they are present and hinder the level of mental vibration until they are 100% cleared up.

I hope that you've come a little closer to knowing the level of spiritual vibration you live in, and therefore who you really are.

The above lines can really help you improve your self-awareness. After all, it's characteristic of Pride and all the levels of spiritual vibration below it that our self-knowledge is partially or completely wrong! From Courage to the level of spiritual vibration of Willingness, our self-view is quite good. Our self-awareness is deep and realistic at the spiritual vibration level of Acceptance and above it. Of course, the trap is that all Humans are convinced that they have good self-knowledge. Yet the Person who lives at or above the spiritual vibration of Acceptance is approximately one person out of 100,000-1,000,000 people. This means that at least 99.99% of People have either incomplete or poor self-awareness. I know this is surprising, but it's true! **So, if you think your selfishness is in check, you are probably living in the trap of the ego!**

After reading these lines, take a few weeks of your life and observe your thoughts and feelings every day. See how often they contain images of the world as I have described them to you at each level of spiritual vibration. It is worth paying attention to your thoughts and feelings about the outside world, because our inner world is usually hidden by our childhood repressions. Moreover, the ego always beautifies reality when it comes to self-knowledge! If you are clever, you can avoid the dark veil of your ego and look behind it in this way. After all, you can infer from the picture of the world in which areas of your soul there are even more or less repressions: shame, guilt, apathy, sadness, fear, etc. If you have this, you will already know where to look for more, and you will strive to heal the soul in order to be happier!

I hope this method improves your self-awareness. Since the ego is an expert "magician" at hiding, you need to be on your guard and listen to your thoughts objectively. You can even keep a small notebook with you so that you can write down what kinds of spiritual vibration you had in your mind in half an hour. Using this method, I found many hidden suppressions, especially those that I thought I had already fixed. Naturally, the internal digging was followed by an external request for help, which made it almost incredible what things I found in myself. This was very good at that time, because when I healed them, my Life became even better afterwards. However, if I had not found them, they would have haunted me from my subconscious all my Life and decreased the happiness in my Life. So, it's definitely worth your time and effort! However, I have one more very important conclusion to make.

At each vibration level, we have a different view of the world, so our view of the truth is also different. Who is right? The answer is: everyone and no one! Only enlightened Humans have the experience of seeing with perfect objectivity. That is why the words containing the basic truths are related to the names of Buddha, Jesus and other great religious founders. Everyone else sees and feels a distorted, narrowed world. When two average people argue about their truth, the fact is that they are both right, but neither represents reality. After all, neither of them has objective perception, even if most of us believe that our truth is objective. At the same time, both parties are right, as it is their truth—their worldview in which they live at that time. If we understand this, we will learn to respect the opinions of others. This is the basis of empathy: learn the basic truth that **no two truths are the same.** As a result, your restlessness decreases and your level of harmony increases. So, no matter how hard it is, respect someone else's point of view, because their point of view is just as true as yours. You don't have to agree with it, just respect it! Mastering this method in your daily life will be an effective way to raise your spiritual vibration level! A more detailed understanding and elaboration of this is provided in the following subsection.

1.5. Signs of low and high mental vibration levels

If you have come this far in the book, you have probably already wondered what your own level of spiritual vibration is. This is very difficult to answer, because when it comes to self-knowledge, our ego usually embellishes reality. Therefore, in most cases we imagine having a higher level of spiritual vibration than we really do. Once, one of my female readers who had been craving for a certain man for ten years without success but with endless passion became convinced that she was living on the spiritual vibration level of Love. She justified this by how deeply she could love. The spiritual vibratory level of Love exists in one in millions of Humans lives, so it's very rare. She didn't realize that ten years of hopeless yearning could only be achieved by a Person living on the spiritual vibration level of Desire. The lady's ego had surpassed her self-image by an incredible amount, and the man she desired had become an obsession in her Life. Obsessions are most often symptoms of a psychic vibration level of persistent craving. At the same time, I have seen a case where a man suffering from deep self-doubt thought of himself as having a very low level of mental vibration, while an outstanding value came out for him. In his case, the dominant emotion of the ego was self-doubt.

You can find a free self-knowledge test on our website, the availability of which is indicated at the beginning of the book. The test will help you determine your level of spiritual vibration, but it will only give you a realistic picture if you are honest enough with yourself and able to see beyond your ego. That's why a good kinesiologist will measure your mental vibration, but I'll come back to that later in this book.

In this subsection, I'll discuss the behavioral symptoms that indicate low or high levels of mental vibration. Of course, without being exhaustive, I just want to introduce you to some of the forms of appearance typical of today's society. It is important that if you are thinking through this article about the level of mental vibration at which someone around you lives, then look at the average of their daily behavior and don't just highlight a negative or positive characteristic. This is important so that you don't get a distorted picture of yourself or someone else. It's therefore a good idea to take a few weeks of your life to observe yourself in the following ways. Join me for this little voyage of self-realization!

Patience: Today, the world is telling us to want everything immediately, so we live in overdrive. As a result, everyone is impatient with others and often with themselves. Many people do not make spiritual progress because they want everything immediately and are not willing to devote the necessary time and energy to their spiritual development. Spiritual growth isn't an easy path, but it's the best investment to make. Impatience is a sign of low mental vibration. The more patient you are, the higher your mental vibration. Of course, this is true only if it comes from an instinctive inner peace of mind and not from restraining oneself.

Desires: Enhancing and arousing desires is also the hallmark of our society today. We are subject to constant temptations that are almost ingrained in us. However, our desires betray our level of spiritual vibration. The more extreme our desires are, the lower our level of mental vibration usually is. At the highest levels of spiritual vibration, People are desire-free because they experience the perfection of the present moment. As long as we are longing, our soul cannot really live in the present. Desires pull our consciousness, emotions, thoughts into the future and thus steal the joys of the present moment from us. After all, the feeling of longing gives us an inner energy and that's why we think it's right; it's because we take it seriously that it drives us forward. Unfortunately, this is a mirage. In truth, the more desireless you are, the higher your mental vibration level.

Labeling and Acceptance: It's scary how unpeaceful people are today. Everyone has a negative opinion of everyone. Everyone fingers everyone, reviews everyone, hates everyone. We do this in a unique way because we feel worthless inside and thus try to compensate ourselves and the world in order to feel different by disparaging others. The more critical you are and the more inclined you are to label, the lower your mental vibration. Conversely, the more accepting you are, the higher your level is.

Restlessness: We can judge the extent of our restlessness mainly by observing our thoughts. After all, you don't necessarily have to fight with physics every day to be restless. Please observe how many times a day you think hostile thoughts. Of course, hostile actions should also be included here, but thankfully these will be only a fraction of our hostile thoughts. The more restless you are, the lower your spiritual vibration level, and the more peaceful it is, the higher it is.

Emotional fluctuations: You must know a lot of people who are suddenly angry, or who are extremely cheerful at one moment and fall into depression after a few hours. Surely there are also those on your horizon who cannot control themselves and do not have conscious control over their desires. The extreme version of these People is the infantile Person, who is childish in their inability to control emotional swings. The more extreme our emotional fluctuations of this kind are, the more easily our environment can throw us out of our mental balance, the less time we can exist in mental balance, and the lower our mental vibration level. As the endurance of the inner balance increases, it indicates an increase in the level of mental vibration.

Self-control and Power: The feeling of powerlessness and helplessness is a sign of low spiritual vibration, while the sincere inner feeling of power, manifested in true self-control, is a sign of high spiritual vibration. Those who strive with powerful bodily force to achieve their goals and impose them on others are actually weak and have low levels of spiritual vibration. A good example of this is when someone raises their voice more and more in a debate to assert their truth, or when a man hits a woman when they get into an argument with each other. These are clear signs of a very low level of mental vibration. So, please don't consider the word "power" in the traditional sense; it's about the degree to which you have self-control and concentration.

Fluctuation of thoughts: The orientation of thoughts to the present is a sign of a high level of mental vibration. Notice that 99.9% of our thoughts are unnecessary and meaningless. These negative and superfluous thoughts ruin our lives. The lower our mental vibration level, the less control we have over our thoughts and their quality. The more negative thoughts we have, the more worries we have about the imaginary future or the past, fictional realities or the Lives of others, and the lower our spiritual vibration level. To keep our thoughts positive and focused on the present, we need to practice. Unfortunately, the more undisciplined our minds are, the lower our mental vibration level and the more unhappy we are.

Order and cleanliness: Being mindful of our environment can contribute to balancing us, but an obsession with order and cleanliness is an addiction. But if this obsession doesn't occur, the greater the order and purity in your Life, both in your surroundings and in your soul, your conscience and in the way you conduct your Life, and the higher your spiritual vibration level. Unfortunately, this statement is also true in reverse. If you do not have the strength to keep order around you, if you are undemanding of yourself or your environment, if your conscience is not clear, if your Life is disordered, and if there is no system in your Life, it's a sign of low spiritual vibration.

Joy, peace, gratitude, acceptance: Please notice how long you are genuinely joyful, peaceful, grateful, or accepting on an average day. The less time spent this way, the lower your mental vibration. I know: the ego immediately turns on and starts to list reasons why this cannot be done. But these are the subterfuges of the ego, which is the enemy of your happiness. Reasons are unimportant; just address the fact of how long you are joyful and peaceful on an average day.

If you've read this book so far, I have a request for you. You probably have a tendency to focus on the external reasons why you are this or that when reading these lines, or you use it to justify why you can't be this or that. We often tend to respond to such questions by thinking "I will be there when this or that happens". **Please remember: these are your ego's self-defense reactions!** Since it is essential to know your ego thoroughly in order to raise your spiritual vibration, there will be a chapter later in this book that will be exclusively about the ego.

1.6. Our daily activities and mental vibration levels

As I briefly mentioned, the state of your soul depends to a great extent on your doing activities that either destroy or build it. The choice is in everything we do. However, we often choose unconsciously and are not aware of the spiritual consequences. The point is that if you are doing low-vibration activities, they will take your spiritual vibration level down, but if you are doing high-vibration ones they will take you up. At the same time, it's also a good mirror of our mental vibration level what kind of activities we eagerly do. It doesn't matter what hobby you choose, how you have fun, or what books you read. For example, if one Person's hobby is hunting and another's is meditation, it's quite clear that the latter Person has a much higher level of spiritual vibration. If someone gets drunk and carouses at every party, they have a much lower level of mental vibration than someone who has a good conversation at a peaceful, harmonious dinner with friends. If I read a horror novel, it pulls me down. Conversely, my previous book lifts me up (*Dittrich, 2021*), since the latter's psychic vibration level has been measured at 703, which is at the lower limit of Enlightenment. I therefore recommend it to you from the bottom of my heart, because even just reading books with high spiritual vibration raises your own.

One of the most popular forms of recreation for today's Humans is watching movies or series. Therefore, through this activity, I would like to show you how important it is how we spend our time. If we look at what we want to watch and what we don't from the point of view of our soul, we may not get the same answer that our desire to have fun "whispers" to us.

We've been watching American-style action movies in droves for decades. The movie plot is always the same. There is a protagonist who is enraged by an unconquerable evil, and the hero destroys all evil and thus saves Humanity. Of course, there are also romantic and erotic threads in the film, and the protagonist regularly loses his relatives or friends, meaning that he (the protagonist is usually male) pays a great price for winning. The well-proven recipe goes like this: positive hero – action – fight – many murders – suffering – fight – romance – erotica

– exciting visuals and, in the end, the triumph of good.

Now let's watch this kind of movie from the perspective of spiritual vibration levels. I am captivated by these films, either in their full length or in some of their details. After all, we really enjoy the movie when we emotionally identify with the story. Thus, our soul will work at the level of spiritual vibration projected by the film. In a typical action film, Good and Evil fight approximately 60% of the duration of the film. There is a war, a massacre, or a struggle. The psychological vibration level of these scenes is resistance (Anger), which has a value of 150. The film presents the "good guys" as being ideal—both externally and internally. The love object of the protagonist is also usually the most wonderful-looking woman. The emotion between the protagonist and the girl he adores is the perfect love. These ideas, which the film reveals to us, push the psyche to the level of spiritual vibration of craving—without our realizing it—for about 20% of the duration of the film. This value is 125. In order to identify deeply with the good in the film, it's necessary to present evil as infinitely bad and scary. In these scenes, our mental vibration level drops to the level of Fear, which has a value of 100. That's about 15% of the duration of the movie. When good triumphs and we experience catharsis, it reinforces the feeling that "yes, we are on the right side" and thus, at the end of the film (for a period of approximately 5%), we rise to the spiritual vibration level of Pride, which is 175. If we take the weighted average of the values assigned to the psychic vibration in the durations thus obtained, then we get a rounded average psychic vibration level value of 140, which is a strongly Life Destroying value.

What this means for our soul is that we went to the cinema and paid to sink into a sufficiently Life-destroying level of spiritual vibration between Anger and Desire. The film ruined our souls for 1.5 hours. I watched these movies for decades and couldn't understand why I felt deep down that it wasn't right. It was so much fun! Why did I feel inside that these American-type action films were wrong? I couldn't explain it—I just felt it. That makes the correct answer pretty clear, doesn't it?

These films also have another strand, which we call the denial of evil (*Bradshaw, 2015*). This is the ethical aspect of the film. In these films, there is usually almost no distinction between good and bad when we look at the two sides in terms of their actions. Good also kisses and kills and is above any and all Human or ethical rules, because in the fight for good the protagonist must use anything against evil. Unfortunately, in every film, we identify with this evil while also denying it. This is the most insidious spiritual trap. We don't even realize we're on the wrong side. As you know, there is no good or bad side in these films; both sides are bad, but only one is portrayed as being good. Just because

I kill for a good cause doesn't mean I'm not a murderer. Most action heroes are ordinary mass murderers. They are the "good guys" purely because they're on the right side.

If you put together the thought process of spiritual vibration levels with the denial of evil, it becomes perfectly clear why it's so bad to watch these films. It will be clear and understandable why such a pastime destroys the soul every day.

But let's not stop at a simple American-type action film. Now let's look at how much harm we do to our souls by "consuming" average media products:

- Advertisements: the psychological vibration level of Desire is 125.
- Horror films: psychological vibration level ranging from Fear to Shame, value: approx. 50.
- Sex films, soft porn films: psychological vibration level of Desire, value: 125.
- Thrillers: psychological vibration level of Fear, value 100.
- Porn depicting perverse desires: the psychological vibration level and values of Shame, Guilt and Desire: approx. 50.
- Excessively intense romantic film: the psychological resonance level of Desire, its value is 125.
- Action films: psychological vibration levels ranging from Pride to Fear, value: approx. 140
- News: a wide range from Shame to Anger, with an average estimated value of 90.

If you look at how many commercials and soul-destroying shows the TV channels broadcast to you, you may understand why you feel energy-deficient and lazy when you get up from the TV after one or two hours. The TV has literally drained your soul.

I once monitored a popular Hungarian television channel for how many Life-supporting or psychologically elevating programs (or parts thereof) there were during that day's programming. When I searched as open-mindedly as I could, I found no more than one hour within the 24-hour period. It was no accident that I used the TV for this experiment; I very rarely turn it on in general. They are constantly destroying our souls through their channels. What do I need it for? Advancing one's spiritual development is challenging enough even without TV. So, for the past 15 years I've almost never watched it.

The world of the Internet is an even tougher one. Because here, the most exciting seductions are available to us at the touch of a button. These are usually downward-moving temptations and are not uplifting. It's always easy to fall back, but hard to get back up again. In this case, the simplest way is not the right way. In addition, here we are quickly trapped by pleasure or ideas, as we do not limit our desires.

I used to get two reactions from People to the above observations and analysis regarding films. One was: "these things don't affect me that negatively because I'm psychologically strong" and the other was: "if this were all true, then People would not enjoy these films and shows so much". Both are reactions of an ego that wants to protect and justify its habits. This is an instinctive and natural reaction, but it doesn't necessarily make it right. However, I will point out why both reactions are wrong.

The answer to the first is that everything depends on what your basic level of spiritual vibration is. For example, if someone lives at the psychological vibration level of Guilt, they experience a positive catharsis as a result of a typical American action film, as it raises their psychological vibration level from 50 to 140. That Person will come out of the cinema with a soaring lift. That's great to hear! Thus, for them, watching action films is a serious help in their spiritual development. Go for it! Watch a lot of them! If you live on the spiritual vibratory level of Desire, you may not realize that commercials or soft porn are draining your soul because they are at the same level as you are, preventing you from moving forward. I used to love action movies and porn. Today, if I look at either one of them, then

I feel bad for a while. I am especially repelled by the sight of aggression in action films. Even if porn increases sexual desire for a short time and temporarily brings about a pleasant condition, a few hours later I still become mentally worse. Today, I feel the differences well because from a mental vibration level below approximately 300, the deviations become hard to perceive. So, even if you don't feel it, there's still a problem. The fact that you don't feel it just shows that it's time to improve. Living on a Life-destroying level of spiritual vibration is not very happy.

In fact, the response to the other reaction can already be understood from the thinking so far. Today, there are many Life-destroying spiritually vibrational People on Earth—much more than the number of Life-supporting People. The media serves the masses, as the media is only interested in audience size. Unfortunately, they don't concern themselves about dragging people back spiritually every day. Today's media is one of the main obstacles to the spiritual development of Humanity. Of course, more Life-supporting programs and even whole channels are starting to appear. This shows that the change has begun. However, these channels have lower ratings, as they attract a smaller audience (for now).

The conclusion is clear: it's up to you what kind of fun you choose! Reading this book is also Life-supporting. After all, it was written out of complete altruism with the intention of helping you, and its only purpose is to help you achieve your happiness, which is increased by your spiritual development. By reading such a book, you have made a serious effort to raise your spiritual vibration. There are plenty of soul-inspiring books and movies to choose from, though it's true that this requires purposeful selection.

Another closing thought: Why is it easier to click on a soul-destroying series or action film than to read a soul-raising book? The answer is simple: developing the soul works in the same way as training the body. Training hard and keeping fit is hard work, while slumping in front of the TV and eating chips is easy. After a hard workout, we are full of good feelings. After watching TV and chips, we feel stagnant, lacking in energy, and lazy. We're not in the mood for anything. You have to train your soul too! This takes hard work and attention. Climbing is also difficult, but the higher you get, the better you feel and the wider your field of vision will be. This is how it works with spiritual vibration levels, and also with spiritual development. It is also a kind of mountaineering in the metaphorical sense. Just as it's wonderful for a climber to reach the top, it's so wonderful for you when your soul has reached a higher state. It's worth the work and the investment, so go for it. The only rule is that once you take this path, you never stop! There will be relapses, but they should not be interrupted, because they will only be temporary if you persevere!

This chapter isn't suggesting that you don't watch soul-destroying things from now on. It wouldn't last! Sometimes I am "guilty" too; sometimes it feels good to be a little bad or to identify with something bad. Rather, this article wants to tell you to pay attention to the proportions. Try to choose more Life-supporting activities than distractions. If the proportions are positive, then the change starts in the right direction. Gradual change takes time and patience. Changing our habits isn't easy, but it's worth it!

It's even important to point out that our spiritual vibration level cannot only rise but also fall. If we don't take care of ourselves and avoid things that pull us down, we will unfortunately sink. You have already learned from this book, but the following chapters will especially prepare you to clearly see what is a psychic vibration level lifter and what pulls you down. The first step is to acquire knowledge, but then persistent awareness is very important. Happiness falls into very few people's laps, but with the recipe of the L.I.F.E. method it is available to everyone. It's true that you have to do it consciously every day. It's also important to clarify that your mental vibration level is an average value. We live on the spectrum of our emotions above and below it. Only our emotions close to the mean value are more common, while those farther away are less common. Finally, I would like to give you the closing thought of the chapter, which is perhaps the most important: it's a fact that if your spiritual vibration level increases, your happiness level also increases! This is important to emphasize because our ego always protects the current state, so it tends to make us believe that we don't even need a new worldview or reality image for a higher level of spiritual vibration. But don't let your ego fool you: your level of happiness is constantly increasing with the increase in your level of psychic vibration, whatever your ego is saying as a counter-argument!

CHAPTER 2

Vibration levels of the mind

2.1. States of consciousness and brain waves

The activity level of the brain can be determined from its vibration levels. After all, it has been observed that the brain works at different levels of vibration (frequencies) in different states of consciousness. This has long been known by medicine and can be measured by a brain EEG, while the extent of mental vibration levels can only be quantified by physiological methods (muscle testing) (*Uwe Albrecht, 2012*). Because we are not yet able to measure such subtle frequencies physically, brain vibration levels associated with states of consciousness characteristic of the functioning of the mind can also be measured with an instrument (*Joe Dispenza, 2020*). From the development history of the measurement range of physical frequencies (*which you can find in* **Appendix 4**), it is astonishing to see how extensive the frequency range that can be measured by humans has been in the last 100 years. So, just because something cannot yet be measured by physical measurement, it still exists. Therefore, we use the kinesiological method of muscle testing to determine mental vibration levels, but I believe that humanity will be able to measure this frequency range in the near future. **Appendix 4** also explains how effective creation works and how the entire Universe is a collection of information.

Because it's important for our future discussion, I would like to take a brief look at the physically measurable vibration levels of the brain and the associated mental states:

Delta (1–3 Hz): This is the lowest frequency level of the brain; it occurs during deep sleep. At such times, we sleep without dreaming. Meditation masters are in this state when they seem to be unconscious. However, they are still awake at those times. In meditation, this is a state of deep inner silence, when the only thing that exists is one's inner peace.

Theta (4–7 Hz): This condition is characterized by a short transition period before falling asleep, after waking up, and during dreamy periods of sleep. It is also a very deep and calm state. Meditation practitioners are able to remain in this state permanently. It is also used in Theta Healing (*Vianna Stibal, 2017*) and other hypnotic healing techniques. In this state, we have access to our subconscious and our intuition is strengthened. Therefore, dream interpretation is also a good self-knowledge method, since we dream in the Theta state. Dreams are nothing more than images released from our subconscious which can be translated in a way that we can understand them through symbolic interpretation. Various universal motifs appear in the dreaming phase (Theta-state), to which both Freud and Jung paid immense attention (*C. G. Jung, 2022*). (I will discuss this in more detail in my next book.) Numerous scientific analyses confirm that dreamers also see motifs in their dreams that they have never seen before in their lives (of course, these observations are from before the world of the Internet). This is proof of the existence of the large, common universal field of consciousness perceived by many spiritual gurus, from which our brain is able to extract information while in the Theta state. This is also proof that the Human brain is not only capable of independent thoughts, but is also a "transmitter-receiver". Unique, creative thoughts are not our own "products", but "signs" drawn from the universal consciousness. Only our ego makes us believe that they are our own creation. That is why humility and modesty are so characteristic of the great masters; they know exactly that they are only mediating. At the same time, with the Theta and Delta states, we have seen the scientific basis of effective meditation and its key to success as well.

Alpha (8–12 Hz): This is the calm attention state of wakefulness. In such cases, we are peaceful and do not really think about things. The brain is simply in a receptive state and does not appreciate what it sees. We are often at this level when it comes to directed mediation, but unfortunately well-prepared advertisements also take advantage of this. People stumble upon the advertisement, the contents of which reach their consciousness without evaluation. Thus, they influence us very well and skillfully without us realizing it. The Alpha state is also used in mind control, and the very fashionable 'mindfulness' is based on this state.

Beta (13–40 Hz): This is the state of focused active wakefulness. Within this frequency range, the higher we get, the more stress we have. Within the Beta frequencies, there is a thin range when the stress level is relatively low, as high stress, anxiety, irritability or overheated states above 18 Hz are the signal factors. This is why, for example, many computer games have such a bad effect on children; they keep their minds above 18 Hz almost constantly. This will increase their cortisol production and keep it high.

Gamma (41–100 Hz): These brain waves appear during the REM phase of sleep and sweep through us during strong visualization and extremely high levels of brain data processing. These brain waves are experienced for a short time in average people. Spiritual masters are able to remain in this state of concentration for a long time. After all, they actually become masters of concentration through their meditation. Such brain activity requires pinpoint concentration and incredibly focused energies. In the samadhi state, when the mind takes full power and the sensations of mind, body and soul cease (i.e, the state of enlightenment), we can be in this state permanently. In this case, the energies of consciousness dominate the whole Human

Being. These are unbelievably high energies that the common Human cannot even imagine. In my own experience, my body shook faster than the frequency of a hummingbird's wings for at least half an hour after such an experience—so much so that there was even a sound of resonance. In the world of the ego, it's only possible to activate such high-level energies for moments, and it can only be permanently activated in a self-absorbed consciousness. The enlightened great masters could be in this state of hunger for days—often weeks—and yet they will not have had any health problems (*Judyth Reichenberg-Ullman, Robert Ullman, 2016*), contradicting all the claims of medicine.

In general, the more persistently your mind is in a state of high Beta consciousness, the more stressed you are, and the weaker your immune system is. If this becomes your lifestyle, this condition will reach a more durable state, and more and more chronic diseases will appear in your life. There is therefore great truth to the Hungarian saying "tranquility is the secret of a long life". This means avoiding high Beta states! Unfortunately, the whole Western way of life pushes us in the other direction. But let's look at how persistent stressed states of mind cause our illnesses. You will also get a more detailed picture of brain waves through the example in the chapter below.

2.2. Melatonin or cortisol?

The main role of melatonin in our body is manifested in our sleep cycle. The body produces serotonin when it is awake. This substance is necessary for our bodies so that we can deal with space and time and live the waking and conscious part of our Life. In this state, the brain works on the Beta wavelength. When our sleep cycle begins, melatonin production begins instead of serotonin production. Melatonin production is normally brought on by a decrease in light. This is why, under natural circumstances, our sleep cycle adjusts to the sunrise-sunset time intervals of the given place. Melatonin production causes the brain to first enter the Alpha state. This brings a feeling of drowsiness. In such cases, we don't have the desire or power to think and analyze. After that, our brain picks up Theta and Delta brainwave states from the Alpha state. During sleep, the Delta and Theta states alternate, during which our sleep time is divided into dreaming and deep sleep periods, and REM phases interrupt these cycles for short periods of time. The Delta state is the period of the organization's revelation. This is a state of deep sleep when not only our brain is resting, but also our body is slowing down and all our cells are regenerating. This is why those who reach the inner peace level of meditation age more slowly and practice this regularly.

Now comes the most exciting part! Doctors have discovered that melatonin production and cortisol produced by the adrenal glands are complementary to each other. If cortisol production increases, melatonin production is reduced or stopped. This is a logical conclusion. After all, cortisol is the stress hormone in the body that evolution has developed to fight for survival. If a caveman was being chased by a lion, it would obviously have cost him his Life if he had dreamed even for a few seconds. The problem is that in today's modern, "civilized" world, we do our best to make our bodies produce a lot of cortisol. Our overexcited lifestyle (a state of high Beta brainwaves) keeps our body under constant stress, causing it to produce large amounts of cortisol. The production of cortisol inhibits the production of melatonin. This is why we may not be able to fall asleep at night, or we wake up after a little sleep and are unable to fall back to sleep due to the constant clicking of our minds. Our brain and entire nervous system are accustomed to being ready to jump as soon as we wake up, so cortisol production starts immediately. My colleague is a doctor who, due to decades of hospital work, has accustomed himself to being alert and ready to act immediately if he is awakened, as People's Lives may depend on it. Thus, your body is accustomed to starting cortisol production immediately after the first thoughts of waking up. Therefore, he wakes up easily, but in return he often cannot go back to sleep—even when he would like to.

In fact, most people with sleep disorders have a common main cause: a body that is accustomed to producing cortisol immediately. The irony is that in the evening when we want to relax, most of us actually do things that increase our cortisol levels. Action movies, a lot of aggression in the news, the effects of certain types of advertising, and most of the computer games and websites create a lot of tension in us. We think it's fun to watch an action movie when it actually has a harmful effect on our soul and body (as we've already seen). It's also known that these activities increase or maintain our cortisol production.

It is worth supplementing this knowledge with the fact that cortisol production turns off all body-regenerating functions—even genetic ones. Oops! This is why cancer and many chronic diseases are closely associated with prolonged stress. Near-continuous cortisol production does not allow the production of melatonin for enough time for healing in the body, which "directs" its regeneration at the genetic and cellular levels.

For a deeper understanding of this process, read the following scientifically proven facts about the beneficial effects of melatonin (*Joe Dispenza, 2020*):

- ▶ It prevents excessive cortisol excretion due to stress (in a normal case).
- ▶ It improves carbohydrate breakdown (aids in weight loss).
- ▶ It reduces the level of triglycerides (acts against cardiovascular problems).
- ▶ It prevents the hardening of the arteries (acts against blood pressure disease).
- ▶ It enhances the immunity of the body.

- ▶ It inhibits the development of some tumors.
- ▶ Increases Lifespan by approximately 25%.
- ▶ It activates the nervous system of the brain.
- ▶ It stretches the dream phase.
- ▶ It stimulates the accumulation of free radicals (anti-cancer effect).
- ▶ It promotes DNA regeneration and division (effective against cancer and other chronic diseases).

Let's translate the knowledge gained in this way into our Lifestyle. Most people react to stress by eating extra carbohydrates. But because cortisol prevents the production of the right amount of melatonin, the efficiency of carbohydrate breakdown is impaired. Thus, we have already identified one of the main causes of obesity. On the other hand, if you produce more melatonin and less cortisol, you crave fewer carbohydrates, and the carbohydrates you consume are broken down more efficiently. Thus, body fat formation is reduced. Have you noticed that the largest percentage of obese People are also poor sleepers? (Of course, this is not always true.) Have you also noticed that the more stressed we are, the more often we go to the fridge looking for something to eat?

Most moms have some degree of sleep disturbance. During the breastfeeding period and while their children are young, the mother's nervous system is always ready to be activated. If the child cries, the mother needs to be ready and active in seconds. Mothers have programmed themselves so that their first thought upon awakening would be accompanied by immediate cortisol production. However, when the children are older and their mother's instant attention is no longer needed, this years-long program remains fixed. In this way, women consider their sleep disturbance as a natural basic characteristic, although it can be changed. It's true that counter-programming is at least as difficult as it was to switch to the current active program with the first child. If mothers think back to how difficult their first breastfeeding period likely was, they must still have in them the spirit needed to switch to a hitherto unknown Lifestyle. Either way, it's a lot of work.

Sleep disturbance also occurs in those who take work-related stress home or are exposed to stress at home. Thus, their cortisol production does not allow the production of melatonin, and sleep disturbance is guaranteed. The problem is further aggravated by the fact that fatigue is widely combatted with a lot of coffee during the day, which can inhibit or reduce the production of melatonin for up to eight or ten hours.

Melatonin is basically produced in the twilight—in the dark. However, People may also work in the evening, which works against this. No wonder we have trouble falling asleep in our bedrooms with lights on or a laptop glowing. Melatonin production only starts when we are finally in the dark. Many people fall asleep with the lights or the TV on, which in most cases causes restlessness and also sleep disturbance.

But this is still just the beginning! If we don't have sufficient length of sleep and regular melatonin production on a daily basis, the regenerative ability of the body is ruined. At the DNA and cellular level, the body will not have time to repair the damage caused by intraday stress. Thus, chronic diseases, blood pressure problems, nervous system problems, and ultimately cancer can be the result of decades of an improper Lifestyle. Melatonin is also responsible for protecting the nervous system. Thus, if our melatonin production is not persistent or regular enough, our ability to withstand stress is also reduced. If it decreases, our body produces even more cortisol and we will have even less of a chance to produce enough melatonin, so we go into a downward spiral. Of course, this also affects our behavior. We get angry suddenly, we get out of control more easily, we make hasty decisions, we make mistakes more often, and our movements become more undirected. Of course, this causes more reactions or generates guilt and anger in us. Thus, the stress is further exacerbated.

This self-exciting spiral magnifies itself downward. Among the beneficial effects of melatonin is the strengthening of immune responses, so if our body cannot produce enough of it or not regularly enough, our immune system will also weaken. This makes us more prone to catching all kinds of bacterial diseases or viruses. That's why you need to get enough sleep every day. But think of how many workaholics are "cool" with how little sleep they get! For the same reason, we have to sleep a lot when we are sick. And that's why it's such a big mistake not to rest from our illnesses. Unfortunately, in today's Western society, we don't even have time to be sick. We keep ourselves energized with treatments to mask the symptoms and drive ourselves onward when we're sick. I remember how proudly I told everyone during my workaholic period that I even carried the flu while on my feet because I couldn't afford to get sick. At that time, I was not aware of what kind of self-destruction this was— and how I shouldn't be proud of it.

More importantly, melatonin also increases the length of our lives. It is no coincidence that generally calm People live for a long time. The Hungarian saying "walk slowly, you will mature longer" also illustrates this well.

Here are the conclusions that can help you transcend some of the negative symptoms of your Life. Obviously, it is difficult to incorporate all of these into our Way of Life, but if you successfully follow any of them your Quality of Life will improve:

1. Put a system in your sleep cycle; always go to bed at the same time and always get up at the same time.
2. Sleep in the dark, never with lights on and never in front of the TV.
3. For a minimum of one hour before going to sleep, do not watch anything that generates excitement or do anything that causes stress or tension.
4. During the period before going to sleep, do things that wind you down and relax you, for example meditation,

reading a relaxed book, doing some needlework, listening to soothing music, making love, getting a massage, having a good orgasm, etc.
5. Make sure your sleep time is never less than what your body actually needs. For average people, this is 6–9 hours, but for individuals it may differ more markedly in either direction.
6. Holidays are important! It is important to choose a stress-free holiday and one that is long enough. Prolonged stress-free vacations are a good way to "reboot" your body. It is essential that the holiday is not too active, that is, there should be a lot of rest to maximize melatonin production.
7. It is forbidden to deal with work or any stress factors on weekends, so these can be guaranteed to remain stress-free! The two days of the weekend are just enough to roughly fix the destruction caused by the five-day spin in your body. But that's only true if your weekend is truly stress-free and comes with plenty of sleep. In this regard, snoozes after lunch are very effective on the weekend.
8. Spend as much stress-free time as you can. Every stress-free minute prolongs your life and reduces the chances of many of the negative things you've read about above!
9. The best way to be stress-free is to meditate—a method that can be practiced and developed throughout life. But even at the most beginner level, it heals because you do nothing, you slow down and your body becomes free of cortisol production. By the way, during meditation, melatonin is produced in your body. As you meditate, your body's ability to heal itself is also enhanced.

10. Minimize your consumption of coffee or energy drinks and do not drink them within eight hours of going to bed.
11. In the two hours before going to sleep, it is forbidden to engage in work or anything that is a source of everyday stress.
12. Slow Down Your Life As Much As Possible!

To sum up, let's de-cortisolize and maximize melatonin! But of course, it's not good to go to the other extreme either. Anything that irritates or causes tension or stresses unfortunately produces cortisol; this is the result of activities that generate high Beta brainwaves. At the same time, any activity that calms you down, creates peace and brings balance will help your body to produce melatonin permanently during your subsequent rest phase and be able to regenerate and heal well. Therefore, the main goal is to reduce the Beta state as much as possible. Your Lifestyle is up to you! Change first requires the emergence of an internal need, so you must first be honest with yourself about how much you want to change. Then, go over which of your activities regularly and permanently elevate you to the high Beta range. Start your Lifestyle change with these.

So, the goal is to achieve the smallest possible duration of high Beta brainwaves in our everyday lives! While we need to raise our spiritual vibration, we need to lower the vibration level of our mind. However, the two go hand in hand and are related. Persistently low levels of vibration in the mind raise the vibration level of the soul, and vice versa.

CHAPTER 3

Vibration levels of the body and the relationship of body-soul-mind vibrations

The relationship of your mind and emotions (soul) with your body appears in the realm of your hormones. In the previous section, although we only talked about three types of hormones, this important relationship nonetheless became clear. But your body makes a lot of different hormones. Each sensation generates a different production of hormones in your body. So, if a person stays at the psychological vibration level of shame for a long time, their feelings generate related problems, through which the hormones of shame are produced in their body. In fact, there is a completely unique hormone cocktail in every Human's body, as it is caused by the unique compositions of their thoughts and emotions. Hormones reach every cell in the body and thus shape the state of the body. Based on the example of cortisol described in the previous chapter, cells are unable to regenerate due to the constant effect of cortisol. Thus, if the situation persists, the deterioration of the body's condition at the cellular level begins. So far, you can see that there is a clear connection between the mind-soul and the body: hormones. Through hormonal balance, our emotions and thinking are clearly reflected in the body. However, the condition of the body can be measured by its vibration level. Consequently, it's not just our minds and souls that have vibration levels, but also our bodies.

Ever since Einstein, we have known that every energy and every living or non-living thing vibrates at a different frequency. Recent discoveries in quantum physics and the validation of string theory have further strengthened this view. Thus, it is quite natural that our body also has a vibration, and its "quality" depends on its condition.

For example, the vibration level of a healthy Human is between 62–70 MHz, but if it falls permanently below this, diseases will appear. Cold symptoms, for example, are already present at 58 MHz, and tumor cells start to form at 42 MHz. Death starts at 25 MHz. It is therefore in our best interest to do everything in our power to bring our bodies into a state of high vibration. It is no coincidence that healing procedures using multiple frequencies have been developed over the past decade. Thanks to the results of quantum physics, it is now certain that our organs that become unhealthy become distorted in frequency, so by harmonizing them, the organ is also healed. Therefore, these methods are very suitable for maintaining and restoring our health.

The vibrations of our body are closely related to our feelings, so we can do a lot for ourselves with high-vibration emotions. Emotions associated with high psychological vibration raise the vibration level of our body, while emotions associated with low psychological vibration lower it. After all, through these we produce hormones that lead to a healthy body or the opposite energetic state. Thoughts work in the same way—just the other way around. Our mind causes a decrease in the vibration level of the body in a high Beta state, while it causes an increase in it in a low state. Therefore, soothing, peaceful, or harmonious thoughts raise you to the vibration of a healthy body, while thoughts that increase stress pull you down, but you will learn more about how this works in the following chapters.

However, the things described so far also work in reverse. Specifically, if you raise your body to a higher vibration, it will also have a positive effect on your thoughts and feelings. The body, the soul, and the mind interact with each other. This is illustrated in **Figure 2**.

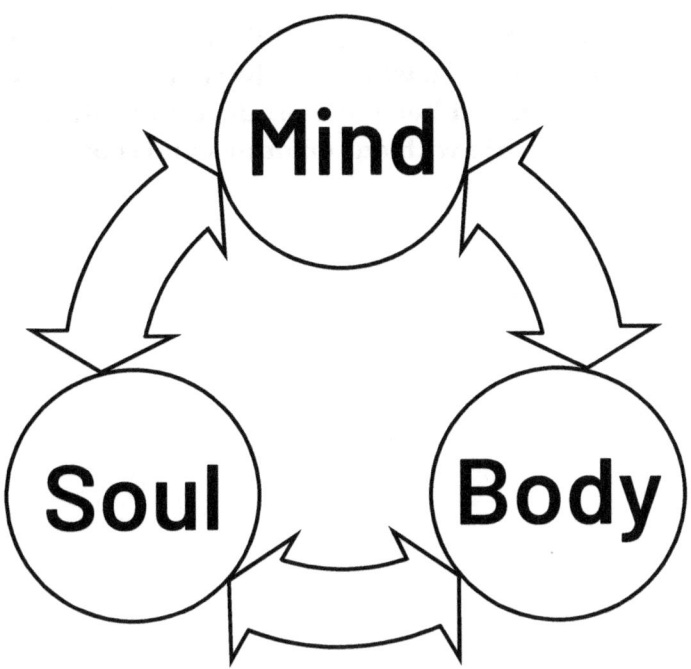

Figure 2: the Body-Soul-Mind Relationship

Therefore, an important principle of the L.I.F.E. method is that in order to be successful in our pursuit of happiness, we must deal with the body, the soul and the mind. The vibration level of the body can be increased by—among other things—proper nutrition, adequate rest, sports, or drinking a sufficient amount of fluid. Basically, it can be said that what serves physical health raises the vibration level of the body. At the same time, unhealthy things such as smoking, coffee, alcohol, drugs, heavily processed foods, excessive sugar consumption, etc. reduce the vibration level of the body. In the practical part of this volume, I will write to you in more detail about these in order to raise your body to the best vibration and thus set your vibrations and your health in the right direction.

You can find an exciting and detailed summary of this issue in Annex 3, which also introduces our body's energy, nerve, and hormone production centers, and their relationship with our emotions and thoughts.

CHAPTER 4

Ego and vibration levels

4.1 Levels of awakening

The first step on the road to happiness is awakening, which can be described with the words 'recognition' and 'realization'. This is the moment when you realize that **you are the only one responsible for most of the bad things that happen to you!** Of course, this statement is only true if you are already an independent adult; the situation in childhood is different. But since this book is primarily for adults who are interested in finding happiness, I will say it again: **you are the cause of most of the bad things that happen to you!** Please don't put the book down! Keep reading! I realized the above when I was 26 years old. At that time, I had not read any spiritual literature and did not really know what spirituality was. (Many consider spirituality to be an over-mystified thing, but the word means nothing more than "spiritual growth"). Before the age of 26, I didn't understand why so many good things happened to others and so many bad things happened to me. I didn't even understand why I couldn't attain what had just seemed to have fallen into others' laps no matter how much I struggled. I couldn't figure out why others were so lucky while I was unlucky. I thought back then how unfair it was of Life that I was born under such an unlucky star. I have good news for you: it has nothing to do with stars and luck! When I was 26, I suddenly realized that I was responsible for a lot of the bad things that had happened to me. At that time, I thought that I couldn't have been responsible for everything, as many of those things were the result of reasons beyond my control, but getting that far was a big step forward! This is the first level of awakening.

Then, as I gained a higher level of spiritual development and deeper self-knowledge, I came closer and closer to the now-clear realization that I am responsible not only for the majority of all the bad things that happened to me, but for all of them. This is the second level of awakening. Among these unwanted situations, there are some for which I am directly responsible and some for which I am indirectly responsible. Obviously, the immediate things are easier to notice, as they can often be seen and accepted even by the ego. Detecting the indirect things requires deeper self-knowledge and a higher level of spiritual development, which can only be achieved through long, gradual work. The point is that through awakening and deepening self-knowledge, the proportion of things we blame on others will decrease.

If you look more closely at People, you will find that most of them are always blaming others for what their lives are like. If they are divorced, the other party was the reason for the deterioration of the relationship. If their living conditions are bad, then the social order, evil politicians or the People who dispossessed them have all done this. If a woman has been through more than one bad relationship, it is always the men who are to blame (and vice versa, of course). Most Humans always shift the responsibility onto someone else. These Humans have not yet reached the first moment of awakening. They are spiritually unconscious. They are not yet guided by consciousness, so as prisoners of their addictions, games and destructive egos (more on these later), they live their lives as unconscious beings. Obviously, this does not mean that they are uncivilized and do not use their minds. In fact, many of them were educated and highly professional people. I know many scientists and educators who have not even reached the first level of awakening. This only means that they have not yet entered the path of consciousness and are not even aware that this "blindness" is the main obstacle to their happiness.

4.2. What the ego really is and the 3 main types of ego

Many years ago, Eckhart Tolle in his book *The New Earth* made it clear that my ego is not me—that there is a real self behind it. That's when I started researching and searching for what the ego really is and how to separate it from myself. Reading many books, learning from a master and my own experience brought me closer to the answer, but there was always a mistake—a vague part or a contradiction in my idea. Tamás Miron Varga (whose YouTube videos and lectures I wholeheartedly recommend to all advanced searchers) greatly opened my horizons about understanding the ego. Then I was fortunate to have often meditated with Sri Chimnoy's disciples. My experiences there provided the missing parts. So, let's see what your ego is and who your true self is. First, I will describe the definition to you, and then I will explain it in a little more detail:

Your ego is a part of your body, your mind, and your soul. All the sensations and changes you detect that are different from the state of a perfectly healthy and relaxed body are your ego. In your mind, any thought that is not pure intuition or a product of the inspiration sent by the Universe is your ego (the word 'Universe' can be replaced by 'God' or any other word that matches your creed). All the feelings and emotions of your soul that do not come from a perfect union with the Universe or a selfless neutral emotional state are your ego.

Now let's see what this means when translated into the practical level of our lives. Surely it also has happened to you (or it will surely happen in the future) when an intuitive notion swept away all rational thoughts and you knew it was the truth. Or it could have happened that there was a powerful intuitive notion that you pushed aside because it didn't seem logical. After taking the logical steps, you realized that you should have listened to your gut. Several famous universities have proven the existence and outstanding efficiency of intuition. The part of you that presented the intuitive notion in these cases was your ego-free true self. This is called consciousness, or in some cultures the word 'ghost' is applied to it. Therefore, your mind (or spirit) is your true, non-egoic self.

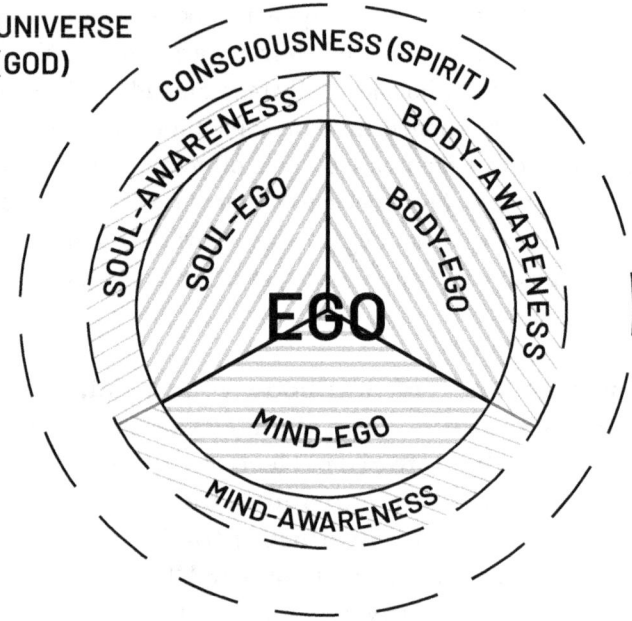

Figure 3: The connection of the ego and consciousness with body, soul and mind

Figure 3 illustrates the relationship between the ego and consciousness. In the figure, the boundary of the ego is marked by a continuous thick black circle. The part of your body-soul and mind that is within the thick black circle is dominated by the ego. Your consciousness is the part between the ego boundary and the dashed outer outline. The continuous circle at the border of the ego indicates the almost impenetrable boundary between consciousness and ego. The boundary of the ego is strong and continuous, and does not want to be aware of the consciousness around it. Therefore, the Person living in their ego is convinced that they exist as a separate, independent being. However, consciousness surrounds the ego and tries to influence it through intuition. The outer boundary of consciousness is torn, beyond which is the Universe. Consciousness lives in unity with the Universe (as mentioned above, you can replace the word 'Universe' with 'God' or any other word that fits your belief system). This is indicated by the dashed line, which shows the permeable connection between the two entities. The more a person is connected to their consciousness, the more often they can experience the feeling of unity, which makes it clear to the experiencer that they are safe because they are not alone. The ego is in a separate solitude, which is why it is afraid and why a Human with a strong ego strives to maximize their security. After all, according to their perspective, they can actually count on no one and nothing but themselves.

It's even more helpful to understand whether you can identify and separate the real you from your ego. Your real self is the perfectly relaxed, healthy and unselfish state of your body. Every tension in your body—every positive or negative state other than being relaxed—is the ego. It's also part of your ego when sexual pleasure gives you a sense of physical pleasure, and it's also part of your ego when you suffer from illness. Each is a specific type of tension that differs from a perfectly relaxed bodily state. That's why we always begin meditation by turning our attention to all our body parts one by one and relaxing them. You cannot become ego-free in a tight posture. For example, I strained in traditional meditation sessions for a long time— which did not lead to success—because my posture is quite crooked due to a lack of self-confidence in my youth. And for me, having a straight back is unfortunately associated with great physical tension. Mediation should always be done in a comfortable, relaxed position if you want to find your true self.

Every thought in your mind—positive or negative—is part of your ego if it doesn't come clearly from intuition. Those who live in the ego rarely experience the power of intuition and thus do not believe in its existence. The real self (consciousness) constantly sends thoughts to us, but these can only rarely penetrate the strong ego. It is important to know that your ego is not concerned with anything other than strengthening and maintaining itself. This is true even if it's not good for you. That's why the ego uses your body, soul, and mind. That is why the holders of strong egos will sooner or later become sick and have worn-out bodies and minds. The ego trap is a slow poison that slowly destroys us on a scale of decades. The first serious symptoms in most people appear in their 40s and 50s. Until then, the regenerative capacity of the youthful body during nightly rest can still roughly repair the daytime destruction of the ego (*as we saw in Chapter 2.2*). As you know, the basic vegetative processes of your body are all controlled by your true self. The beating of your heart and the jobs performed by every cell are not controlled by your ego, but by your consciousness. Your cells die and new ones are born every hour to keep the whole system healthy. They work selflessly for the good of the whole—which is you—serving the interests of the whole you. Cancer is exactly what happens when some cells become selfish and begin to proliferate by quitting their selfless tasks. This is the result of your ego! If your ego is constantly teaching you to be selfish, why would you expect your cells not to adopt that attitude from you? For decades, your ego has been constantly radiating selfishness to your cells. After a while, the ego can completely take over some of your organs, and this unfortunately results in cancer or other chronic diseases. The stronger the ego, the greater the part of our body, soul, mind under its control. Your ego first achieves this through the mind. Observe your mind! Its wheels are constantly turning. Sometimes it dwells in the past, sometimes it analyzes the alternatives of the future, sometimes it regrets, sometimes it boasts, sometimes it generates future fears. The point is to be aware of the constant noise of the mind. Why? Because the impulses of the real self can be suppressed by this internal noise, and thus the ego ensures its existence! The overly rational Human scoffs at people deeply into spirituality for being out of their minds because they themselves have never experienced anything similar, so they're convinced that it's stupid. However, the person who calls others 'stupid' is the one who lives imprisoned by their ego. Of course, they are not stupid either; they only perceive the world through a narrower field of vision, but with greater conviction. So strong is the over-rationalized noise of the mind that it cannot hear its true self. For these Humans, the ego is equal to themselves, and this results in an unhappy, spiritually unsuccessful Life. It is known that every Human on Earth is born with specific Life Tasks. The impulses of the real self seek to turn the body, soul and mind towards the experience of these Life Tasks. However, the ego only wants to deal with self-affirmation. Since this is generally inconsistent with our Life Tasks, the ego does its best to intensify the noise of our minds and distract us from what is really important. Therefore, if you want to reconnect with your real self, you first have to learn to exist again without your mind buzzing. For example, when we do things in public without thinking about anything, today it is fashionably called mindfulness.

Finally, let's also separate the real self and the ego in your soul.

The real self can only be completely ego-free in a state of enlightenment. In this state, the individual exists in perfect unity with the Universe. All other feelings that appear in you are the world of the ego. But it doesn't matter how you feel, because depending on it, you can live in the world of the destructive ego, the neutral ego, or the creator ego. I will return to these ego types soon.

Now, if you look again at **Figure 3** and think back to what you learned about the psychic vibration levels, it becomes clear and understandable how the ego is weakened by raising oneself to each psychic vibration level. However, during the increase in the level of mental vibration, the ego is not only weakened, but also transformed. I will return to this a little later. The higher you rise in spiritual vibration, the more often you will be able to connect with your true self and the more likely you are to complete the Life Tasks for which you were born. The more you know, the more lasting happiness you will live in!

In the first stage of my spiritual development, I experienced it as a serious revelation when I realized that the destructive ego in me was the source of all my troubles. These insights prompted me to look for ways and methods to dismantle the ego as completely as possible. From **Figure 1**, you can clearly see that the right way is not to eliminate the ego, but to gradually transform and weaken it, since the ego ceases to exist completely only in a state of enlightenment. However, in our time, incredibly few Humans reach this state: about one in a billion Humans.

The ego is nothing more than your body, soul, and thinking together. The main driving force is identification, that is, the ego gives things a sense of self. Thus, the ego is nothing more than the parts of your body, soul and mind identified with the sense of self (*Eckhart Tolle, 2022*), which are also in symbiosis with each other so that the ego can more strongly structure itself. This also shows that the body-soul-mind affect one another, since the ego also tries to exert the greatest possible influence on all three. If the ego method works, why shouldn't it work the other way around? If we want to strengthen the "power" of consciousness within ourselves at the expense of the ego, we have to work with the mind-soul-body triad, since all of these are in the sphere of influence of the ego. How does the ego's sphere of influence work? Thoughts generate emotions, and emotions produce different hormones and other chemicals in the body. These hormones and other chemicals are important for our cells, so the cell membrane becomes sensitive to them in order to absorb them effectively from the blood. Cell walls (cell membranes) will always be sensitive to the hormones they receive a lot of. This is essential for the body to adapt. This is how thoughts and feelings arising from our sensations have a physical effect on the functioning of cells. However, if the cells get used to a certain hormone blend, which is a unique cocktail of emotions in different proportions, they will need it constantly. It follows that if our thinking and emotions do not produce enough of any hormone, then the cells transmit the desire to the nervous system such that we can't bear not to replace them. For example, if someone grew up in a family where their parents burdened them with a lot of guilt, they unconsciously provoke life situations where they can feel guilty as an adult. Under the influence of the desire radiated by the cells, those thoughts arise from our subconscious that replace the missing part of the usual hormone cocktail. This self-reflective feedback system is the physical explanation of the ego itself. Thus, the ego cannot just be destroyed because it is made up of our thinking, our feelings and our body. It can be gradually transformed, weakened and reshaped. The ego is an important part of Life on Earth, so basically, the problem is not with the ego, but with the nature of it. Based on this, you can immediately see why the ego always protects its current state—the things it believed to be true until now. Our old truth awakens the old thoughts that give rise to the familiar emotions and hormone cocktail. In this system, all reactions affect all cells of the body, since the sensitivity of the cell walls affects the ability to switch to other chemicals in all such cases. The ego protects its old habitual hormone cocktail until the end, but when the body receives a permanently different hormone cocktail and the cells get used to the new one, the ego will protect that one instead. That's why, for example, when a porn addict heals completely from their addiction, they can no longer have a relapse because their body is no longer excited about those hormones. If, on the other hand, they just suppress their desire, after a while the suppression is broken through and they sink deeper into their addiction. This is how it works for every type of addiction.

What is the difference between relapsing and quitting? The answer is simple: the Person experiencing a relapse forcefully suppresses their addiction because they are aware of its negative effects. But unfortunately, in these cases the ego always wins. It is not possible to resist the hormone deficiency of all cells in the body for a long time. This only works effectively if you start to acclimate your ego to the hormones of a positive emotion. This also provides a sure-fire recipe for quitting addictions, which I will detail in Chapter 5.4.3.

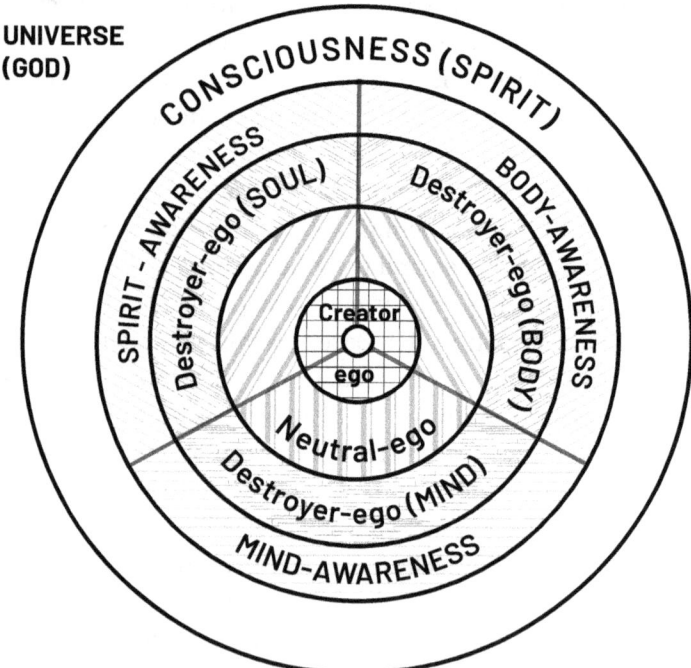

Figure 4: Main types and layers of ego

Now that you understand what the ego is and how it works, stick with me please so you can understand why it's worth changing the ego—that is to say, getting it accustomed to a different way of functioning. Different basic feelings were built into the ego at different levels of mental vibration. Conversely, at our characteristic level of psychological vibration, we have accustomed our cells to the hormones of that basic feeling. I have already shown you that the psychic vibration levels below 200 (Shame, Guilt, Apathy, Sadness, Fear, Longing, Anger, Pride) are life-destroying, while psychic vibration levels above 200 (Courage, Impartiality, Willingness, Acceptance, Rationality, Love, Joy, Peace, Enlightenment) are life-supporting. But these levels of psychic resonance can also be grouped in terms of the impact the ego has on the personal life of the host individual and the world around them, which defines the three main types of ego. This is illustrated in **Figure 4**:

Spiritual vibration levels below 200 are characterized by the destructive ego, which means that it selfishly takes a lot of energy away from the environment in order to sustain itself. At these levels of spiritual vibration, the individual does not have the power to deal with others—certainly not to perform some Life Supporting action. It may happen that such a Human does good to others, but they do this only because they expect some kind of advantage (reciprocation, for example) from it. Unfortunately, these levels of psychological vibration are also characterized by self-destruction, which often results from the involvement of unconscious but "accidental" bad events. From anorexia to alcoholism, this could be anything; the toolbox of the ego is almost endless. In this range, the personality is not pure or mature, which means it is led by games, addictions, and other such programs. The individual does not move towards the Life Task assigned to them by their consciousness, so in their lonely moments they escape from the inner emptiness into some kind of activity. In **Figure 4**, this is the outer layer of the ego that dominates part of the body-soul-mind triad.

The neutral ego is characteristic from the levels of Courage to Reasonableness. This is already a wonderful level of spiritual development. After all, here the ego no longer just draws life force from its environment, but also gives it. In this way, the individual not only destroys, but also builds and heals. Thus, the balance is evened out in the Lives of the People who are living at these levels of spiritual vibration. Self-destruction at these levels of psychic vibration is already lessened. If it does occur, the person will quickly recover from it. The personality is already quite suppressed and the individual gradually gets rid of their addictions and games and other programs. The individual turns to their Life Task. In **Figure 4**, this is the middle layer of the ego, which dominates part of the body-soul-mind triad.

The creator ego is characteristic of Love and the levels of spiritual vibration above it. At these levels of spiritual vibration, the inner need for perfect altruism appears, and thus the person already gives more to their environment than they take from it. Such People are supporters of Life. They also have a positive impact on People's Lives and the Natural Resources in their environment. At these levels of spiritual vibration, the code of destruction has already been minimally incorporated into the ego. Here, the ego is already a supporter of the development of the Person. The personality has already fully matured and developed. The individual is free from games, addictions and programs, is fully aware of their Life Task and lives their life accordingly. In **Figure 4**, this is the outer layer of the ego that dominates part of the body-soul-mind triad.

Only the enlightened Person can be ego-free because they are already living in the unity of the Universe at every moment. Their body and soul exist as part of the Universe, which is perfect as it is. The enlightened Person is thus ego-free, for there is no longer any you-and-me or good-and-evil, but only the perfection of existence. There are no truths in it that support self-justification;

they only know the eternal and generally valid truths. For them, everything else is just an unnecessary overcomplication of Life. This is indicated in **Figure 4** by the inner empty small circle, which I call our 'inner core of light' and which is within all of us. From the point of view of understanding the ego and your soul, it is important to emphasize that it is always the outermost ego layer that is active. Until the destructive ego is transformed, the neutral and creative egos that lie dormant inside you cannot assert themselves to the extent of fulfilling your true self. When you transform the destructive ego, the layer of the neutral ego becomes active and the layer of the destructive ego is taken over by consciousness. When the neutral ego ceases to exist, consciousness takes its place and the creator ego becomes the guide of our Life. Finally, consciousness and our inner core of light come together. This takes effect when the creator ego ceases to exist and we reach a state of enlightenment.

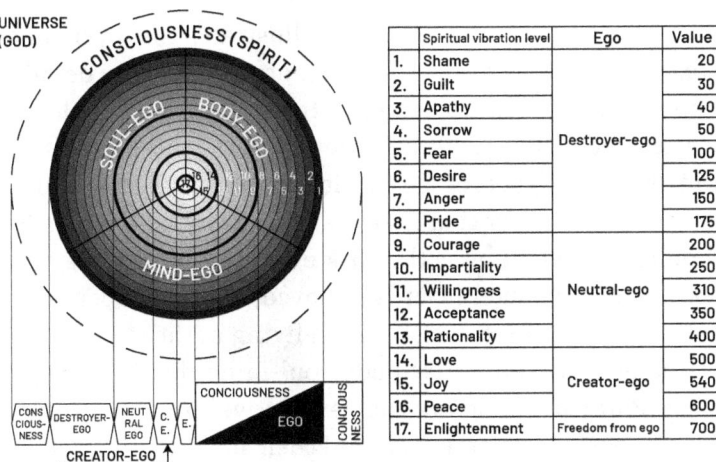

	Spiritual vibration level	Ego	Value
1.	Shame	Destroyer-ego	20
2.	Guilt		30
3.	Apathy		40
4.	Sorrow		50
5.	Fear		100
6.	Desire		125
7.	Anger		150
8.	Pride		175
9.	Courage	Neutral-ego	200
10.	Impartiality		250
11.	Willingness		310
12.	Acceptance		350
13.	Rationality		400
14.	Love	Creator-ego	500
15.	Joy		540
16.	Peace		600
17.	Enlightenment	Freedom from ego	700

Figure 5: Relationship between ego-consciousness and psychological vibration levels

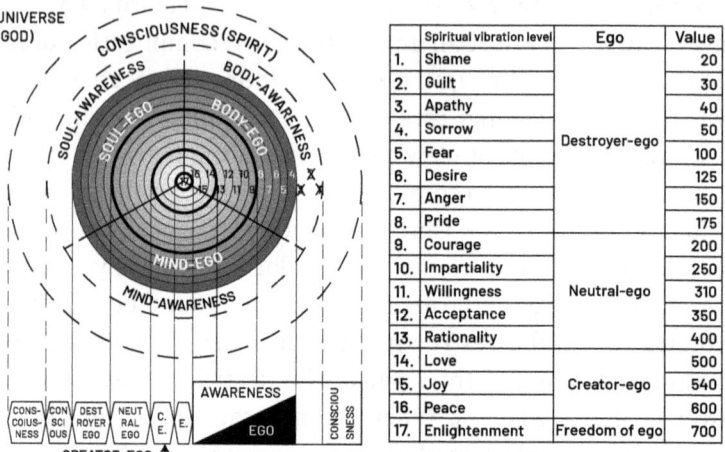

	Spiritual vibration level	Ego	Value
1.	Shame	Destroyer-ego	20
2.	Guilt		30
3.	Apathy		40
4.	Sorrow		50
5.	Fear		100
6.	Desire		125
7.	Anger		150
8.	Pride		175
9.	Courage	Neutral-ego	200
10.	Impartiality		250
11.	Willingness		310
12.	Acceptance		350
13.	Rationality		400
14.	Love	Creator-ego	500
15.	Joy		540
16.	Peace		600
17.	Enlightenment	Freedom of ego	700

Figure 6: Relationship between ego-consciousness and psychological vibration levels at the psychological vibration level of Sorrow

The lower left half of **Figure 5** illustrates the layers of ego presented so far. However, here I'll present in more detail the construction of our inner world. In the figure, layers learned at the psychological vibration levels have been added to the already known layers of the ego. It remains true that it is always the outermost layer that is active and covers all the rest. This should be thought of as the bark on a tree or clothing on the body. Until the outer layer is removed, the one underneath is not visible. For example, a Person living at the spiritual level of Shame has their entire body-soul-mind dominated by the most powerful version of the destructive ego. Such a person lives in perfect separateness and their mental vibration level is low, so their thoughts and feelings are constantly very negative. The mind is constantly clicking and is characterized by a Beta state with high stress levels most of the time. With the hormone cocktail formed in the body, the body is sick and its physical vibration level is low. In fact, **Figure 5** shows the entire structure of a Human living at the level of spiritual vibration of Shame.

When someone heals their soul so much that they step out of the spiritual vibration of Shame, this outermost layer is released into consciousness. The destructive ego weakens and the consciousness can exert a slightly greater influence on the body-soul-mind, although this is still small. Thanks to the psychological vibration of Guilt, the mind is still very noisy but less burdened than before, and the body's hormone cocktail is shaped accordingly. The body breathes a little; its vibration increases slightly.

Thus, the process continues to change with the increase in our spiritual vibration level by exceeding the spiritual vibration levels of Apathy, Sadness, Fear, Longing, Anger, and then Pride. For example, the next figure (*page 130*) shows a Human living at the psychological vibration level of Sorrow:

In the lower left half of **Figure 6**, you can see that by overcoming Shame, Guilt, and Apathy, this Person's destructive ego band has decreased relative to the spiritual vibration level of Shame. The "space" thus liberated comes under the jurisdiction of consciousness. Thus, consciousness can have a greater effect on the body (body consciousness), the soul (soul consciousness) and the mind (mind consciousness).

As our spiritual vibration level continues to rise, the destructive ego ceases to exist when we reach the spiritual vibration level of Courage. A serious part of our body can already be affected by consciousness. Our mind is less busy, and sometimes quieter periods appear. During the work of the mind, the periods of the high Beta range are already much shorter. This state is shown in the figure on the next page:

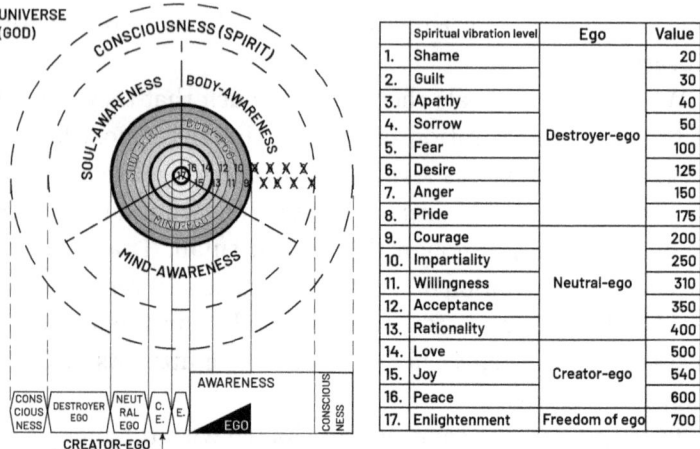

Figure 7: Relationship between ego-consciousness and psychological vibration levels at the psychological vibration level of Courage (initial level of the neutral ego)

If you compare the lower right half of **Figure 7** with the previous two figures, you can clearly see how much the power of the ego has already decreased and how much awareness there is in the individual's Life. It is important to emphasize that people living in Rationality misinterpret the word 'awareness'. They believe that consciousness means that the individual logically thinks about the given problem and acts accordingly. This would seem to be logical thinking. But consciousness means what it literally means: that we exist by giving space to consciousness. A conscious Person does not give in to their rational thinking, but rather to their hunches and intuitions. They live in the present, i.e. they just do what they have to do without thinking.

With the further continuation of spiritual development, the disengagement from the spiritual vibratory levels of Impartiality, Willingness, Acceptance and Rationality weakens, the neutral ego and creative ego become active, the first active layer of which is the spiritual vibratory level of Love. This state is reflected in the figure on the next page:

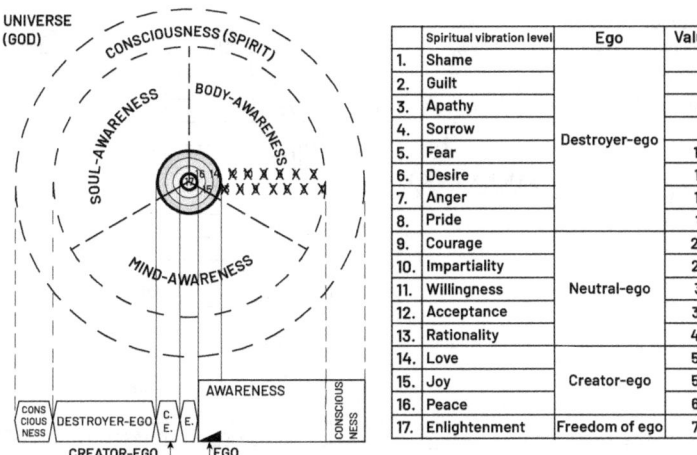

Figure 8: The relationship between ego-consciousness and spiritual vibration levels at the spiritual vibration level of Love (the initial level of the creator ego)

Here the mind is already silent and seldom resides in the Beta state—even in the waking state. Positive emotions dominate our souls. Tensions disappear from our body and the body regains its full health through cellular regeneration. If you compare the lower right part of **Figure 8** to the previous ones, you can see how little impact the ego already has on such a Human Life. Here, consciousness is almost completely in control. The "pollution" of the ego is almost negligible.

If we continue to raise our spiritual vibration and step by step leave the individual layers (Love, Joy, Peace), we will enter a state of enlightenment. Consciousness takes over the soul-mind-body and the ego ceases to exist. There are no more emotional swings of the soul, constraints of the mind or problems of the body. The individual exists as pure consciousness in the unity of the Universe and does not need an independent identity. You can see this status in the diagram on the next page:

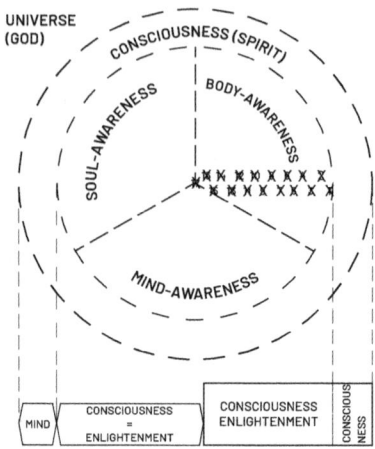

	Spiritual vibration level	Ego	Value
1.	Shame	Destroyer-ego	20
2.	Guilt		30
3.	Apathy		40
4.	Sorrow		50
5.	Fear		100
6.	Desire		125
7.	Anger		150
8.	Pride		175
9.	Courage	Natural-ego	200
10.	Impartiality		250
11.	Willingness		310
12.	Acceptance		350
13.	Rationality		400
14.	Love		500
15.	Joy	Creator-ego	540
16.	Peace		600
17.	Enlightenment	Freedom of ego	700

Figure 9: Relationship between ego-consciousness and psychic vibratory levels at the psychic vibratory level of enlightenment (the ego-free state)

If you compare **Figure 9** with the spiritual vibration of Shame, you will see a huge simplification. With the increase in the level of psychic vibration, we think more and more simply, our emotional life becomes less and less erratic, and our body becomes more and more stable and relaxed. In conclusion, you can clearly see that it is worth choosing the path of spiritual development and raising your spiritual vibration level! The ego is thus transformed and your Life becomes more peaceful, harmonious and happy.

Until you are enlightened like Buddha, Jesus, or Krishna, you cannot be completely ego-free. Thus, the path to your development is not to destroy your ego but to transform it, which you can do by raising your spiritual vibration level. Meanwhile, your ego becomes weaker and less in control of your being. If you are so lucky that you become enlightened, then your ego will become nothing, but since this is given to very few, you should work on transforming your ego in the meantime. Reform the destructive ego first into a neutral ego, then into a creator ego. How? For this, too, I will provide all the information. Some of these details are included in this volume. However, this journey is long, so I will also provide exciting information in the next book, which builds on it.

4.3. Some features of your ego

Now I'm going to show you a sentence. Please notice how reading it makes you feel. It's important to stop for a few minutes after reading the sentence and only pay attention to your feelings and mental reactions:

"I feel that I am perfectly equal to all Humans; I am neither more nor less than anyone else."

Thank you for observing yourself! How did that sentence make you feel? Did you feel that this statement is perfectly true, or rather that it is absolutely untrue? If you felt that it's not true, did you have any thoughts about how much you are better than others? Or did you have thoughts about how much weaker or lesser you are than some People?

Anyone who could read this sentence with perfect agreement has a very weak ego or no ego at all. I congratulate them. There are very few such Humans on Earth. I presume that if you are one of them, then you are a happy, peaceful and balanced Human! But, please, don't confuse that state with reading the sentence and not being self-involved, because the conclusion led by the protective-ego reaction will be misguided! Lack of self-involvement means that you don't bring your feelings into the process, but you distance yourself emotionally from it out of instinctive internal self-defense. At the lower psychic vibration levels, many people are characterized by this self-defense, which is a natural thing. After all, if we have a lot of internal problems, we try to escape from this burden, and anything that can break through this is dangerous or causes unnecessary problems. This is why many people develop a self-defense strategy where they distance themselves from and suppress the hard-to-digest parts of their own emotions. People tend to focus on differences and feel internal resentment and tension when reading the sentence. This check is a confirmation of the presence of the ego in you.

There are two main stages in our lives. Until we reach middle age, we look for our place in the world and want to leave a mark. Few People at this stage of life notice the many harmful effects of their ego. After all, a strong desire for self-assertion stabilizes and strengthens the ego, and thus the person can easily get into symbiosis. However, in the second half of our lives, many of us realize that we have gone down the wrong path. Spiritual development becomes a major theme in the lives of most of us, and then we realize how stupid and narrow-minded it is to live hiding behind the ego.

The ego is constantly comparing us to others. It is always looking for how we are different or distinct. Diversity can be both negative and positive. For example, if someone is more attractive than you, your ego triggers envy in you and creates cravings. Or it may even idealize why their looks are already "too much" and thus reinforces your difference from them. It may also be that the ego makes you feel subordinate to the "greatness" of others, resulting in the integration of a negative difference into your false self. For example, because I had a strong lack of self-confidence, I tended to regard others as almost divine, while I considered myself a worthless person. At the same time, when something I did was successful, I thought highly of myself compared to others (i.e., I went to the other extreme). Because of my lack of self-confidence, of course, these were short periods, followed by situations when life slapped me in the face. The ego cleverly "stepped in" and indicated that it would protect me from such people next time, and thus it further strengthened itself in me.

It does this to everyone; it uses every spiritual wound to justify the importance of its own existence and obtain permission to grow even stronger in your soul, mind, and body.

Some People make money because of this effect. They gain power or fame, maybe extra attention—the list goes on. This is what makes the ego (especially the destructive ego) feel safe. However, the gradually strengthening ego demands a high price in return. We believe more and more that we are different from others, and in doing so, our Human relationships become more and more superficial. This way, we become more and more lonely inside. If we are not honest with ourselves, why would our Human relationships be? But how can we be honest with ourselves when we have already lost our true selves and see our egos as ourselves instead? For example, conceit and arrogance are good examples of a strong form of the crusty, hard ego. Here we are completely disconnected from our true selves, and we no longer have any knowledge of who we really are. This is the level at which the ego has completely detached us from our real personality and we believe that our real self was adapted to some system of external compliance needs. Conceited Humans all believe themselves to be special or different, while most of them are typical and template-like. But, of course, they can't see that until they dare to look behind their egos. But these qualities were only illustrative examples. As in the layers of different levels of spiritual vibration, the ego is embossed with different characteristics.

So, the stronger our ego is, the less we know who we really are. And the price is inner spiritual isolation. How many People live in relationships where they are lonely on the inside? How many People live in work or school communities that are lonely inside? How many People go with groups of friends to places of entertainment feeling lonely inside? This inner, excruciating loneliness is the price of the strengthening of the ego! This is a spiritual detachment from ourselves and also from others. This is emotional distancing. The consequence of a strong ego is also a distance from God (or the Universe, etc.). After all, the ego makes it believe that it exists only on its own. This further enhances the internal uncertainty, because as a result of our ego, there is no force that we can count on; our ego is the only one that protects us. It is this inner uncertainty that the ego clings to, sustained by the necessity of its existence. This is the main reason why there is no real happiness with the existence of a strong ego—only short-term pleasures. Thus, our human relations, which are becoming increasingly superficial, are changing faster and faster. After all, only novelty can bring an adequate escape from inner loneliness. This constant desire for novelty is the cause of the many extra pursuits of pleasure that are characteristic of Western society. It doesn't matter if you're thinking about shopping, traveling, gaming, sex, drugs, alcohol, a new relationship, or constant work. The list could go on and on, but the real reason is always the same.

Of course, the ego often makes us believe in happiness. When you buy a better car, or a bigger house, or a trip to an even more exotic place, the ego makes you believe that this is happiness. Temporarily, you also feel joy, but then a new desire comes along because something inside you still remains empty. You are fleeing from inner loneliness into another possession or another ego-boosting desire. The bad news is that this process will eventually come to a terrible end!

Politicians with an infinite thirst for power have ended up in suicide, conviction, assassination, or perhaps in a mental hospital when their power unexpectedly collapsed. This is a typical manifestation of the collapse of the incredibly crusty destructive ego. Think, for example, of the execution of Nicolae Ceaușescu in 1989. The ego, if it is over-skinned, can only be gotten rid of at the cost of great work or hard failures, because it will be crushed in the most unexpected way at the cost of incredible suffering. My ego was completely broken three times. Unfortunately, in the first two cases I grew an even stronger, more skillful and prudent ego. It made me believe that everything would get better from now on! After the third total collapse, I didn't want to rebuild an even stronger ego! By that time, I could clearly see the destructive function of the ego and its parasitic system against the spirit. My ego was strong and presumptuous. I was convinced that everything I had figured out and wanted to carry out was the best, most correct and most effective. I was incredibly stubborn and always knew exactly what the right path was. I was also convinced that I did not need external help, whatever it was called: God, the Almighty, the Universe, luck, etc. I thought these were only for the weak. "I am strong, and even without external help I can overcome the challenges of Life with my own strength. I can't count on anyone, but I don't need anyone." From this perspective, it's understandable that my Life was a constant struggle with much anguish and deep waves, and my deep spiritual corpses were accompanied by a lot of suffering. Living in the world of the ego is like looking at the world through the narrowed field of view form the circular opening at the end of a tube. Through the ego, we become incredibly purposeful and focused on a very small detail of reality. We are convinced that what we experience is the only existing reality, and that anyone who thinks or feels differently is stupid or abnormal. After all, what I experience is the only real truth. Through the ego, we lock ourselves into a narrow and presumptuous world, which not only destroys our Life, but also lowers our efficiency. How is this possible when the Person with a strong ego is convinced of the opposite?

Dr. Joe Dispenza (whose books I wholeheartedly recommend) was asked in one of his lectures how he could be so modest when he was such a famous Person? (He is currently one of the most famous spiritual leaders in the Western world.) He replied, "I've put an incredible amount of work into weakening my ego. I don't feel like doing this work over and over again." The ego always wants to reintegrate itself into our soul. It's a spiritual parasite that needs a host. The ego cannot exist without you, but you can exist without your ego. Imagine a living creature inhabited by parasites. Do you think it can be more efficient, healthy or fruitful than its partner who exists without a parasite? Of the mistletoe-infected tree and the mistletoe-free, healthy one living next to it, which one do you think is growing? Which one is fresher and more vigorous?

But how does the ego parasite make us lame and less effective while making us believe the opposite? I would like to answer this with several points:

A. Tunnel vision

I've written about this before, but let's now focus on the downside. If I see a narrow part of the world and I am convinced that it's the only reality that exists, then a lot of opportunities pass me by without my even noticing them. If I have fewer options to choose from, my efficiency decreases drastically, as I may be getting to my destination by the most complicated route, while I have no idea that there are much shorter routes. I used to experience this without understanding why I had to work ten times harder to achieve the same goal that fell into someone else's lap. Life seemed unjust. However, it was only thanks to my crusty, hardened destructive ego that I ended up thinking like that. I felt unfortunate and unlucky, and as a result I grew an even stronger and more destructive ego. The ego always makes us believe that it is there to protect us and to make us more effective. In fact, the ego is only concerned with self-realization, and you are only a host for it to exploit.

B. Negative feedback of unnecessary thoughts

The ego keeps you in constant fear, as it can make you believe that it is the one protecting you. That's why your brain is constantly scanning for possible alternatives in the future and trying to think through the direction that works best for you. At the same time, 99.999% of your thoughts when analyzing the future never happen! Thus, 99.999% of your thoughts about the future are completely unnecessary. That means that out of 100,000 thoughts, only one makes sense. Those with weak egos trust the future, so they don't scan it all the time. Thus, they can use those 99,999 thoughts for much more meaningful purposes. Brain work burns more energy than running. It's no coincidence that we're so hungry after a lot of creative work that requires a lot of thinking. This is compounded by the fact that the ego (especially the destructive ego) often encourages you to think about the past. If you did something wrong, it makes you think about it a thousand times so you don't do it again in the future. This again strengthens the ego in you, but the point is that 99.999% of your thoughts in the past were also unnecessary. This means you were wasting an incredible amount of internal energy. Imagine if you could use all that energy to make your life better. How would your Life turn out?

Back then, as long as I had a strong destructive ego, I was constantly struggling from a lack of energy, but I didn't understand why. It's clear now. I wish someone had explained this to me, just as I am trying to help you now. Almost constantly, I felt like I didn't have enough Life force to accomplish my goals. I abused myself just for that reason and proceeded towards my goals at the cost of my overall health. This, of course, plunged me into a downward spiral of energy. Getting up every morning was torture. Every night's work, in order to be able to get more done, was a separate suffering. But I did it. My strength was drained by many, many unnecessary thoughts without me realizing it. Today, living in the world of the creator ego, I do more in 8 hours than I did in 16 before, and I am very rarely tired. I wake up feeling energetic in the morning. I feel good almost all day. I always focus on the task that Life is bringing me. Even though I work a lot, I'm almost never tense, and my effectiveness is many times greater than it was. So, in retrospect, it has been well worth transforming the destructive ego into a fruitful one over the past few years.

I used to plan my day precisely. If anyone or anything wanted to divert me from my original schedule, I was angry—even furious—and just kept going according to my original plans. All this anger, rage and forced scheduling also drained a lot of energy. Why did I do all this? Because I was convinced that the way I had imagined the future was just right. Wow, I was such a dope! Life (you can substitute any other word from your faith) takes care of everyone who is open to it! It is an all-pervading energy system that organizes every aspect of Life. Only the ego is blind to it, but you and anyone else can be open to it! It is only the ego and the excess of rationality that drives you out of it. In the biblical tale, the serpent and the apple threw Adam and Eve out of paradise. The apple is a symbol of excessive rationality and an excessive belief in knowledge, while the snake is a symbol of seduction and ego.

C. Health Effects of Incorrect Thoughts

As we've seen in the previous chapters, diseases arise from incorrect thought patterns. If we live with a lot of permanently negative thoughts and consequently experience a lot of negative emotions, sooner or later our bodies will get sick. One of the destructive ego's favorite tools is to evoke negative emotions. For example, if we are afraid, it can tell you even more that it will protect you. This is true of all negative emotions. Shame, guilt, apathy, grief, fear, longing, anger, and most of all pride are embedded in our destructive ego. The ego is strengthened by these negative emotions. It achieves this with thoughts that lead to such emotions (and vice versa). I remember that I used to constantly think (unnecessarily) about future alternatives in which I would have to defend myself or avoid criticism from others. At the same time, I was constantly angry when something didn't turn out the way I had imagined. And if something did happen to turn out the way I'd predicted, I was damn proud of myself. My ego was constantly labeling others and comparing and criticizing. It either shamed me, guilted me, or made me proud. If I felt better than someone else, it strengthened my pride. If someone *did* something better than me, I felt shame or guilt. Do you think all these negative feelings can go away without a trace? Please take a look at most People over the age of 40! Look at the state of their bodies! See what's showing in their faces! Most of them were beautiful and healthy at a young age, full of hope and goals. You may not feel the effects of all that negativity yet at a young age, but over the decades this process slowly consumes your health like a poison. In your twenties you ignore any signs, and in your thirties you don't yet address your mild symptoms. Then, in your forties, you start to regret why you've lived so badly. Here come the health issues. It's different for everyone, depending on—among other things—in what proportion and at what concentration you experienced negative emotions from the combination described above.

D. Negative emotional effects of wrong thoughts and the price of suppression

Incorrect thoughts generate negative emotions, as I described to you in the previous point. But also think about what your chances of success are with so many negative emotions. As long as my ego was strong, I couldn't understand why I wasn't happy while doing everything I could for it. I was diligent, purposeful, hardworking. I fought for my goals in such a way that sacrificed myself, but I wasn't really happy. How could I be? I didn't even notice how many negative feelings were inside me, which I mostly suppressed. It was the usual thing to do. In addition, my ego constantly believed that these were not my fault, but the damn world's. In doing so, the ego only strengthened itself in me and actually destroyed me. How deceitful, right? And here I will give you another important piece of knowledge: every repressed emotion will backfire at least 1,000 times later in your life! Therefore, the greatest evil we can do is to suppress our emotions instead of living them!

E. Self-importance

This is one of the trickiest parts of the ego. It makes us think that we are cool, beautiful, smart, etc. As an example, let's take a perfectionist woman's thoughts about her body, and a rich and powerful man. What they have in common is hubris. Each of their egos makes itself believe that it is much better than other Humans. This difference "rightly" makes them feel that they are special. The belief in specialness generates a false sense of happiness. The perfectionist lady is adorned with the vanity of her appearance and the charm of the accolades of many other People. Power and money give comfort and a sense of security, which is what gives the man in this example a sense of happiness. From the outside, I see something else. I was also a perfectionist and I am also an entrepreneur. The reality is that, to the outside world, most of these kinds of People seem to be happy, but inwardly there is a regular burst of inner emptiness. We sweep these aside and we go deeper into our perfectionism, lust for power or other addictive activities—anything but to face that emptiness. It gives us a superficial mirage of conceit and happiness, which we can call compensation from another point of view. This is how the ego makes us believe that we are on the right path. This is the biggest trap, and yet our whole society is based on it. Most Humans try to follow these patterns, wanting to resemble these 'elite' People. But imagine what it would be like to heal the emptiness from within instead of fueling the ego's arrogance. What peace and harmony would come to our lives! This can be achieved by aiming in an ego-free (enlightened) direction, the method of which is to raise your spiritual vibration level.

F. Distorted needs

A typical feature of the ego is that it always plans everything. If you plan what you will do and when even while on vacation, you have a strong and possibly destructive ego. Another feature of the ego is that if something does not turn out as you planned, you experience it as a huge problem. Sometimes I am amazed at how much trouble some people make from not being able to get the coffee they want or their favorite flavor of ice cream. What problems are these, while currently 1 billion people in the world don't have access to healthy drinking water and 3 billion people don't know if they will have something to eat tomorrow? The ego overvalues itself and makes its host's mind believe that its needs are important. I'm not saying that your words aren't important; I simply contend that the ego gives you a distorted view of your real needs. The ego makes you believe that the world of emotions is not important, or that only the satisfaction of my positive emotions is important. At the same time, the ego needs all the good of the material world. And only I matter. Of course I deserve a 600m² house and an urban SUV with an engine the size of a truck's! Of course I can fly to the other side of the world whenever I feel like it! Let me have whatever I want, whatever it is. We don't even realize how much our egos distort our needs. An acquaintance of mine who had suddenly become very rich told me that his desire was to buy anything he wanted. For example, if he wants his 1200th gold watch, he can buy that too. Now, this was the sentence that ended our friendship. True, even though I was deeply spiritual at the time, I judged him. I felt sorry for him, but there was nothing I could do for him. He was blind; his ego made him so. Of course, my ego's reaction was that my own needs were much more modest, so I was much more normal than him. But beware, this is just another tool of the ego focusing on differences.

The ego always gives you the next goal. If you have achieved that, you are a little happy, but the newer one is already starting to stir within you. This way, your needs grow slowly, from decade to decade. You do not even notice that you have changed, because it slowly and gradually builds into your personality. The parasite also grows gently and gradually in the host body, so that it does not throw it off. Please follow your life path in your mind's eye and observe what your needs were in childhood, adolescence, young adulthood, and after about 10 years. Your needs have grown, haven't they?

G. Lack of intuition, decreased creativity

The ego is the eternal, willful designer. Another aspect of this is that we become blind to our intuitions, even though they are much wiser than the advice of the ego. The ego makes us believe that they are nonsense. But it's the other way around: the existence of the ego is the stupidity itself. I am not claiming that there is no need for ego when I am defending myself under a real threat of death. But fortunately, in our modern lives, this occurs extremely rarely, as there is peace and there is good public safety in our environment as of this writing. However, unfortunately, the chances of World War III breaking out are not small. But if Humanity shapes its future wisely, many, many Humans will be able to live their Lives without ever coming close to such a threat. The ego is therefore rarely needed, yet all our actions, thoughts and feelings are controlled by this negative energy system. Meanwhile, as a result of constant planning, we lose two of our greatest strengths: our intuition and our creativity.

H. Stress generator

The ego creates constantly imagined sources of danger on the thought plane in the future. This keeps you in a constant sense of alert. Thus, your body is in full survival mode. This increases stress, and your body is constantly producing cortisol. As a result, you never really feel safe. So how can you be healthy, abundant, and effective? At the same time, your ego makes you believe that you are effective because this inner insecurity keeps you constantly awake. It is also a parasitic tactic. If I feel safe, I can make more prudent decisions. In this way, I get myself into less trouble and achieve my goals with less energy investment.

Imagine how much more peaceful, harmonious, healthy, effective and happy your life would be if you could live without these negative effects! But beware: your ego will generate a million reasons why this concept is crazy, but it is not. I have already reshaped and weakened a part of my ego, so I know for sure that every line you have read is true. However, when I still had a strong ego, I would have swept this idea away for some reason. Obviously, the question now arises: how can the ego be weakened and transformed into a creator ego? The answer is not easy. After all, you have to do this with a parasite that probably got inside you sometime between the ages of three and fifteen, and slowly got absorbed into you. The first step is to reshape the ego to recognize both its existence and how many places in your life it has a strong negative impact on you. This requires deep self-awareness, because due to your ego you probably don't even know who you really are. However, this book will give you all the necessary tools to raise your spiritual vibration level and transform your destructive ego into a neutral and then a creative one. It's important to know that the problem is not the ego itself, but the quality of it! On the planet called Earth, only the enlightened Person can live without ego. Ego is an important and indispensable part of every other Person's life. However, the level of your happiness and the quality of your human relationships depends on what kind of ego lives in inside you.

CHAPTER 5

The main tools of the destroyer-ego

As you already know from the previous chapter, the ego's only purpose is to maintain and strengthen itself. To do this, the ego has a number of sophisticated and refined tools, the most important of which are discussed in this chapter. As I have already mentioned, it's very difficult to see behind the ego. However, doing so is of paramount importance for achieving happiness! That's why this chapter is so important. After all, if you understand the tools used by the ego to hide your true self from you, you will find it much easier to catch it in the act.

5.1. False self-image

If you ask anyone if they know themselves well, they will almost always say 'yes'. But beware: most of the time, this answer is just not true! This is the response of your ego, whose "job" is to hide your true inner self from you, from which your ego was built up by running away from your true self. I know this sounds strange at first. Your ego gets offended that someone dares to assume that you don't know yourself. Obviously, you know yourself in a certain way. But deep self-knowledge means that you are also aware of the part of your personality that your ego hides from you! This is the part of you that you didn't want to accept in yourself at some point, and because of that, you hid it behind your ego so that no one else could see it. Isn't that interesting? You're right to ask why you need to look in there again. You hid it because you couldn't accept it. The solution is simple, because until you know your own soul at the right depths, you cannot be happy! Sorry if this seems harsh, but it was intentional. What's more, you didn't accept your true inner self not because there was anything wrong with it, but because other destructive-ego people who were important to you (your parents, for example) didn't like it. And you believed it was you. However, the problem was with those who formed you in your early childhood, educated you, humiliated you, kept you in check with guilt, forced the feeling of helplessness on you, made you sad, raised you in fear, made you believe that you were not special or lovable... the list goes on.

But let's get back to the chapter title. There are three different levels of self-knowledge, which are presented in the simple diagram below. Let's see what these three levels really mean.

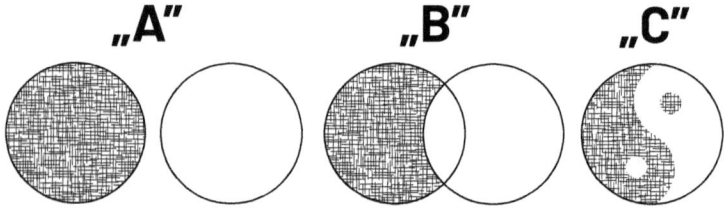

Figure 10: Different levels of self-knowledge

In **Figure 10**, the shaded circles show your self-image, the empty circles show your true self. Self-image means the set of qualities you think about yourself. The real you is who you really are. You must have seen talent shows on TV where there were candidates who knew with incredible confidence that they were very talented singers. Nevertheless, when they sang on stage, it was clear to even non-musical audience members that they had no talent, and even their hearing was terrible. When the jury informed them of this, they either made some excuse ("I performed all night, I barely slept, and that's why..."), or they counterattacked: "This jury is made up of complete idiots! They don't know what they're talking about!" From the outside, this scene seems ridiculous, and it really does make us smile. I think a lot of People watch these shows because they like to make fun of these kinds of contestants. Of course, it's important to note here that everyone's ego (especially the destructive ego) works in such a way that we notice the ridiculousness in others more easily. Of course, this also has sophistication levels. Returning to the figure on page 134, the TV singing candidates I've described clearly belong to Group A, at least in the area in which they were measured. That is, they think of themselves as being completely different from who they really are. There are singer candidates who feel they have some talent, and the stage reveals that they really are natural talents. They are in the fortunate position that their level of self-knowledge belongs to the "B" group and, on top of that, they think less of themselves than they really are. This means they partially see their true selves. Of course, there are also singer candidates who go to the stage with great self-consciousness and their performance for the jury is only slightly better than average. They also belong to the "B" self-knowledge group, but their situation is more difficult because they picture themselves more than they really are. Their self-awareness is also partial. Then there are those who know they are very talented and show it on stage. This is extremely rare, and not by chance. They are part of the "C" group. This is the rarest type of Person on Earth. They are the ones who know themselves well; their self-image is completely correct. As we move from Group A to Group C, our egos weaken. As you may have noticed, truly talented People are modest, cheerful, and pure-minded, with minimal egos. These are all "symptoms" of high levels of mental vibration.

As a young adult, I thought I knew myself perfectly. I would have placed myself in the "C" group with full confidence. But the reality was that I was very firmly in the "A" group. When I took the first self-knowledge tests and they gave me surprising results, my typical reactions were: "The test is lousy; how could you get such a stupid result?" or "What kind of idiot put this test together?" and more. Then, as my self-knowledge deepened, most of the test results proved to be true. I'm not saying that self-knowledge tests are infallible, but the tests put together scientifically are more likely to find their way to the truth. After that, it took about eight to ten years for my level of self-knowledge to go from group "A" through "B" to get closer to "C". But this process is still ongoing. Group C is an idealized goal, by the way! This is something that can never be 100% achieved, since one of the basic questions of Eastern cultures, the "who am I?" is not by accident the most difficult question to answer. When we know a layer of ourselves, another layer emerges underneath that requires deeper self-knowledge. But one of the important rules of the pursuit of happiness is to constantly strive for it. Why? Because the deeper your self-awareness, the greater your chance of happiness! At the same time, it is in your ego's interest that your self-awareness is faulty, because the more this is true, the more your ego can assure you that you need it.

Therefore, whenever you can, deepen your self-awareness with self-knowledge books, self-knowledge tests and courses. Or, you can ask a good psychologist to help you. Deepening your self-image is always a useful investment! There can never be too much of it!

5.2. Comfort zone

A few years ago, I had lunch with an old acquaintance of mine. I remembered how good it was to be with her, and how radiant her balance and happiness were. To my surprise, she thanked me for taking her out of her bad state three years earlier and thus starting her life in a better direction. A truly happy Person sat across from me. I appreciated her thanks, although since I had given her advice out of complete selflessness and with the intention of helping her, I did not expect to ever be thanked for it. But let's get to the point: the key phrase I had said to her was, **"The really good things in your life are outside your current comfort zone!"** The 'comfort zone' is the set of activities, places and habits where we feel psychologically safe. We can get out of our comfort zone by doing something that causes excitement or some stress or fear when we want to start. It's a good idea to take a week or two out of your life and see how comfortable you are. This is an important part of your self-awareness! Generally, adventurers who bravely embark on the new and the unknown are not stuck in their comfort zones. However, those who get along well in their own usual system are People living within their comfort zone. The latter can be divided into two groups. One group is perfectly satisfied with their Life. It is not worthwhile for them to read this subchapter further. After all, they are happy or they make themselves believe it (the latter case is a false trap of the ego). The other group consists of those who are constantly playing in their comfort zone's half of the square, but are not really happy in this "living space". They have desires they dream of but don't step out of their comfort zone to achieve them. Remember what we learned about the ego? It always protects the current state! So, the comfort zone is nothing more than the area of your life dominated by the ego. People trapped in their comfort zone include typical procrastinators and those who can always explain why they shouldn't do a particular thing. This includes those who always forecast the worst future for themselves when they think of doing something unusual. If you belong to this group, then I have a straightforward question for you: if Life in your comfort zone is not really satisfactory, why is it worth staying there? The solution is simple: get out of your comfort zone! Yes, but outside your comfort zone, you can expect not only cool things, but also serious stumbles and bumps on the nose. That's the way it is.

If you step out of your comfort zone and fall on your face, it will be very good for you! It's very rare to make progress without stumbling a few times. Most of the time, we fall into spiritual depths, and then when we process it and become better than we were before the fall. Spiritual depths are used to bring about the crushing of the ego. The same thing happened to the Person mentioned at the beginning of this article (and of course to me—who knows how many times). The fear of getting into trouble only preserves your current unfavorable situation! This doesn't mean you should do everything irresponsibly and run headfirst into a wall. Be careful outside of your comfort zone; it's not worth falling on your nose if you stay that way! But do step out and go play on the other side! If you fail, get up again and learn from it. Once you're on your feet, think again about where the right direction is and be brave enough to keep going. It's no coincidence that the first life-affirming level of spiritual vibration is Courage, and it's not by chance that the last anti-Life psychic energy level is Pride. The ego is the guardian of your comfort zone. Courage is the level where we dare to step out from behind the ego's self-indulgent reflexes and dare to do something to be happier! All it really takes is courage! So be brave and be freer and happier! But never confuse courage with recklessness, because the latter is tied to the spiritual vibration of Anger and does not serve your happiness.

5.3. Compensation

Compensation means showing the world something different about ourselves than what we feel inside. If I want to describe this more accurately, in most cases it can also be said that we show the opposite of what is working in our souls. I have built many of these compensation systems in the past, most of which have now been left behind me.

In most cases, compensation is about wanting to hide some of our features from the world because we are afraid that people will think we are weaker, dumber, clumsier, etc. if that particular characteristic turns out to be true. Thus, the main image of compensation is about the lack of self-acceptance. The less we accept our true selves, the more we compensate towards the world. If we want to translate this into self-knowledge, this statement also applies in the reverse: **the more we compensate towards the world, the less we accept our true self.** Of course, this is very good for the ego. Until you accept yourself, the ego can give you a lot of "help" to "protect" you from the world. This is false of course, because it's actually not good for you; it's your ego—the negative energy system inside you. Let's look at some practical examples:

When I was young, I accepted myself to such a small degree that I literally ran away from the real me. This was obviously due to the fact that my self-esteem was approximately equal to zero. I thought of myself as a stupid, clumsy Person, and completely worthless. Yet the outside world thought of me as a confident, determined, intelligent, capable Person Being. (Obviously, by 'on the outside' I mean the people to whom I didn't dare to show my true self). Because I felt stupid inside, I became a university lecturer, senior manager, expert, and researcher, and I took on a lot of positions that could put smart-sounding titles next to my name. Outward to the world, I compensated for my inner fear of being stupid. Since then, my self-awareness has recovered, and I know and feel that there is nothing wrong with my brain's abilities, but at that time I honestly felt stupid. I remember that when I was in college we all took an IQ test, and I was terrified of having it revealed how stupid I was. I was sure that I would score 80 on the test (it takes a level of 85 to complete elementary school). I remember well the tremendous shock when the result was 142. Of course, the feeling of stupidity was so ingrained in my ego that the explanation was that the IQ test was faulty and must have made a significant error.

Since gaining a good understanding of the spiritual nature of compensation, I look at People differently now. It's shocking how many doctors, engineers, and academic staff compensate every day in front of their students, patients or clients. The intellectual class is imbued with compensation, which is one of the reasons other classes often view intellectuals with such condemnation. Obviously, some academics went to university and studied hard because they wanted to prove to the world (and mostly to themselves) that their fear was false, or that they wanted to appear to be more than what they felt inside. Therefore, this type of compensation among those who are working in intellectual jobs is very childish. Of course, this doesn't mean that all intellectuals are there due to their compensation!

A form of compensation that is often seen (especially in men, although it's becoming more frequent in women) is that we want to appear very strong on the outside. I have met many very hardworking People in my Life who have especially timid souls. Some women also like to look tough, while they can't wait to finally trust a man so they can feel like a weak woman next to him. I know some People who are loud and like to be the center of attention, thus appearing outwardly as People with high self-confidence. Meanwhile, deep down, they have a deep lack of self-esteem. Then there are those who have grown great in power, while deep down they are afraid and insecure. A very common example (especially for women) is someone constantly posting more and more beautiful pictures of themselves on Facebook. These People usually don't think of themselves as attractive enough or lovable enough on the inside, so they try to fill this sense of lack in their souls by collecting a lot of 'likes'.

Of course, compensation cannot be criticized and the compensating Person must not be judged. If you recognize it in someone, don't judge them please, and don't do the same to yourself. Compensation is about the need to get a lot of recognition from the outside world in order to believe that we are more than what we feel inside. The compensating Person actually needs a lot of help, whether they realize this about themselves or not. If a person feels stupid and goes to university as a lecturer, they need to get feedback from a lot of students about how smart they are. In this way, rationally processed experiences can gradually be integrated into our egos, so in principle, our inner sense of deficiency is reduced.

However, there are serious problems with this strategy! The main root of the problem is that **change is only successful if it comes from inside.** I used to get recognition from thousands of students for how smart I am. However, the thousands of accolades only changed my rational thinking. That is, I knew rationally that I was a smart Person, but at the same time, deep down, the feeling of stupidity in my soul did not disappear. I wanted to prove myself more and more to the world, which is an endless process with little success. When did this change? It came when, as a result of many years of spiritual self-improvement, my self-esteem was restored to its spiritual place. In this way, my self-image has become real, and today I think of myself in a way that's in keeping with reality. I don't think of myself as being any more or less than what I am in this field. What's even better news is that I also feel this way! So, I'll confidently say that earning millions of accolades from People does not bring true spiritual healing either! This is the big trap of social media. With it, we can only deceive ourselves, and we adorn ourselves in front of our egos. However, internal change modifies everything in the right direction—a process that results in a realistic self-image and realistic desires. This first requires deep self-knowledge! In what areas do you compensate? What feelings will these compensations cause? What are the causes of these feelings—from family or other experiences? Once you have these answers, you are past the first step and you know what the problem is. Whoever reaches this point is already a special Person. Most People don't reach this self-awareness level in their lifetime! Then, with appropriate spiritual development methods (the second half of this book is covers these), you will begin to realize the miracle when you will truly feel yourself as you are, and all this will be imbued with a feeling of total inner self-acceptance. I'm committed to getting you there, because it's wonderful to live like that! I know your reaction now is likely to feel that it's impossible. I thought so too for decades, but there is a Person speaking to you now who has succeeded. True, it takes hard work and dedication. However, this book was born with the selfless purpose of helping you get there.

5.4. Addictions

5.4.1. Addiction basics

Those who want to embark on the path of spiritual growth must be clean of their addictions. I don't want to bore anyone with scientific definitions, though I know that in my past, many kinds of addictions ruined my Life, from each of which I was able to come out permanently. I know the right way to get out of these. This book will unselfishly help you do this completely, and all you have to do is follow its instructions! The L.I.F.E. method is a powerful, efficient system. I hope you will experience this too.

Understanding addictions and then recognizing them in yourself is an important step to healing. Most People are either unaware of their addictions or believe they are okay. This is why most alcoholics don't want to give up alcohol. For example, when I was a party drinker (this is a form of alcoholism where one can only have fun in a nightclub under the influence of alcohol),

I was sure that it was cool and acceptable to get drunk at every party. I was convinced that everything was in order. But to identify your addictions well, you have to first understand what addiction really is.

Addictions are also called bents or dependencies. In my experience, addictions are psychologically rooted processes and activities in which we suffer long-term losses in return for short-term pleasure. Another characteristic of addictions is that we can't control them at all, or only for short periods. That is, they dominate us. The short-term source of pleasure must be obtained in increasing doses, otherwise tension, irritability, fatigue or other negative symptoms will start in our body. When we look at addictions on a spiritual level, their common root is the feeling of craving. People who are addicted are always craving something. However, it is very rare for someone to have only one addiction. In general, we live with several addictions, one of which intensifies as the other subsides, so they burden our life stages in waves. Another characteristic of addictions is that after achieving the craving goal (e.g., by drinking a lot), they are always followed by a stage of lack of energy and usually imbued with shame, guilt, apathy, grief, or fear. For a brief sense of happiness, we pay an incredible price.

There are many addictions. I'll list a few of them for you to give you the real picture: eating addiction, alcoholism, drug addiction, workaholism, shopping addiction, series addiction ('binge watching'), gambling addiction, sex addiction, porn addiction, speed addiction, internet addiction, obsessive tidying, body perfectionism, etc. Addiction can also be the opposites of any of these, like when we are abnormally detached from something, such as anorexia or sexual anorexia. These are the addictions I see most often in my surroundings. I suffered from several of them over the course of decades.

The first level of self-knowledge is to determine which addictions are characteristic of you! Beware: there are levels to addictions and your ego always embellishes reality. Continuing with the example of the alcoholic, you very rarely see realistically that anything is wrong. Your ego justifies why you need to drink and why you don't have a problem when you do. This works the same for all other addictions. It's also important to understand that although workaholism and body perfectionism are seen as positive things in society, they are no different from drug addiction in terms of their spiritual root. Each Person suffers the consequences of their addiction, the only difference being that the drug addict is condemned by everyone, while a body perfectionist, by receiving a lot of positive feedback, even believes that they're on the right track. Perfectionism becomes a crystallized part of your ego and you don't realize how wrong your Life is going. You are chasing a false mirage with total commitment—which unfortunately will carry a very harsh price.

Let's move on to the feeling of craving that permeates all addictions. It's no coincidence that most addicted People live at or below the spiritual vibration of Craving. The drug addict craves the substance and the released state caused by the substance. The alcoholic wants to be constantly depressed so that they don't have to occupy themselves with the difficult things in Life. Workaholics set themselves ever-greater goals that they crave to achieve. The body perfectionist will do almost anything to achieve an increasingly beautiful and perfect body image.

It's important to emphasize that setting positive goals (e.g., wanting to be more fit) is a completely healthy thing to do. The difference between addiction and the pursuit of positive goals is that one is already pathological and has long-term negative consequences, while the other increases the real happiness level. This can be distinguished by the fact that by the time the workaholic achieves their goal, they will have set new goals, and are therefore only briefly happy (if at all) with the achievement of their previous goals. Here, the pathological aspect can be seen from the fact that there is always a need to struggle for something. The craving is the engine. Another main feature of the pathological condition is that we move towards our goals at the cost of self-destruction or exploitation of others. The workaholic, for example, works nights and weekends and is even proud of it. However, in doing so they actually suck out their body and soul, that is to say, they proceed with self-destructive actions. In the case of a healthy goal and its healthy achievement, we are permanently happy with the goal achieved and we feel grateful for having achieved it almost throughout our lives. At the same time, the path to achieving that goal is also joyful, exciting, and fully life-affirming. Why do we need to recover from our addictions? The answer is very simple. Although addictions in the short term give short-term well-being (for example, a sex addict feels happy for a few minutes or even a few hours after a good romp), in the medium and long term their life is sinking deeper and deeper. For example, a sex addict will not be able to have normal, psychologically functional Person relationships, so they will experience loneliness and suffering; they will also want to experience increasingly extreme perversions.

Knowing your addictions is important in order to get behind your ego because the ego always deceives you with illusions and window dressing. For those more deeply interested in this topic, I highly recommend Gábor Máté's book *In the Realm of Hungry Ghosts*. I have read quite a few books on the subject, but I find this book to be extremely good.

My bucket list used to be quite different than it is today. There used to be a lot of forbidden and perverse things on it. With the enhancement of my peace of mind, these wishes disappeared by themselves because what's desired at a low level of spiritual vibration is no longer attractive at higher levels. Conversely, what seems less desirable or unrealistic at lower levels of mental vibration will become desirable at higher levels of mental vibration. I remember thinking that rule-makers who never did anything forbidden or bad were boring and gray. At the time, my soul needed extremes. Obviously, anyone who follows the rules purely out of good manners and lives with constant repression really is lackluster. However, the direct consequence of spiritual development is that our thinking and our desires become less and less extreme. For example, in the eyes of a Person at the level of spiritual vibration of Craving, this seems boring, and they can't understand what is good about it. (This line of thinking can be deduced in the same way for most of the Life Destructive psychological vibration levels.) After all, their soul is fueled by intense longing and craving; it's a fiery, strong, powerful spiritual "engine". Their ego immediately reacts to all this in such a way that a balanced Life, where there are no extremes, would be uncomfortable for them. But it is not, because extreme thinking and extreme desires are replaced by something else. They will be replaced by more peaceful forces, which are also more powerful and Life-supporting. They allow us to experience miracles that are much more significant than craving. While craving squeezes the body and soul and thus makes the individual self-destructive, the enhancement of inner peace makes it possible to experience Life at a deeper level and thus become fuller. It is precisely this Life-destroying craving that generates the extremes. After all, craving stirs you up, generating positive extremes, then squeezes you out and pushes you into negative extremes. Then the body and soul rest for a short time, usually at the spiritual vibration level of Apathy or even deeper, and the cycle of extremes begins again. This is the working process of all addictions. As a result of the increase in my mental vibration level, different things were added to my bucket list—mainly cultural—as well as Nature- or Human-supporting ones. From the point of view of my old ego, I became a gray, boring Human, the result of a distorted and erroneous filter at the time. And when I reached a higher level of mental resilience, the bucket list ceased to exist in my life. Today, I feel clearly that Life always brings me what I need most for the development of my consciousness, so I simply entrust myself to the miracle of Life and let it come through to me at whatever cost. A Life without a bucket list is available in the world of the creator-ego, and it is a wonderful physical-spiritual and thoughtful sense of freedom which permeates every minute.

In *The Lord of the Rings* (a book I recommend to everyone), the ring is the addiction—a wonderful symbol of this dependency—and it accompanies the whole story. Gollum is an extremely addicted creature. The ring is his "precious thing" that he never wants to be apart from. Yet the ring squeezes his body, sucks out his soul, and thus enslaves him. The wise magician Gandalf the Grey said to Bilbo the old hobbit at the beginning of the story: 'then you can go and be free' after asking him to put the ring down for good. It's a wonderful half sentence that has everything you need in order to have a deep understanding of addictions. The ring binds you to itself and prompts you to do unnatural things. The ring/addiction analogy illustrates this incredibly well. The object of addiction (alcohol, drugs, porn, work, eating, cigarettes, shopping, speed, play, etc.) makes you a spiritual slave and do Life-destroying things. This is the huge problem of addictions: spiritual slavery.

In Gollum's eyes, the ring became such a wonderful "my precious" that the other motifs in his Life no longer mattered. There was only him and his "precious". This symbolic world perfectly reflects the way addiction works. I recently saw a documentary about very fat People. They all had one thing in common: they all said that their sense of taste gave them so much pleasure that they would sacrifice anything for it. For them, eating was the ring that had distorted itself to become a "wonderful precious" in their souls. All other pleasures of Life were dwarfed by the joy of eating. In the aforementioned documentary, several interviewees mentioned that they also sacrificed their sexuality in order to experience more flavor. They no longer cared that their excess fat would make them undesirable to other People. In *The Lord of the Rings* trilogy, Gollum was also disfigured by his "precious" Lifestyle.

Gandalf, the old magician, said it perfectly: if you put the ring down, you will be free. The parallel is also true here: if you put down the object of your addiction, you can live a freer and fuller Life. Therefore, when People periodically put down what they depended on before, they felt enthusiastic and liberated. But in fact, most people don't want to eliminate what they crave from their lives because they are as attached to it as Gollum was to the ring.

However, if you do decide to drop your addiction, unfortunately, unlike Bilbo, most People will either relapse or replace their addiction with another one. What could the reason be for this? There are psychological reasons behind every addiction. In most cases, lack of love, lack of self-acceptance, repressed guilt, shame, fears, and unresolved grief are the most common psychological causes. If a person gives up their addiction by force and does not heal the spiritual cause of it, sooner or later they will fall back. The subconscious is incredibly powerful; it always beats the conscious self! However, it is important to emphasize that relapse is nothing more than gathering the strength of the soul before trying again. Thus, the recidivist should not see failure in it and thus feel guilty again, but a new chance! It is very important to be aware of this point of view for your whole Life. If you can do this one thing, a wonderful change will begin in your life.

For me, the thought of getting rid of my computer addiction helped me ask myself: "How unhappy would I be if I didn't play my favorite game anymore? My answer was that I would not be unhappy at all; in fact, I would be happier without it. But even with this understanding, I could only moderate the amount of play, because the "solution" from the brain is never enough. It is always the spiritual cause that needs to be healed, and then the addiction will disappear from our Life by itself. I haven't thought about playing any computer games for a few years. It feels like a life-destroying, worthless and irresponsible pastime, while a few years ago I sat fully engaged in front of the computer for several hours a day.

5.4.2. Intergenerational addictions

I first read the following statement in Eric Berne's book (2009): *"Whoever dissolves an addiction in themselves will save generations after them"*. Since then, quite many books exploring this issue have been published, and not without reason. Addictions and other mental illnesses are transmitted to our children, who then carry our burdens. Unfortunately, this is the case even if we are aware of our addictions and consciously raise our children not to be like us. For example, when I was a young adult, I was overly perfectionist. It's a very heavy psychological burden. I didn't want my first daughter to suffer from this in adulthood, so I invested a lot of effort in her upbringing so that she would not be like this, but I could only moderate this effect in her. She too had become a perfectionist, albeit not in an exaggerated way as I had been. Her perfectionism was truly relieved when my spiritual wounds healed; I changed, and it radiated through her.

The child considers their parent as God. They don't choose between their parent's characteristics. The way the parent does something is perfect. If it makes children feel bad or they don't like it, then they would rather question their own personality (and can even break up with it), but they still want to be like their parent. Children are thus like the perfect "copying machines"; they copy and reproduce every behavior pattern—both the good and the bad. Since they are incredibly sensitive, they also copy the characteristics you consciously try to hide from them! I was always accepting of my daughter so that she would not be a perfectionist due to a sea of parental expectations. At the same time, I was not completely accepting of myself at that time, and the result of this was that she became like me. I hid it from her in vain. She copied me, in spite of the fact that I was not worthy of it. Most parents unconsciously live their parental attitudes and are unaware of the responsibility of being a parent. But it's a huge responsibility! At the same time, it's a very great opportunity to raise happier, more balanced children than ourselves. But this is only possible if we solve our own—mostly transgenerational—programs and raise our psychological vibration level. I know from experience that when I started to rise dynamically, my children immediately followed me on this path. It's never too late to change! Our children take the good from us just as "professionally" as the bad. Therefore, it makes a difference which path we choose.

Obviously, there is no perfect Person and therefore no perfect parent. But by consciously developing our soul, we can improve not only our own Life but also the future of our prospective or existing children. In my own life, I see many examples that prove this unequivocally. When my soul went through an incredible healing process through complex spiritual development, my relationship with my children also changed a lot. It was good before, but it got even better. At the same time, my children were also affected by my spiritual development, because they are much more balanced spiritually than they were before. My partner did the same. Seeing my "pattern", she went down this path as well. The spiritual development of her children soon followed the transformation of the parent's position. I could write many other examples from my environment, but the point is already clear from this. If the parent breaks with their addiction and develops their soul, they do a lot in order for their child to live happier than them.

Intergenerational addictions should not be understood to mean that, for example, if the father was an alcoholic then the son will also be an alcoholic (although this is possible, of course). In our family, for example, this was the case. In my father's family, wine was a basic "consumer product", with a basic level of alcoholism permeating the family. My father also became an alcoholic. But because of the shame he had brought from his family, it had become even stronger than the level he had brought from his parents. His alcoholism was one of the main pillars of his suicide. Of course, his mother blamed everyone else for her son's death. It never occurred to her that she was one of the causes of her son's death through having put her shame on her child. Yet the cause-and-effect relationships are so clear, whether we flee from them or dare to face them. How could a mother be expected to cope with the guilt of being the indirect cause of her son's death? This is how you can understand her self-defense reflex, which blamed everyone else. Looking in the mirror honestly can be a painful thing, but it's useful. Of course, it should also be mentioned that our fate is in our hands, so my father had the chance to change, and to realize that this should not have happened to him. The child has grown up and is already carrying the burden; there is no more blaming the parent! We are on our own path and only we can put down what we have taken on ourselves! We all have the potential for a happy Life, just as I no longer follow my father's example. Through putting a lot of strength, energy and perseverance into improving my Life, not only am I happy today, but I heal the souls of others with selfless love, for which I am grateful to Life for every minute. The power of my healing comes from the very fact that I came from the depths and transformed those depths into high emotions. In this way, I can give you not just things learned from books, but from good, well-functioning experiences.

Recently, I was relaxing with my partner in a hotel with all-inclusive catering. At the table next to us was a very obese couple with their two children. We ran into them many times, so we instinctively "observed" them. It was clear that the two adults were addicted to food. We received an unlimited amount of food five times every day (breakfast, brunch, lunch, snack, dinner), but this family even asked for a couple of large piles of French fries between 10 am and noon, a cooked meal between lunches and dinners, and ice cream after dinner. Their children were constantly stuffed: "Eat more, son." "Try it—isn't it delicious?" You could see in the children that they didn't want any more food (or girth), but they ate it anyway because they saw that this was how they could earn the love of their parents. Despite their young ages, the children were also already very obese. They were developing the food addiction burnt into them by their parents. After all, in the children, taste perception had been linked to parental love. They received caresses, smiles and words of appreciation when they ate another meal. This would make it the most pleasurable factor in their entire lives. Those poor children have little chance of a happy future unless they take matters into their own hands and undo the addictive program that their parents have burned into them. It works the same way with any addiction. It's passed on to the child because they think that this is how they can earn the love of their parent. However, it's very important that you know that in every addiction and trauma there is a chance for change and thus a happy Life! You're the helmsman, and this book is the map.

At the same time, it is much more common for a parent's addiction to appear in a different "disguise" in the child. Recently, I was in talks with a businessman who was in the mood to pour his soul out to me. He told me that he had worked hard all his life, that he'd always been hard-working, and that he'd recently hit his adult son in anger because he was a useless, work-averse, lazy human, and that this had made him unbearably angry. He didn't understand where he went wrong—how his child could be so different from him. This is an example that is as common as it is typical. The parent is a workaholic who is strict with himself, who suppresses his own personality, and who wants to prove himself to the world. And as a workaholic, he has a positive addiction in the eyes of society. He is the hero of the capitalist world. Regardless, this is still a very serious addiction. His son had become a "reprobate." He was not interested in challenges and couldn't meet any expectations. Instead of workaholism, computer gaming addiction became his "choice". Obviously, from the point of view of social judgment, the father is the "good Man". In fact, the father's addiction was copied by his son, whose soul was wounded, and the suppression was passed on. It was only because he couldn't compete with his perfectionist dad in the world of work that his soul went down the path of other addictions. Father and son do not differ from each other in any way. The depth and degree of addiction are similar; only the "disguise" is different. True, there was a good chance that the boy couldn't meet his father's perfectionist expectations, so his shame continued to destroy his soul. He has a good chance of having an even less happy Life than his father. But as I said, he gets a chance every day to pick up a book like this and start on the path of change!

There are plenty of other examples out there, but you can also find one in your local area. Every family is imbued with a chain of addiction. They are transmitted from generation to generation as negative energy waves. My grandparents lived through the two World Wars; they were regularly starving. My grandfather was one of the few soldiers who survived the horrors of the Don River disaster and made it home alive. My great-grandmother was raped by six Russian soldiers. She let them do this so they wouldn't notice that her 16-year-old daughter was also hiding in the house. The pains generated by the huge psychological wounds caused by the war were realized in addictions and then passed on to the next generations. However, if we consciously work to raise our mental vibration, the negative energy waves across the generations will be quelled more and more, just like the waves of the sea when the wind stops. One of the main tasks of our generation is to finally calm this turbulent sea and turn future generations towards inner peace and happiness.

Fortunately, there is peace in Europe as I write these lines, although the Russo-Ukrainian war is raging hard. But if you understand this intergenerational chain, it is immediately clear why there are so many mentally ill People around us. Since the World Wars, four or five generations have been able to only slightly mitigate the mental illnesses transmitted to our children. It is true that the main reason for this is that our society has moved away from spirituality. Our technocratic, over-rationalized development did not help, and even further destroyed the chances of Human healing. But it's time to change all that by working together, setting an example, and changing the main direction of our own Lives. If we understand and clearly see our addictions as negative waves of energy spreading from generation to generation and we feel the responsibility of it, this will give us the strength to invest more energy into healing our souls. With this, we protect not only ourselves but also future generations from the negative future generated by the past.

5.4.3. A sure-fire recipe for quitting addictions

Each addiction is associated with one or more levels of Life-destroying psychic vibration. This means that one or more negative feelings are the main driving force behind each addiction. For example, an alcoholic or a junkie usually feeds on feelings of shame or guilt, since on the surface the goal is to reach a stupefied state, while the real subconscious goal is to become ashamed in front of other People or to feel guilty for what they have done. This line of thinking is true for all addictions! On the surface, there is a huge difference between a rationally-known desire and a real subconscious goal. For example, a computer game or porn addict usually thinks they're doing it because they enjoy the pleasure of playing a game or watching porn. Their body is flooded with excitement and they feel better in the short term. At the same time, the porn lowers them to the Life-destroying spiritual vibration level of Desire, but if they were strongly influenced by their upbringing and religious dogmas in childhood, then behind it are hidden mixed emotions of shame and guilt. The computer game addict also generates craving, which is accompanied by anger as they constantly have a desire to defeat their opponents or the computer. But in fact, shame, guilt or fear are working in the background, which they are escaping through their gaming addiction.

Hormones produced by addiction-related emotions also cause long-term physical diseases, so it is also very important to protect or restore our health to reduce our dependence. The second step in quitting is to understand how your body and soul work in this regard. Consider, for example, the feeling of guilt, but you can replace this word with any negative feeling. Every sensation generates the production of certain hormones in your body. For example, if you often feel guilty, your body will often produce the hormone blend it associates with it. The consequence of this is that your cells are affected by the hormones generated by guilt. Cells are perfectly adaptable machines. In other words, the hormones they get more of long-term are the ones their cell membranes adapt to the most. Cells don't distinguish between good and bad; they just do their job; they adapt to what they are trained to do. This is appropriate from an evolutionary point of view, since the body's job is to adapt itself to the environment as much as possible. If your parents made you feel guilty a lot when you were a child, your subconscious mind will do everything to put you into situations that cause you to feel guilty, even if you know in your brain that this is not good for you. Think about how many times you've "accidentally" drifted into unexpected guilt situations when you didn't want to. This is because your cells are dependent on the hormones produced by guilt. That's why we feel guilty even if we don't want to. Your subconscious has made sure your cells get what they want. This is why addiction itself develops, as it's a tool to replace what our parents no longer carry out in our lives. Our cells are constantly craving these hormones, so your whole body subconsciously radiates them to you to finally feel guilty because it needs the hormone cocktail that causes the addiction.

The good news is that your cells can be adapted to a hormone cocktail generated by positive levels of psychological vibration (Courage, Impartiality, Willingness, Acceptance, Rationality, Love, Serenity, Peace, Enlightenment) although this can only be achieved gradually. After all, the membranes of the cells must be transformed to be more sensitive to these hormones. Therefore, if you start to consciously focus on positive feelings on a regular basis, then the cells will receive these hormones more and more, and after a while they will start to crave them. The cell membrane begins to become sensitive to these hormones as it receives more and more of them. It is at this point that the hormones of guilt or other life-destroying mental vibration levels become less interesting to your body, so you will hardly feel any temptation. In fact, with this, I have given you a surefire recipe for quitting addictions. This is the third step: you need to train your body to crave the hormones of positive emotions by practicing positive emotions and thoughts!

But it's important to know that every beginning is hard! At first, you will find such exercises boring. It could also be that your ego is sweeping you away by saying that it's nonsense, or that it will never work anyway. You need to know that your ego is nothing more than a psychological mechanism to protect your current hormonal status. Your ego is the subconscious impulse of all your cells! It does nothing more than want to preserve the current situation; it wants to receive the hormone cocktail your body has become accustomed to so far in your Life. That's why you shouldn't believe your own ego! Your ego doesn't want you to change. The good news is that the ego will slowly get used to the new, and then it will protect the new at all costs. When I underwent major soul healings, I no longer understood how I could have lived as

I did before, and my soul no longer wanted me to fall back there. After a while, the subconscious desire for this also disappeared, as my cells got used to it. I have experienced this process many times, so what I'm sharing here has deep experiences and deep, selfless energies to help you on this difficult path!

Why do so few people give up their addictions? As a result of the above, you can probably guess the answer: the ego does its best to preserve the existing state! That's why the **first typical mistake** is that most People don't even recognize their addiction! Even if others hold a mirror up to it, the addicted Person still brushes it off by not understanding why it's such a big problem. The "owner" of the addiction always sees the problem as much milder, as their ego defends it with every argument. So, the first pitfall is that you either don't even recognize your addiction, or you trivialize it so you don't have a chance to do anything about it.

The **second typical mistake** is that when someone finally recognizes and realizes that their addiction is a barrier to their happiness or even their health, they think that they have already solved everything. They try to mentally avoid addictive situations. A typical example is when a smoker decides to quit smoking. Thanks to their enthusiasm, careful storing and conscious attention, they can endure it for two or three weeks. Then, "unexpectedly," something happens that forces them to light a cigarette. The ego and the subconscious do their best to give the body the hormones it's addicted to. But here, too, nicotine addiction is just the surface. True addiction is a self-destructive emotion in the deep layers of the soul. In two or three weeks, every cell feels a deep craving—a lack of what it is expecting. This huge inner effect cannot be overcome by the brain! Not even the most strong-willed Person can do that! It's therefore a big mistake to hurt an alcoholic by telling them that they don't have enough willpower to give up alcohol for good. No one has the willpower for this! You can't permanently take action against your own cells! (There are some people who have been able to succeed, but they usually switch to other addictions). So where is the error? The Person who consciously wanted to quit was able to remove the hormones of negative emotion from their cells, but didn't give them anything else in return. Quitting will be more effective if we engage in activities that create positive emotions so that our cells begin to depend on those hormones instead. On the one hand, you need to heal deep psychological wounds, and on the other hand, you need to "feed" your cells with positive emotions and thoughts.

The **third typical mistake** in getting rid of addictions is a lack of perseverance. There are relapses in every quitting process. In such cases, it's a huge mistake to feel guilty and beat ourselves up! After all, with the help of the ego, our cells reach the goal of receiving certain hormones. In this case, we lose our strength and enthusiasm, and we fall back to our original state. But this is where you have to persevere! The most important thing is to feel the joy of relapse when relapsing, but don't feel guilty or other negative emotions. Accept that this is how it turned out! Acceptance already produces positive hormones. In the meantime, be aware that if your cells have picked themselves up, you will start again and continue to develop consciously by practicing positive emotions. The quitting process should be seen from the perspective of returns. If you develop in the right direction, the falls from the wagon get smaller and shorter, or they remain deep but become less frequent.

It is important to ask for help in quitting addictions! The **fourth typical mistake** is not asking for help or pushing away the intention to help! This is no coincidence, because the ego also serves to maintain the original state. Family and friends can help you, as you can experience positive emotions with them. A psychologist, a kinesiologist, a therapist, or spiritual leader can help you too. But I will come back to this in more detail.

The **fifth typical mistake** is not changing the way you spend your free time. Please also replace your pastimes with ones that elevate you to a higher level of spiritual vibration. For example, it matters what you read, what movies you watch, and what content you consume online. This book is also at a high level of mental vibration, so even reading this will help you live a happier life.

A deeper understanding of this issue is provided by the exciting summary of **Appendix No. 3**, from which you can understand which addictions are related to which hormone producer and which nerve center.

5.5. Games

I am sure that most readers are aware of the psychological meaning of the word "game". However, some people may not know exactly what this term means. At the same time, I'll try not to bore you with definitions here. I hope this subchapter will be interesting for you even if you are already aware of this issue.

Eric Berne was the creator of the theory behind *Games People Play*, and I recommend his books to everyone who wants to better understand the functioning of the Human soul. By the way, the book *Born to Win* (Muriel James-Dorothy Jongeward) discusses this subject in much simpler language. I recommend it too from the bottom of my heart to anyone who wants to learn the basics of understanding the functioning of the Human soul and to develop their own self-knowledge.

When I was about 32, I read the referenced book by Eric Berne, and although I found it very interesting, I was convinced that I didn't have any 'games' myself. How tricky the destroyer-ego is, right? I needed around two years for the content of the book to mature in me, then I started to realize —Wow! I too must also have one or two games! Then I read the book I've just recommended— "*Born to Win*"—when I was 36 years old. I already had a full map of games about myself and I have to admit that I played a lot of different games at that time. By that time, I had an accurate picture of this, and I also understood which type of game had a spiritual root and what its cause was from my past. These insights were key milestones in the development of my self-knowledge.

Since then, I have met a lot of People who are aware of what these games mean and who can see other People's games well, but they don't have any knowledge of their own games. They are simply not aware of them. It's also true in general that we have a basic blindness to our deeper self-discovery. This is actually not blindness, but the ego's own game against us. It's no coincidence that the destroyer-ego uses this tool to maintain its own existence.

For the sake of simplicity, in the example of Eric Berne I will call a 'transaction' any method of communication between two or more People, or any act towards another Person or Persons. Transactions are required to create People Games. That is, the games are created during our transactions. The game means that the target on the surface during the transaction is different from the real target. It's not that we intentionally lie, but that we actually want to achieve something other than what we say in the transaction. So, for example, there is a conversation between two People that has a purpose on the surface, but actually under the surface a different spiritual purpose represents the real motivation. This may sound complicated at first, but it's about to be clarified.

In order to have a thorough understanding of the games, one must first have a good understanding of the true spiritual purpose. For example, Hungarians typically have a system of complaining. When I lived in the USA, I realized the huge difference between Hungarians and Americans. Hungarians always complain, and most of the time they walk down the street in a sad or neutral state. Americans almost always try to smile and almost never complain. If an American begins to complain to another Person, it's because they need help. This is a completely straightforward, game-free transaction. After all, I complain because I want the other party to help me. So, if the other party offers to help, the complainant will gladly accept and be grateful. In this case, an average American Person wants to give a helping hand. In Hungary, on the other hand, in most cases, complaining is a game. We start to express our grievances, and then when the other person sympathetically starts to give advice or offer their help, we shake them off with something like: "Ah, let it go, there will be a way". It's a game, because the transaction on the surface is a request for help, but the real spiritual goal is to get confirmation of the worldview that Life sucks. We Hungarians like to believe—through our losing throughout history over many generations—that Life is hard and sad, and we can stick to this worldview. However, it is thankfully true that in the last one or two decades this mindset has started to change.

Let's look at another example. One of my many games was that I always had to suffer much more than others for a little success. Everything was always much harder for me. This appeared in my communication (unconsciously, of course) by shaping the conversations in such a way that I received confirmation of this worldview. If someone wanted to shed light on how it could be simpler or easier to live, I ignored these suggestions or convinced the speaker that "my case is actually special". My subconscious goal was to gain self-righteousness and "deserve" the pity of others because of my "special" difficult situation. Even though my case was not special, I just didn't want to deviate from my established worldview. The essence of the gaming system is that we like to talk to People who give us this spiritual "gain". If someone doesn't participate in our game, we will avoid them the next time because those People are not sympathetic to us.

I would like to use a third example to show how complex and diverse the world of games is. I recently helped a family solve a problem with their child. The mother and her adolescent daughter quarreled quite a bit, which poisoned the family climate. I talked to the mother, who told me that her daughter's empathy skills were approaching zero, which makes her crazy, since the parents were not like that and they did not raise their children that way. However, after deeper conversations, it turned out that the mother felt guilty for days every time she scolded her daughter. At the same time, her daughter felt guilty because once again she could not do enough for her mother. The lack of empathy on the surface was the cause of the quarrels, but the real goal was to experience guilt regularly. The mother carried a lot of repressed guilt from the child that her parents blamed on her. The subconscious reason for these quarrels was that the mother could receive the packages of guilt that she received from her own parents as a child. The irony of Life is that with this game, she gave her child the guilt that she suffered from as a child. This is what the previous section was about: how harmful habits and addictions are transmitted from parent to child. In fact, guilt addiction is also an addiction that develops at a subconscious level, even though the person suffers from it. And games are the perfect way to provoke these negative emotions. Therefore, the real purpose of the games is, on the one hand, to always gain self-reinforcement. On the other hand, we want to receive the "reward" radiated by our subconscious mind. No matter how wrong, erroneous, or self-destructive the worldview you feel is, the goal is still to reap the spiritual "gains" of self-reinforcement. It makes sense why alcoholics and workaholics can't be told that what they're doing is wrong, doesn't it? With the help of their games, they get multiple self-reinforcements.

I once knew a lady who was a very reputable Person. I mean this in the sense that she would only be able to get into bed with anyone if true love and trust had already developed. Despite this, her behavior towards men was highly flirtatious and blatant. Her transactions on the surface incubated the image of a sexually easy woman. The men who ignored her were, in her eyes, evil People because they didn't pay attention to her. The men who had been involved in her flirtatious behavior and who had, sooner or later, turned on their masculine fantasies, had been rudely thrown off by her and labeled as disgusting creatures. On the surface, the essence of the transaction was "Come, flirt back to me, and get a wonderful reward in return". However, the real purpose of the transaction was for the lady to receive confirmation of her worldview that all men wanted the same thing and therefore they couldn't be trusted, further reinforcing her fear of deep Human relationships. This is called spiritual intimacy inhibition.

All four examples show the same thing. On a spiritual level, we want to get affirmations of our view of reality from others. However, if you look at these examples from the outside, you would probably have an idea of what childhood grievances could have caused the Person's current playing system. Getting to know your own games will also open up a lot of deeper gates of self-knowledge within you, which makes this all the start of an exciting process. In any case, it can be stated that the lower the level of spiritual vibration a Person is at, the more they "maneuver" in Life with a system of games. After all, they have to invest lots of energy to strengthen their mistaken worldview, which they believe to be real.

I could write about many more types of games and examples, but the scope of this article does not allow this. With this article, my goal was to encourage you to delve into the related literature and thereby broaden your horizons, your Human- and Self-knowledge. I trust that I have piqued your interest in this interesting journey that I think is important and useful in every Person's Life. Imagine that most of my relationships—before I was finally ruined by them—were ruined by my games! All this happened in such a way that I didn't even know about my games. Today, most of my Human relationships are free of games. Of course, I'm aware that it will never be perfect, because then I would be a fully enlightened Person. However, with the decrease of my games, a lot of my Human relationships became peaceful, harmonious and honest. This increased my happiness. The first step for everyone is to incorporate a complete mapping of your own gaming systems into your self-awareness system! I wish you every success on this journey. Don't forget: your ego will start by saying that you have few or no games, or why what you have is justified. But please don't let yourself be fooled!

5.6. Rationalizing mind

People are never capable of perfect objectivity until they reach the level of spiritual vibration of Rationality. All you need for that is pure rational thinking. Most People think of themselves as fundamentally objective and rational. This is especially true for People who, leaving the world of spirituality, are willing to live only in the rational world of scientific facts, considering it the only truth. The corollary of this is atheism, as belief in God or other religious icons is incompatible with objective thinking. Despite the fact that there are so many of this type of People, very few of them are actually objective or rational. The level of spiritual vibration of Rationality is so high that only one in millions of People in today's Person population will get there during their lifetime. However, lots of people believe this about themselves.

This is because 99.999% of People are not actually *rational*, but *rationalizing*. What the individual decides emotionally on the subconscious plane is subsequently supported by "rational" thoughts in order to strengthen their reality. It's true! But how does this process work? Suppose that you can choose from many competing products in a store. We select a specific product. Usually, there is already some positive emotion stored in our subconscious about the given brand, which could be caused by, for example, an advertisement seen on TV in early childhood, or the satisfaction of our parent with that brand. So, in our subconscious, in a fraction of a second, it was decided which one to choose. We don't even notice it because the process is so fast. When the choice is made on the subconscious plane, it radiates a feeling. As a reaction to this, our brain starts to "create" explanations that argue in favor of the given product. The purpose of rationalization is to validate the legitimacy of the code burned in at the subconscious level. We therefore list the positive arguments in favor of the product and the negative arguments against competing products. The thing is, we do the same thing in other areas, from how we respond to our partners, to our behavioral decisions, and to our self-expression. All our decisions are rationalized with thoughts after the fact! It's a good task to observe yourself doing this. The emotion "takes care" of the attachment to a decision direction in a fraction of a second, but it is difficult to catch it because of its speed. However, the more emotionally attached we are to our decision, the more true it is that we are rationalizing and not rational. It's a wonderful journey of self-knowledge, but it's not easy! It's an even more sophisticated tool than ego games to capture your current reality. It's in the ego's interest that this should survive, because that is how it ensures its own existence within you.

Let's look at another example. For about ten years, a woman has been craving a man who doesn't care about her at all. Despite all the rejection, this lady clearly "knows" that she is the other half of his soul, but he has not realized it yet. This "knowledge" of reality is a rationalization, the huge disadvantage of which is that the lady cannot realize that this is the main reason for the unhappiness of the obsession. She is stuck on the spiritual vibratory level of Desire, and until she realizes that her reality is false, she has no chance of being a happy Human. But why can't she realize reality? The answer is simple: because she is emotionally attached to a reality of her own world. She is convinced that her soul can only tell her the truth, and she "knows" with 100% certainty that the man she wants is really her other half. In fact, there is no rational basis for this, yet her ego defends the current reality with rationalizing thoughts. Thus, the destructive ego maintains itself in the woman as a host, which, due to its gullibility and controllability, is ideal for an ego parasite. The lady is under the hypnotic influence of her own ego, like everyone else who lives at a spiritual vibration level below 200. The problem is that although at least eight out of ten people currently live at this level of spiritual vibration, they are convinced of the opposite. It's no coincidence that Courage is the first Life-supporting psychological vibration, as it takes a lot of courage to face the fact that our reality is a false mirage, guided by programs formed from deeply burned childhood pains, rather than from ourselves.

This above example shows how dangerous rationalization can be, and is the perfect tool for the destroyer-ego to ruin our lives. Those who are able to see behind it will move towards a freer and happier Life. Maybe there will be suffering ahead of them, because most of the time it takes suffering to get rid of emotionally-attached reality images. This is the process of breaking the ego. However, the important thing is **not to build an even stronger ego afterwards!** This is the biggest mistake People make. When they "finally" shatter a part of their ego, they pick up where and what they did wrong and instinctively build an ego with an even stronger capacity for self-defense. Unfortunately, this will cause even more suffering after a temporary feeling of happiness. Instead, once your ego is broken, be glad that you are partially rid of it and protect yourself from it becoming stronger again!

Please take the time to catch your rationalizing emotions and their anchors in the act. This way, you will find out which of your reality images are wrong. With all this, you become more genuinely objective and rational, and weaken your ego! By the way, you are getting closer to the gateway to a happy Life.

CHAPTER 6

The L.I.F.E. Method

6.1. The Ego Streams, or the Three Basic Rules of the L.I.F.E. Method

Congratulations on making it this far in the book! You did what I asked, didn't you? You didn't devour the book in a short time, and you did the self-knowledge analyses I've asked you to do up to now, didn't you? This is very important in order for our work together to be successful! If you didn't do so, please do not proceed further until you have fulfilled the requests I've made to you so far! If you have done these things, it is with great joy and Love that I give you the basics of the L.I.F.E. method, which gives you the tools to make your life happier.

As you can clearly see from the previous chapters, the ego can be found in three places: the body, mind, and soul. Let's see how you can find out how powerful your ego's presence is.

Let's start with the **body. Your ego is stronger the more symptoms your body produces and the more you deal with them.** An ego-free body is perfectly healthy and neutral, **so the stronger your ego is, the more your body deviates from its healthy and tension-free state.** In other words, the egoless body does its job without you being particularly aware of its existence. The body is there to be a tool for your consciousness (spirit) to experience your Life Task. It's a wonderful and perfect tool for that, but it's no more than that. I would like to compare what has been described so far to the water supply network. It is natural for People that when they turn on the faucet at home, the water flows. They don't think about the huge infrastructure behind it (several kilometers of pipe networks, water purification works, wells, the devoted work of many People, etc.). People only think about the system behind the tap if the water doesn't flow, in which case they complain to the utility company. The body is a similar kind of tool. A stress-free and healthy body does its job without any symptoms, without us having to think about how it works or how many millions of cells do their job so that it can be the way we want it to be. When the body starts to work differently than we expect, we think many things about our body. There are body warning symptoms that something is wrong. All the symptoms that make you deal with your body are part of the ego. This includes pain, tension, inflammation and diseases, but also anorexia or obesity, and today, things like physical perfectionism. These are all swings away from a neutral and healthy body.

Now let's deal with the **mind. The ego-free state of the mind is a state of silence of the mind. At these times, there are no thoughts in our minds; we only have intuition—nothing else.** Echart Tolle said that we move our hands or feet whenever we want. Our brain is our one organ that we cannot command! We think about millions of useless things even when we don't need to think. This is why mediation has been such an effective technique for thousands of years; it seeks a thoughtless state of mind. That is, it introduces you to the ego-free state. My master, Tamás Miron Varga, said that only he who is the master of his mind can be the master of his future. And the master of his mind is the one who can exist in perfect thoughtlessness for at least four or five minutes. No matter how easy it seems at first hearing, I succeeded only twice in my first year of practice. But let's return to the basic question: how strong is the ego in your mind? **The more thoughts the ego has during a given unit of time, the stronger it is! So, the more occupied your mind is, the less you can slow it down, and the stronger your ego is.** For example, many people can't even sleep because they are constantly thinking. This is a sign of a very strong ego. It can also be that the experience of a wonderful moment is mitigated by unnecessary thoughts that come to us. It's also common that during sex we think about other things or about some sexual perversion to make it easier for us to reach orgasm. These are all signs of a strong ego dominating the mind. Of course, the examples could go on and on.

Now, let's get to the **soul.** Our emotions arise in the soul. Spiritual People often fall into the trap of being controlled by their emotions. However, the soul is also the "playground" of the ego. We are convinced that what our soul is saying is right. Unfortunately, this is also an ego trap. **The ego-free state of the soul is the neutral emotional state.** I would like to emphasize that this is not the same as insensitivity or apathy. The latter are signs of a strong Life-destroying state of mind. For example, in the state of neutrality, we deeply sympathize with our fellow humans, but we do so from a neutral point of view. True selfless love is also neutral in its reality, as it loves everyone and everything without direction. Selfish Love, for example, is anxious and possessive, radiating negative energy to the loved one. Unselfish Love doesn't worry and possess; it just empathizes and supports. A neutral soul is infinitely selfless. Swaying from neutrality is always caused by selfish self-interest. This means that **any negative or positive emotion that does not come from a neutral and unselfish state is the result of your ego.** How can you tell how strong your ego is in your soul? The answer is very simple: the more powerful the non-neutral emotions (positive or negative) appear in you and the less you can control them, the stronger the ego is in you. So, the easier it is to get carried away, the more you worry, the more inclined you are to go from one romance to another, or the more you make decisions based on emotions, the stronger your ego is in your soul.

But what good is all this knowledge? I have developed a way to raise our mental vibration and gradually reshape the ego. I call it the "L.I.F.E. method". In the Hungarian language, the name of the method comes from the abbreviation É.L.E.T., which stands for "Life-Supporting Soul-Mind-Body." For English readers, I have chosen the abbreviation L.I.F.E., or "Living Intuitively, Feeling Energized". In order to reach toward that happy state, it's important to also keep in mind the meaning of the method's Hungarian name, as it emphasizes the importance of the Soul-Mind-Body connection.

From the knowledge transferred so far, here are the three basic rules of the L.I.F.E. method:

Rule #1: You can't change just by polishing your body or mind or spirit. All three "ego playgrounds" need to be upgraded in order to achieve lasting success!

Rule #2: Any activity, or method that reduces body-soul-mind swings belongs in your Life and raises your spiritual vibration; that is: it weakens your ego.

Rule #3: The power of emotions is 100 times greater than the power of the mind, and the power of the body is 10 times greater than the power of the mind. So the power ratio of the three "ego playgrounds" (soul : body : mind) is 100 : 10: 1.

Let's look at an example for understanding the first rule. How many People have failed to lose weight successfully? Newer and newer consumer methods come out almost every week, yet 98% of people do not achieve successful weight loss permanently. And why is that? Most people are enthusiastic about finding another method, and understand in their mind how it works. Then, with the power of enthusiasm and understanding, they achieve huge results in the short term. Then, a few months later, they find themselves gaining back all the weight they had previously lost through their painful efforts. What happened? The mind was taught the right way, but the mind and body were not taught the same. In the short term, the mind may triumph over the soul and body, but in the medium term, the mind has no chance. The basic feature of the ego is that it always protects itself. So, in the medium term, it retains the original state surrounding the ego, which is in these cases the obese state with the accompanying unpleasant feelings and thoughts (mostly shame), as well as physical symptoms. Since the power of thoughts is weak because they are in a 1:10:100 ratio with the power of the body and the soul, the chance of success when wanting to institute change from the mind is the weakest. At the same time, we need to change our thinking if we want to change, because thoughts are also the focal point of our emotions and physical reactions. Due to the interplaying cycle of body-mind-soul, you have to deal with all three parts of yourself in order to succeed!

Let's look at some examples illustrating the second rule. In the case of the body, everything that enhances your health raises your mental vibration and weakens your ego. At the same time, everything that is unhealthy takes you down by strengthening your ego. For example, if you eat a lot of sweets, drink a lot of coffee, drink alcohol, smoke cigarettes or consume chips in front of the TV, it strengthens your ego and reduces your physical—and indirectly your spiritual—vibration level. Exercising regularly, eating fresh vegetables, taking vitamins, drinking herbal teas, and drinking crystal clear spring water raises your mood and weakens your ego. Watching a romantic or an action movie strengthens your ego in your mind and soul. Instead, meditating or practicing on a forest walk to be present without thought raises your spiritual vibration and weakens your ego.

To understand the third rule, please think about the following. When you want to suppress an emotion, how many thoughts does it bring? You have to go through something at least a hundred times—but often up to a thousand times—before you can suppress the feeling in your soul that causes the problem. So, with a single emotion, you neutralize at least 100 thoughts. That's why affirmations, or otherwise called mantras, don't work when we feel something other than what we say about it. Or they only work if you repeat them at least 100 times after each feeling appears. So even if you tell yourself that you will be rich, if you feel deep down that you don't deserve to be rich or that you think money is disgusting, you will never be rich. Your emotions go against the expectations generated by your mind. It's no use telling your body that you're healthy when deep down you're overwhelmed with guilt and don't feel like you deserve a life without suffering. A confirmation of health spoken at least 10 times is dissolved by a single bodily sensation. The conclusion from Rule #3 is that healing or the desired change is most effective if it starts from the soul, because there you can neutralize a minimum of 100 thoughts and a minimum of 10 physical projection opportunities by changing a single emotion. That is why I have dealt most with psychic vibrations in this book. The greatest strength is achieved by internally transforming our emotions into higher ones.

6.2. Optimize your vibrations!

We combine the three basic rules of the previous chapter with the fact that both our mind-body and soul are composed of vibrations, and as you have already read, their state depends on the level of their vibrations. From the basics you have learned so far, it's clear to you that to increase your happiness, success and health, you need the following:

I.   Raise the vibration level of your soul!
II. Reduce the vibration level of your mind!
III. Raise the vibration level of your body!
IV.

You have gained a lot of exciting knowledge about these in the chapters so far, and I especially recommend the interesting and useful summary of **Annex 3**.

Now you understand that the purpose of raising your level of spiritual vibration is to move from your current level of spiritual vibration toward Enlightenment. Actually reaching enlightenment is not the goal, as it's very rare in today's Human population. But the further you go on this path, the happier, more peaceful and harmonious Life you will have.

You also understand that the more time your mind spends in the high Beta range, the less happy you are. It's therefore important to slow down your mind consciously. The less noisy your mind is, the less it buzzes, and the happier you will be. I know that this world and your ego suggest the opposite. But from the chapters you've already read, it should've become clear to you why I'm right. Now, try a short self-awareness exercise: Sit down, relax, take a few deep breaths, and then command your mind to be quiet. While you're giving yourself this order, check the time for an hour. Close your eyes and open them when the first thought crosses your mind. Today's Western average person can only be literally thoughtless for seconds. It's not accidental to be set adrift through the control and effects of others. They have no control over their own minds, so they cannot realize a happy present and future for themselves. It takes a lot of practice to be able to command our minds. Western People are infantile, which means that their thoughts and emotions are riddled with desires. The average Western Person has almost no self-control, so they want everything immediately. Our whole society and way of life radiates this. Self-mastery development is achieved through our mastery of the mind. So, consciously slow down your mind when you don't need it! Obviously, if you need to solve a rational problem quickly, it's necessary for your mind to work quickly. But in all other cases, the millions of thoughts generated by our minds appear in our heads as meaningless and surplus noise. So, when you don't need your brain to be spinning, slow it down. Do activities that help you do that. The ideal ranges are outside the Beta brainwaves. The longer you stay in a state of deep brainwaves, the more connected you become to happiness.

Your body's vibration levels are reduced by stress, poor eating and lifestyle habits. You have to consciously work at it every day so that your body regains its health and vitality, which is to say that its vibration level increases to a healthy 60 MHz.

6.3. Methods of the L.I.F.E. method and their grouping

Now you understand the essence of my method, right? Obviously, the next question that comes up is: okay, but how? In the remainder of the book, I will give only the answers to this question. In my work on self-improvement and helping others, I have collected about a hundred ways to help you achieve this. I will give you 21 of them in this volume—the ones I recommend for beginners because they're easier to learn. There are methods that raise the vibration level of the body, others that raise the vibration level of the soul, and there are also methods that lower the vibration level of the mind. I have either tried most of these methods, or trustworthy People have achieved impressive success with them.

However, I have also observed that People at different levels of happiness-seeking are capable of different things. For example, although the great spiritual masters say that anyone can meditate, I know from my own experience that it's impossible to try meditation until a certain level of spiritual vibration is reached and a certain level of control over the mind is achieved. I have also witnessed that meditation has made someone obsessive or

METHODS (BASELINE)		Gratitude	Me-time	Ventilation	Love languages	Balloons and clouds method	Do not color!	Best scenario	Confirmations	Daily balance method	Order and system	Self boundaries	Neutraliz of your fears	Balance method	Kaleidoscope	Meal (baseline)	Symmetry and holding	Melatonin-production	Breathing (baseline)	Sport (baseline)	Smile	Water (baseline)
		METHODS OF LIVING						MIND METHODS								BODY METHODS						
1.	Shame																					
2.	Guilt																					
3.	Apathy																					
4.	Sorrow	Destroyer-ego																				
5.	Fear																					
6.	Desire																					
7.	Anger																					
8.	Pride																					
9.	Courage																					
10.	Impartiality	Neutral-ego																				
11.	Willingness																					
12.	Acceptance																					
13.	Rationality																					
14.	Love	Creator-ego																				
15.	Joy																					
16.	Peace																					
17.	Enlightenment	Freedom of ego																				

Table 1: Summary of the methods to be presented in this book and their recommended application

depressed because it was started at an inappropriate time i.e., when their personality couldn't handle it correctly. Therefore, I've divided the methods of seeking happiness into several groups. For the remainder of this book, I'll only introduce you to beginner-level methods. Obviously, there will be some that are already an integral part of your Life. Be proud of them and keep them! Please focus on those that you don't routinely use. There is a lot of emphasis on this word here. It's not enough to know what's right! Change will only be successful if it's an integral part of your life. That is, you need to practice until it becomes instinctive. When you get to the point where you feel bad about a method if you neglect or omit it, you'll know it has really become a part of your Life.

In other respects, I divided the methods into three main groups:
1. Soul Level Raising Methods (hereinafter referred to as Soul Methods)
2. Methods to reduce the average vibration level of the mind (hereinafter: Mind Methods)
3. Methods to increase the vibration level of your body (hereinafter: Body Methods)

In this volume, I have collected a total of twenty-one proven methods (three groups times seven items) to help you effectively move towards a happier Life.

In the table on page 171, I have summarized the exercises, methods and tools that I recommend for beginners and I will present them in detail in the rest of this volume. Please look through this table:

6.4. Method of application of the tools of the L.I.F.E. method

To apply the tools, proceed as follows: 1. Start with the first step in the Soul method, then continue with the first step in the Mind method, then turn to the first step of the Body method. Continue in this way until you get beyond the 7th group of methods. If you have made them part of your life, then look back at the self who started using this system. If you see a clear change and improvement in your life and want to increase your happiness even more, I will be happy to see you among the readers of my intermediate level book or in my courses. If you don't succeed, please reach out so that we can work together to find the root causes that continue to hold you back.

6.5. Always have a helper!

We can't achieve change on our own! The reason for this lies in the functioning of the ego and the immense power of the subconscious. Unfortunately, most People overvalue their own abilities in terms of how well they can change certain bad habits or absorb their psychological problems. We usually make the mistake that when we recognize the causes of the psychological problems in ourselves and understand what we need to do, we think the rest will be easy.

The reality is that this is just the beginning of the journey. I could also say that recognizing and exploring the problem in detail is only one to three percent of the way. Change is much more difficult than realization itself. Most of the time, we don't ask for external help for internal change because our egos make us believe that we can do it ourselves. In most cases, this is just a mirage; our ego is lying to us in order to maintain its importance, so it tricks us and pulls us back into our old pathways.

The other main problem is that we tend to underestimate the situation and make ourselves believe that we don't need help. However, it's also common to be afraid to ask for help. We are afraid of being ridiculed, or we're ashamed to talk about our real problems. We often feel that our problems would be a burden to others. The truth is that most spiritual helpers are imbued with altruism. They are energized when they can help someone. This is why I'm writing this book, too—because it feels so good to have this selfless inner power to support people. At the same time, spiritual helpers have seen problems much worse than yours, so you won't be able to surprise them. Because they deal with people like you every day, they also won't judge you. Moreover, the spiritual helpers know exactly what Christ also proclaimed: that there is no incorruptible sin, so there is nothing that cannot be corrected.

Often this attitude is also heard: "I don't go to a psychologist because I'm not mentally ill". My response to this is that apart from the enlightened ones (whose number is currently approximately less than ten worldwide) *everyone* has psychological wounds, pain and problems. Almost everyone needs spiritual help. Spiritual helpers know this, so they will always be accepting and open about any problem they encounter. Asking for help is therefore neither a sin nor a shame. With help, you can usually achieve results in your search for happiness more effectively and in a shorter time. Therefore, I encourage all People who want to improve and change to **ask for help!**

You have many choices when it comes to spiritual helpers.

I think of the following people who can be recommended at a basic level:

- ▶ Your soulmate
- ▶ Your true friend
- ▶ Your priest or religious leader

- Your spiritual guide
- A psychologist
- An integrative psychotherapist (they are also psychologists, but they are only trained in special methods)
- A kinesiologist
- A Soul Support Group
- A coach
- Your community

I would like to share some thoughts about when to choose a spiritual helper, in case my own experiences can help you.

Your soulmate (if you have one) is capable of helping you only if you have a maximally honest relationship and help each other on the path of spiritual development with complete openness and affection. In my experience, less than one percent of relationships are like this. Most of the time, men are too rational and absolutely closed to spiritual questions, but I have also seen cases where the woman in the relationship was like this. Unfortunately, few of us men are open-minded and therefore capable of a more serious approach to spirituality. The reason for this hiding is in our upbringing; society expects us to be tough macho people who don't care about spiritual problems. This is burned into us at a very young age and we try to comply with this completely inappropriate social conditioning.

But back to the main point. If your soul mate meets the above requirements, they are only suitable to help you on your journey if you have an appropriate level of psychological sensitivity and a certain level of professional knowledge. They can best help you if they themselves have already gone through the change that you are in right now. This way, they can be understanding and give a lot of advice along the way. At the same time, you need to be able to put aside your pride and accept that your partner supports you. Most People feel this to be a lecture and it hurts their pride.

Thus, the partner cannot help even if they are otherwise suitable. So, the ideal situation where all these requirements coincide is very rare. That's also why they say that such a thing doesn't work within a family; it's also important that there is no adult-child transaction between the assisting party and the assisted party. The basis of a good relationship is to treat each other as equal adults. To do this, it is necessary that the helper does not order the other from above, that is: they help with humbleness. And those who receive help should not be subordinated to the other, but should walk the path of development with a straight spine and good self-esteem.

Good friends are there to help each other with their problems. However, it's very rare to have friends who can give unbiased advice beyond simply listening. If you just want to be helped to the extent that someone listens and understands you, or you feel that if you could tell someone your whole problem so that it is clearer in you, then a friend is great for that.

Your priest or religious leader is best suited to mitigate your guilt and shame if you are a true believer. Shame and guilt are the two deepest and most destructive feelings, and are at the root of many mental illnesses. It's therefore very important that we mitigate these feelings in ourselves as much as possible. The feeling of divine forgiveness can be a very serious remedy for our souls. I do not belong to any religious denomination, but at the same time I have tried to get spiritual help from a priest. Unfortunately, my experience was negative in that the priest was unable to exclude religious dogmatism from spiritual assistance. I respect any priest who is an exception to this effect. Unfortunately, I see religious dogmatism as a problem that distorts social development, but I will write about this in detail in one of the next volumes, and I have detailed my opinion on its harmful social effects in my book *Future=Life?! A Solution for Climate Change and World Peace*. Don't get me wrong—I have great respect for all world religions! The foundations of world religions were formed by the eternal words of wonderful, enlightened people. However, dogmatism has been imposed on religions over the centuries through the distorting effects of low spiritual vibration religious critics. I am a great admirer of all world religions because they radiate wonderful life affirmation in their foundations. So, if your faith is tied to a religion, its dogmatism is also acceptable to you or at least does not cause negative overtones in you. In this case, a good priest, blessed with spiritual sensitivity, can be an effective helper.

Some People turn to spiritual leaders for help. I was able to meet a Zen master once (unfortunately only once) and it was a wonderful experience. I think that the mere proximity of spiritual leaders at a really high level is a spiritual vibration-level-enhancer, and you can clearly understand the reason for this from the previous chapters. Unfortunately, there are many quacks in the world of "spiritual leaders" and many abuse Human gullibility, so choose with due care and objectivity. However, spiritual leaders can often provide insights, messages, and help that far exceed the abilities of a traditional psychologist. This mostly depends on the level of spiritual vibration of that particular spiritual guide. As you have read, at and above the spiritual vibratory level of Love, People are already capable of real miracles. Which, in fact, are only really miracles when seen through the filter of ordinary People. Such a master can have a huge impact on our spiritual development path and on the increase of our spiritual vibration level. Two examples are Gyöngyi Spitzer and Mamagésa Soma (whose books and courses I wholeheartedly recommend to all seekers), with whom a six-hour meeting opened my heart so much that it raised me from the spiritual vibration level of Rationality to the spiritual vibration level of Love! I will be grateful for it for all my life. Since then, I have experienced her power and high spiritual vibration several times, and many others have too. Even the time spent near her is transformative in itself, even if she doesn't speak to you. It is a great honor for me that she read this book and wrote a recommendation for it with all her heart.

I recommend psychologists who engage in "traditional" talking-type therapy to those who either want to improve their self-knowledge or cannot see the forest for the trees, that is, they are confused by the vortexes of their problems. For those who are just starting to open up to the path of spiritual development, this may be the best choice to start. True and deep soul healing is not their place. They are more like good spiritual counsellors who help to untangle the threads, form diagnoses, find the right directions, and provide Lifestyle and behavioral advice that can reduce problems. The method is very good and very useful. The only problem with it is that the real cause of the mental problem does not heal the spiritual wound itself; these are left up to time and to the patient. I have also visited such a helper twice, and both experiences were useful and valuable. However, there is a certain level of development above which this method no longer helps, but it is highly recommended for "beginners".

Integrative psychotherapy is a very serious and effective method.Among psychologists, you can find someone who has turned to integrative therapy. I myself participated in this therapy in two stages. I went for a total of two and a half years to a therapist who is considered to be at a high level within their own profession. I am very grateful to them, as they made incredible progress with their method. With this method, I achieved more in those two and a half years than in fourteen years of other methods earlier, so I can confidently say it works! By the way, it has not only worked for me, but also for others to whom I recommended the method and who applied it persistently, which resulted in significant spiritual development for them and thus an improvement in their quality of Life. It's also important to say that of the many methods I have tried in my life, this was by far one of the most effective! I have been dealing with self-awareness and spiritual self-development for 22 years, but the biggest development was my two and a half years in integrative therapy. Today, I know even more effective methods, but this is an excellent springboard for using them. These will be discussed in later volumes.

The great thing about this method is that it builds on one of the greatest insights of my life: **spiritual problems cannot be healed or overridden by rational thinking** (at least not if there are effects in your soul from early childhood that have not yet been healed by anyone). Our spiritual problems are rooted in our subconscious, so methods that can help us on the subconscious plane are the most effective. To understand the essence of the method, imagine that all the repressed negative feelings you have experienced have formed a deep well in your soul. If your self-knowledge is at the right level, you have probably experienced this deep well. It's what makes you feel empty, or fearful when you are alone and doing nothing. This is the feeling that People unconsciously flee from. That's why we always have to do something: type on our phones, go online, do our work—something always has to be happening. Because if nothing is happening, that strange, scary feeling of emptiness comes over us. The deeper someone's "well" is, the louder, brisker, and more complex a life they live. After all, they have to escape better than those whose "wells" are not so deep.

The essence of integrative psychotherapy is that the "well" is filled with positive feelings from week to week. Imagine that every positive feeling you experience is a pebble that you throw into this well. If you persevere in therapy and put in a pebble like this every week with the help of your therapist, that well will fill up week by week. As the depth of your well decreases, you will become more peaceful inside, more accepting of yourself, and as a result, you will have fewer conflicts with the world and yourself. The method is effective because it performs the experience of positive feelings on the subconscious plane, so it will surely fill the well of your soul. Among the methods used, Katathym Imaginative Psychotherapy (KIP) was the most effective tool for me, because we really worked at a subconscious level. Such results can never be achieved with independent work! Therefore, I consider the use of this method indispensable for all people with childhood trauma. If there is a lot of suffering in your current Life and you want a more peaceful, happier Life or you want to develop on a spiritual level, then choose this kind of therapist to help you. Be persistent! Your progress will not be continuous. Spiritual development is never linear. There will be setbacks in the process, but this should not discourage you! The downturns will never be as deep as they were when you started! The method is also very good in that it works even if you don't believe in it! I didn't believe in it either, but it worked. Furthermore, the method doesn't require deep self-knowledge; it works even without it. The only necessity is to start and do it persistently, week by week! You can find out more about therapy and therapists on this website: **https://www.makomp.hu/**

A kinesiologist can also be an effective helper. Kinesiologists are very good at uncovering repressed things hidden in the subconscious, through which our self-knowledge can be developed to incredible depths. At the same time, they also have effective ways to change the bad habits that arise from mental problems. I myself went to a kinesiologist for one and a half years and enjoyed working with them very much. You can already read in detail about the operation and raison d'être of kinesiology at the beginning of this book. The bottom line is that while you can't use your brain to retrieve your body's deep subconscious signals, a kinesiologist can. With a simple body response method, they can check your body response to any question. What is this method good for? A lot of things, because your body is much, much wiser than you (sorry!) and your body never lies (sorry again!). You, on the other hand, even if you don't lie to others, you are sure to lie to yourself (sorry!). We often lie to ourselves because it's easier to believe someone else's truth than to look inside ourselves. But we also often lie to ourselves out of a desire to please others. It is very rare for a Person to be able to be completely honest with themselves, even if everyone usually believes this about themselves. (This erroneous belief is, of course, a mirage of the ego, about which you have read a great deal in this book.) Then there are our mental repressions, which we find very, very difficult to look into. Our body, on the other hand, knows exactly what is suppressed in it. It is no coincidence that after a while it can signal us intensely with psychosomatic diseases.

A kinesiologist is good for deeper self-knowledge, and for opening and dissolving psychological wounds. The kinesiologist knows so much more than the psychologist because they always work from the truth. In traditional "talking" psychotherapy, the patient often twists and beautifies things in a way that is more favorable from their point of view. For example, there may be factors behind their problems that they don't even dare to admit to themself, let alone to their therapist. In contrast, a kinesiologist cannot be lied to because they work from an honest body response.

The method is complicated by the fact that the body can only answer 'yes' or 'no'. That is, you can only ask your body a decisive question. But a good kinesiologist can still peel off anything you want to face in a few minutes. The kinesiologist is thus like a ruthlessly honest mirror, so think carefully about what you're asking. Only ask questions for which you are prepared to receive an answer. For example, I was about 44 years old when I learned that I had been an unexpected child. However, this revelation didn't wear me down because by that time—after 18 years of self-improvement—I was able to handle such spiritual burdens well.

If you choose a kinesiologist, I recommend that you look for someone who is not only a kinesiologist, but also a psychologist. The reason for this is that if the tool of kinesiology falls into the hands of a Person who is not sufficiently prepared and sensitive on the spiritual plane, they can unfortunately cause more harm than good. I have heard of People who have been ruined by kinesiologists. Excessive honesty isn't always beneficial! There may be situations where the patient can only gradually process the truth. In such cases, psychological expertise and sensitivity are also required on the part of the kinesiologist to know to what extent someone can be psychologically burdened in their particular condition.

Psychological support groups can also be effective. They are certainly very good for learning from the experiences of others and for seeing that others are also walking in our shoes. This can help us not fall into excessive self-pity or self-loathing. At the same time, we can help others when they're in a difficult situation. Compassionate support has immense power!

Whatever spiritual support you choose, make sure that your helper's spiritual vibration level is higher than yours. Obviously, you can't measure it, but if you're near them, you can feel it. For example, if you feel more peaceful and energetic next to them than when you are alone, there is a good chance that their mental vibration level is higher than yours. It's also important that the person you choose as your helper is experienced and has deep psychological knowledge and sensitivity.

Surprising as it is, a personal trainer can be a good helper; in this book, you will see that sports play an important role in raising our vibration level. If you can't bring yourself to participate in regular sports, a coach or the community coming together as a coach can help you do so.

This brings us to the last type of helper I can recommend for you at a basic level: your community. Community Life helps us to rise spiritually. So, make sure that whenever possible you get involved in your community! Put aside the excuses your ego makes. Human relationships are very important for restoring our vibration level. Obviously, go to a community where the average level of mental vibration is higher than yours, or at least similar. At a certain stage of development, the situation is already reversed, because it is increasingly difficult to find uplifting and non-dragging communities. Then the next level is when nothing can really pull you down. **To summarize:** always choose one or more facilitators. As long as your development is important to you, always have at least one helper, except for periods when you need time to incorporate something new into your Life.

6.6. The Law of Delay: The Virtues of Perseverance, Tenacity, and Patience

When I turn on the hot water tap in the shower, the hot water doesn't come right away; I have to wait one or two minutes for the temperature to be optimal. There is a simple physical reason for this. The water in the wall has cooled down and must flow out of the tap so that the heat can reach there from the boiler. In today's world, we're accustomed to getting everything right away. If we have a headache, we take a pill and it works in fifteen minutes. If you need anything, you order it online and it'll be there in a week. If it takes three weeks, we're already angry that we had to wait so long. Our impatience is heightened, which is a serious reason for our unhappiness, as it's a sign of an undisciplined mind. If we want to heal or change and therefore resort to some method, most of us make a big mistake. We expect that the given mental or physical vibration raising method or the chosen naturopathic procedure will immediately act like the pill we take for a headache. Unfortunately, these remedies don't work that way, but they don't just treat symptoms either. The effect often comes with a long delay and the change is gradual. Since nothing happens immediately in a short period of time, there are many People who give up on well-functioning methods. How many times have I heard "I don't believe in it because it hasn't made any difference to me". All they had to do was keep doing it, and be more persistent. For example, if we drink herbal teas to treat a disease, only persistent and regular consumption can bring success. If we meditate, only persistent and regular spiritual work can lead to results. Even if we use the law of attraction with reinforcements, our situation may continue to deteriorate for weeks or months before the tipping point arrives. The reason for this is the same as for tap water, but on an energetic basis.

Imagine that your mind is controlling you at a subconscious level according to a bad program, so you have bad habits. Your Life is full of problems because of your bad habits. Imagine that your mind starts to become reprogrammed in the right direction. However, the consequences and impacts of the decisions you've made so far in your Life are still functioning. They have to play themselves out. And because of the new program, the boundaries of your correct decisions should slowly be integrated into your Life. In addition, the reprogramming of your mind only works slowly, so that during the transition period, sometimes your old subconscious programs will run, and sometimes the new ones. That is, you will make mixed decisions. At first, decisions according to the old program will predominate, and then the proportions will begin to change. Because of this, the change will be gradual, like when the cold water first becomes lukewarm and then gradually warmer. First, the steepness of the slope decreases, then the low point comes and you slowly start upwards. The change is slow and because of your bad decisions so far; very often the situation can deteriorate even after starting a method. You can't stop there. From the depths of the pit, the road can only lead upwards.

Perseverance and tenacity are not by accident considered by all world religions to be among the most important Human qualities. If you want to change your life, you cannot achieve success without perseverance and tenacity. If you start to change, it's a wonder! The most important thing you can do next is to persevere and not stop! When you feel stranded and your strength is gone, then don't beat yourself up. Put the work aside, take a rest from it, and when you're back on your feet, keep going!

When I was younger, I was told by many people to be more patient, but no one ever explained to me why. Since I didn't understand what it was for, I thought it was stupid. I was a very impatient Person; I wanted everything right away. If something failed right away, I became defiant, angry, tense, irritated, and often mobilized self-destructive energies for my goals. Since I never achieved my goals and desires immediately, I was always dissatisfied. By the time I reached my goals, I had other ones, so I could never be happy about anything. Therefore, my impatience was one of the reasons for my unhappiness. As I never experienced joy, my Life was a constant struggle. It can be read in the wonderful work *The Tragedy of Man* that "The meaning of life is struggle itself". This conclusion was very valuable to me at the time. Of course, I now know that it's not true. This can only be a logical conclusion from a narrower viewpoint.

One of the main causes of unhappiness is impatience. But in order for us to understand this, please look with me a little behind the impatience and to the depth of it. What is impatience, really? The impatient Person constantly wants to hurry, constantly tries to compete with time (and often with other things as well). They feel that everything should be achieved immediately or in the shortest possible time. This suggests the presence of a very crusty, highly selfish destructive ego. Only our ego can be so willful. So, impatience is a symptom of strong selfishness and willfulness. Why is the constant time pressure raging in us? Why do we want to rush everything? The answer must be found in the crusty ego! The crustier, more selfish and stronger our soul grows, the greater the spiritual wounds we have suffered in our past. We build this hard armor so that the spiritual pains we experienced at that time can never happen again, that we never again have to experience such feelings. Impatience is therefore a sign of running away from oneself. We don't want to look deeply into ourselves anymore, so we want to move forward at a crazy pace. As long as we run forward, we certainly can't and don't want to look back.

Most people no longer know what they're really running away from. They have repressed it so deeply that they cannot hope to expose it. The deepest reason for this is separateness. Through it, you understand why we flee so much from ourselves. So the conclusion is clear, as hard as it might be to accept:

- ▶ The more impatient you are, the more hurt you hide in your soul.
- ▶ The more impatient you are, the more you run away from your true self.

Now let's look a little behind the impatience. As a result of my spiritual self-improvement, I became less and less impatient. It's a wonderful thing. While in the past I couldn't force myself to be patient for even short periods of time, today I enjoy being patient and enjoying my existence. This is a huge change that also comes from inside (which is why I couldn't force myself back then!). Behind patience, self-acceptance, a neutral- or creator-ego, and peace of mind live inside us. The more you accept your true self, the more peaceful you are inside and the less you want to hurry. This shows that patience or impatience are consequences, not basic characteristics! If a fundamentally impatient Person forces patience on themselves, they feel like they will explode. This is natural, as it's like a Person who is running from a monster forcing themselves to stop and wait for the monster to catch up with them. With the development of self-acceptance, you will slowly realize that the monster you are running from is actually a wonderful, peaceful, lovable creature. Recently, in a breakthrough moment of walking meditation, I experienced the deep ensemble of feelings in which I felt that all living beings on Earth were perfect and lovable. I experienced this in all its purity, so I know for sure that you are perfect and lovable too!

Patience can be practiced effectively by those who are impatient by habit. Those who have undergone spiritual development but still live according to their old programs are often impatient out of habit. It's a trend to be impatient today. The whole world tells you to be impatient, to want everything immediately. Of course, this is a mirage that destroys the world, which leads Humanity completely in the wrong direction. The more impatient you are, the more turbulent and fast your life is. The faster you live, the more external resources you use, and the more you consume. The more you are like this, the more Life-destroying you are, even though Life-support could be one of your main life goals! Imagine what 8 billion impatient People are able to destroy! Is it so surprising that there is climate change (*Dittrich, 2021*)?

Thus, the real meaning of impatience is running away from oneself and at the same time increasing Life destruction. Patience means self-acceptance and Life support. Therefore, it's impossible to live happily as an impatient Human. Your ego may make you believe that being impatient is trendy and that your Life is good. But impatience only increases your inner emptiness and sense of separateness, so maintaining it is a dead end.

In summary, to enhance your happiness, please do the following with yourself:
- ▶ First, examine yourself, taking the time to ask yourself: how impatient are you? What areas of your life are you impatient about?
- ▶ Then get it into your head that impatience is the enemy of happiness, while patience is the friend of your happiness!
- ▶ Please try to strengthen your patience, as your impatience may be a bad habit and there may not be a serious problem behind it. Try to consciously measure your impatience.
- ▶ If you can't force patience on yourself, then look at yourself: how much do you accept yourself? How much do you love yourself? How lovable do you feel? From the answers, you will know that developing your self-efficacy is the key to your happiness...

Remember, please, your lovability is up to you! Bad events in the past don't mean your future won't shine! So, it's time to start using the methods given in this book on the path where you will feel more and more valuable. Every time you find it difficult to move forward, when you feel hopeless in your attempt to change, please re-read this chapter. Finally, I'm returning to the main purpose of this chapter. It's important that you understand that when it comes to manifesting the changes in your life on the physical plane, it takes time. First, the change appears on the thought plane, then on the emotional plane, then on the bodily plane, and finally it is realized in your life. According to my own experience, when we have eliminated a problem in ourselves, it takes at least two months for the actual effect to appear at the level of our everyday life. So, I wish you a lot of patience and perseverance with the methods found in the rest of this book!

6.7. A few more tips to get you started

Congratulations! If you've made it this far in this book, you've gained a lot of knowledge that can help you change your life. Now for the practical part of this book, I invite you on a journey that will bring your life more and more quality! It's very important that you follow the instructions here, even if you don't like or don't agree with the tasks at first glance. Don't forget: the more your ego opposes you, the more it fears for its existence in you! So don't let yourself down, but hang in there, even when it's hard. I know that each Person's path of spiritual development is unique. But in this system, there are "only" those milestones around which uniqueness can be built. Just as all People have the same general characteristics in terms of their appearance, so too are there also common points in our inner workings. The tasks you will receive on the following pages will make the fixed points in you more clear. Based on these, you will be able to perfect the wonderful unique and diverse mosaic of your soul-mind-body and consciousness.

The chapters so far have made it clear to you that the ego is made up of three parts: body, soul and mind. The cares produced by the mind affect the body and the soul. Emotions generated by the soul affect the mind and body. The state of the body affects our thoughts and emotions (*see* **Figure 2**). When we live in the world of the destructive ego, these three parts interact to pull us on a downward spiral. Our Life-destroying thoughts create feelings of spiritual vibration below 200, which negatively affect the state of our bodies Our physical problems give birth to negative thoughts, and the spiral continues. The practical methods of this book turn this downward spiral into an ascending energy system. In order for this to be effective for the body, soul, and mind, you were given tasks in turn. The order is also important, so please don't skip any tasks unless they're already an integral part of your life. Bad fixations, addictions or other negative behaviors are very difficult to change. But with the right combination and order of methods, you can get to a happier place more efficiently and faster. That's why it's important to follow the order!

If we want to group your issues, an important point of view needs to be highlighted. Examine which era in your life is the true root of the problem you want to overcome. This requires deep self-awareness! There are some psychological problems that we have brought with us from our prenatal life or early childhood. During this period, we do not yet have memory (although we do have emotional memory) and the Person operates at a completely subconscious level. From the later stages of childhood, rational thinking becomes stronger in us, and our conscious memory is already developed. The closer to the time before the age of three the root of the mental problem is, the less likely it will be to solve the problem with methods that approach the question in a rational way. Methods operated through rational thinking are more successful the more recent the event that caused the root of the mental problem. I feel it is also important to emphasize that the deeper the spiritual problem, the more destructive the past events that caused them in you are, and the more necessary it is to involve an external helper. So, if you've had a not-so-deep trauma at a completely rational age, you'll probably be able to get out of it without outside help by choosing some of the right ways you can use yourself. However, if you have experienced severe trauma before the age of three, it is certain that you will not be able to do it on your own. Of course, there is an infinite number of possibilities between these two extremes.

It is also very important to realize that spiritual development is never linearly ascending. This means you'll have some tough setbacks as we work together, starting now! This is because before the ego changes, it always hardens and uses every means in order to stay in its original state. In case of relapses, do not beat yourself up, because this would also strengthen your ego! At the same time, you will be tempted to stop working. Pick yourself up and keep going. The biggest mistake is to stop at this point. The real progress is seen in the fact that these certain relapses will gradually plunge into smaller and smaller depths or will last for shorter and shorter periods of time. So always judge your progress by the durability and depth of your lows.

Now let's get started on this amazing journey together! Please stay with me and be persistent.

To get started, answer the questions below by selecting the most appropriate number from 1 to 10 and circling it. A score of 10 means 'I totally agree' and 1 means 'I totally disagree'.

> ▶ After waking up in the morning, I look forward to the miracles this day will bring me:

1-2-3-4-5-6-7-8-9-10

- My relationships are harmonious, peaceful and characterized by spiritual intimacy, honesty, selflessness. I am not critical of myself or others:

  1-2-3-4-5-6-7-8-9-10

- I have as much work as I can do harmoniously with a flowing but calm activity level. Order and harmony dominate my life:

  1-2-3-4-5-6-7-8-9-10

- I smile a lot, not as a form of self-defense armor, but as the instinctive appearance of my happiness:

  1-2-3-4-5-6-7-8-9-10

- I rarely feel sad, restless, or impatient, and only for very short periods of time:

  1-2-3-4-5-6-7-8-9-10

- I love my Life and I love myself:

  1 - 2 - 3 - 4 - 5 - 6 - 7 - 8 - 9 - 10

- With pure attention, with an open heart, without extraneous thoughts, I am able to live within precious moments:

  1-2-3-4-5-6-7-8-9-10

- ▶ I trust in my future and believe that Life will direct my fate in the right direction (You can replace Life with any word according to your belief system, e.g. God, Almighty, etc.):

    1-2-3-4-5-6-7-8-9-10

- ▶ I sleep deeply and well every day:

    1-2-3-4-5-6-7-8-9-10

- ▶ My physical health is in perfect condition:

    1 - 2 - 3 - 4 - 5 - 6 - 7 - 8 - 9 - 10

Now please add the numbers given to the questions and divide by 10. Write your value here:_____

Thank you!

Now let's begin the most valuable work of your life: the gradual construction of your abundance.

CHAPTER 7

Tools for Your Happiness (Baseline)

The First Step to your happiness (soul): Gratitude

Gratitude is one of the most important, powerful, and easy-to-learn uplifting feelings. This is one of the reasons I'm inviting you to this first challenge. In Western welfare societies, the biggest mistake we make with ourselves is forgetting to be grateful. Prosperity and ego make us believe that everything we receive is due to our own efforts. Meanwhile, new goals are constantly floating in front of us, and in the struggle for them, our soul sinks to the spiritual vibration of Desire. We don't actually feel gratitude at this or any other level of Life-Destroying spiritual vibration. Let's look at why. At the psychological vibration levels of Shame and Guilt, we don't feel worthy of anything, so it doesn't occur to us to be grateful. At the level of spiritual vibration of Apathy and Grief, we don't even have the strength to be grateful. At the psychological vibration level of Fear, all positive feelings are suppressed by the fear gripping our souls. At the spiritual vibratory level of Desire, craving blinds us from gratitude. Anger blinds us to gratitude at the spiritual vibration level of Anger, while at the spiritual vibration level of Pride, we believe that everything we receive is fundamentally deserved.

The feeling of gratitude is one of the gates to higher levels of spiritual vibration. If we want to be happier than we are now, our most important task is to put gratitude back into our lives, make it a part of our daily lives, or increase its amount. The good news for you is that the feeling of gratitude is very easy to learn!

Until the end of my thirties, I was very, very rarely grateful. For example, if I got away with an unexpected car accident, I must have felt instinctively and immediately grateful. However, never on a day-to-day level did I get that feeling. I only felt that way about big things that rarely happen. True, no one had ever taught me how important gratitude is. Our family was not open to spirituality, and we never talked about such things in the first place. I was so busy achieving my goals that even if I achieved something, I didn't have time to feel "grateful" because I was already thinking about reaching my next goals. This is a typical symptom of the psychological vibration level of Desire. But I could have been grateful for a lot of things every day, and today I regret that I wasn't then.

Think about how many People there are on Earth who are unhealthy for some reason. If you're healthy, it's a wonderful thing. Are you grateful for it every day? Please consider that three billion People don't know if there will be food for themselves and their families tomorrow. If you have something to eat every day and you can even choose what you eat, it's a wonderful thing. Are you grateful every day? Imagine tens of millions of people living in polluted cities and industrial areas where every breath literally feels terrible. Is it nice to breathe where you are right now? If so, it's a wonderful thing. Are you grateful for it every day? In the same way, it can be said that a billion people on Earth today live without access to water, or many millions of people live stateless in so-called 'homes' where they are threatened with frostbite.

Obviously, most of us don't feel grateful for these things. Why not? Because our egos make us believe that these are basic things, so we don't even think about it. The result of this is that we experience the miracle of the sensation of taste or the miracle of walking barefoot every day, sometimes the incredible feeling of warm water flowing over our body in the shower, yet we are not grateful for it. With this, we emotionally distance ourselves from the small pleasures of everyday life, which is like closing the tap of happiness. Whether you're grateful for them or fail to engage with them to fulfill your destructive ego is just a matter of attitude. The more you are grateful, the happier you will be! This is stated by all world religions, and it is now a proven fact!

When I was younger, I didn't understand why there were so many more happy people in poorer countries than in prosperous societies. Obviously, there are many reasons for this, but the main reason is gratitude. In poor countries where People have little, they are grateful for every little thing. Thus, their souls are more full of gratitude than in the world of prosperity. They build the house of their happiness every day. In the "developed" welfare societies, on the other hand, our souls become comfortable and we forget to be grateful, although it takes minimal energy and time. And because of our wonderful life, we can be grateful for a thousand times more things. We simply have to rediscover that feeling in ourselves.

The method of this is the gratitude flow, which was developed by two famous psychologists. This method can be found in Barry Michels and Phil Stutz's book *The Tools*. The gratitude-flow method teaches us to activate a feeling of gratitude at any time. After all, the root of this problem is that we have forgotten to be grateful, in other words, the feeling of gratitude instinctively turns on in us very rarely. However, the good news is that with a little practice, anyone can reactivate this spiritual channel within themselves.

The method: Relax your body. Take a few deep breaths. Close your eyes. Choose some things to be grateful for in the last 24 hours. It can be anything small or anything that seems natural. For example, say to yourself: "I am grateful for the fresh air in my lungs, I am grateful for the sun in my window, I am grateful for waking up in a soft, clean bed, I am grateful for starting the day with a warm shower, I am grateful for the thousands of delicious flavors of breakfast food, etc." Think about at least five of these things! At first, you may feel slight tension when you search for these "thank-you items." Then you will feel a sense of gratitude as it rises directly from your heart. When you finish the list, let the feeling of gratitude continue without words. What you will feel then is a stream of gratitude. As the energy flows up from your heart, your chest becomes lighter and you feel the power of endless giving. Let it go and feel it as gratitude gradually pervades every cell of your whole body. Enjoy that your cells can all exist in a feeling of gratitude! Each of them then switches to a self-healing state. Then, completely selflessly pour your gratitude out into the world. Thanks to selflessness, it fills up your soul much more effectively. At this moment, you come into contact with the Universe (you can replace the word Universe with any word according to your religion or faith, like God, Creator of All Things, etc.).

If you want to delve deeper into the subject of gratitude, I wholeheartedly recommend Rhonda Byrne's book *The Magic*. For an example, in this book there is a method that could best be called a gratitude list. Every night, write down at least ten things you were grateful for that day, while reliving those experiences and opening yourself up to gratitude. Even the Person who is really down can find reasons for gratitude in their Life. You don't have to think big. A small flower, a delicate fragrance, a caress of the breeze, or the warmth of the sun bringing light to your life are all things to be thankful for. Gratitude brings light into your soul; it's the most powerful engine for raising your mental level. So, please, don't let your ego belittle this technique!

Imagine a feeling of gratitude as being like a pebble. And imagine the repressed pains, fears and lack of love in your soul as a deep well. This well is the cause of your unhappiness. With every flow of gratitude, you drop a tiny pebble into this well. This way, over months or years, the well of your unhappiness fills up more and more, and you become more and more abundant.

So use the flow of gratitude to make the feeling of gratitude a part of your everyday life. You can never have too much gratitude! There's always a reason to be grateful! As a result, not only is the well of your soul become saturated, but your worldview will also gradually change. In time, instead of looking at the empty half of the glass, you will increasingly look at the full half, which will make your thinking more optimistic and your emotions more positive. Isn't it clear to you that someone who always looks at the empty half of the glass cannot be truly happy?

Here's a summary of what you need to do to complete the first step to your happiness:

Task: Perform at least one flow of gratitude each day. It's best to do it before going to sleep, as this also establishes a more peaceful and self-healing sleep. But the post-awakening flow of gratitude it's also a great thing because it sets the stage for a happier day.

Which part of you it affects the most: the Soul

How long you have to do this task: This is a task for life, as gratitude is the basis of happiness. It is a common mistake for People to get involved in their souls and then let them drift out of their lives after a while. So, slowly and undetectably, the destructive ego pulls these People back into their old ruts. Therefore, it is important to practice regularly enough that it becomes an integral, instinctive part of your life, because in this case it will already be part of your ego, which will then begin to transform into a neutral or creative one.

A few tips: You'll probably find it hard to get started at first. It's also realistic that you will hardly feel anything at the first few attempts of the gratitude flow. But I'm asking you wholeheartedly to keep going. The destructive ego will bring up all the arguments as to why this is stupid or why it doesn't work. Please don't listen to it! Let it know that it's what you want and you're going to do it, so it'd better take it in. When your Life is difficult, it is the most difficult to feel gratitude. But if we don't feel it at those times, we will be stuck in that bad Life. Gratitude is what gets us out of there. Our emotions also affect the decisions of our mind and the state of our body, so it's very important that you practice, no matter how hard it is! Think about it, please: if People in the worst slums are able to feel gratitude, why don't you have the strength?! Please hold on and practice! The most important rule is that once you start, you never stop!

Now, please stop reading this book until you have taken this first step towards your happiness! Afterwards, I promise you that we will continue to work together.

When you can take Step Two: When gratitude flow and a feeling of gratitude have become a part of your life. You will notice this because if one day you accidentally skip it, you will miss it already. The other symptom is that you will be grateful for more and more small things during the day.

The Second Step to your happiness (mind): Affirmations – how to learn to think positively

The good thing about this method is that you can use it to improve any area of your life, which makes it a pretty great way to do a lot of things. Of course, there are limitations to this, but it's still a cool and effective method.

What fundamentally distinguishes successful People from unsuccessful ones is that the group of successful People is positive-minded, while unsuccessful People are generally negative-minded. For example, if something bad happens to a successful Person, they usually try to learn from it and draw the right conclusions in order to prevent it from happening to them in the future, or to grow through the lessons they learned. People who are also successful in the spiritual sense see these kinds of situations as a warning from Life and use them to see behind their egos to find out what they need to live differently, or what the Universe is telling them (the word Universe can be replaced by God or any other word that corresponds to your faith / religion). When something bad happens to unsuccessful People they blame others, or if they have no one to blame they'll blame God or their bad luck, feel sorry for themselves, etc.

Successful People become successful through positive thinking, and unsuccessful People are made unlucky by negative thinking because:

Every thought or spoken sentence is a confirmation.

That is, all our thoughts and sentences affect our future. Words that are thought or spoken really have power! Affirmation, in other words, means thoughts that have an impact on our future. But the point is that all our thoughts have an impact on our future. For example, I used to constantly tell the People around me that I never had enough time and that I was really, really swamped. A friend of mine keeps saying "Life sucks" and his Life really does suck. When he finally starts to make a positive turn in his life, he is always hit by "unexpected bad luck". This is, of course, because:

Every statement or thought made in the present moment shapes our future.

The reason for this, by the way, is the law of attraction, which will be described in detail in the next volume. The point is, if you say every day "no one loves me", then no one will love you, or if you are loved by someone for a short time, you will definitely screw it up at some point. Most people react that this is stupid. After all, if they think that no one likes them (or any other negative thing), it's because this has been their Life experience so far. Anyone who reacts in this way is therefore right in the sense that it genuinely reflects their experience. However, their life experience so far has been caused by programs they mistakenly took on in early childhood, not on their real selves. Thus, in order to change, we need to change the patterns of thinking we already have. After all, most of the time we live according to our parents' bad programs. Confirmations are for transforming these. If we want to change our lives, we must first transform our thinking and speech. Think of every thought and sentence you utter as a seed. Your Life is the soil of these seeds. Some seeds don't even sprout, some die when they are young, and others grow into trees. Now, to use this analogy, please think about your average day. Or even better, observe yourself in this regard for a few days! Look for the answer to the following question: **What percentage of your thoughts and sentences are negative?** The higher the rate, the worse your Life! If you already agree with this statement during your self-examination, please take a few days again and observe what areas of your Life you see as being negative. Some feel negative about their body, some with their work, some with their knowledge, some with their likability, etc. In connection with these, think about how often you think or say any negative things. In general, where we have a lot of negative statements, we are dissatisfied with that area of Life. Some People are dissatisfied with many areas. You may want to put this book down for a few days and hold an investigation. Once you're over it, please continue. Now choose an area of Life that you would most like to change. Of course, you can choose different ones or all of them, but it is likely that from that point you will be able to change more effectively.

From that day forward, after every negative thought or sentence, say five positive ones. Thus, you will "neutralize" each negative sentence with five positive sentences. Also, choose a few positive affirmations to tell yourself several times a day.

You're going to feel stupid at first because you feel your negative thoughts and you believe them, while positive affirmations will seem distant and foreign. Some of the positive statements will be so weird that you'll feel stupid just to be saying them in your head at all. But it's not the positive thought that is "stupid"; it's your bad habits that bring so much evil into your Life. They are the tools of your destructive ego, but you understand this well! At the same time, every beginning is difficult! We don't learn to ride a bicycle by immediately doing it with ease. So, hang in there and do it!

If this all feels silly, the following visualization technique can help, which is a good approximation of reality. Imagine that you are surrounded by a lot of positive energy that Life radiates towards you. However, every negative thought, every negative sentence is a barrier that prevents you from connecting with these positive energies. This barrier separates you from these energies. In each case, when you compensate for a negative thought with five positive ones, you remove this barrier that you have built over many years for a short period of time. As a result, your life will gradually get better as you open up more and more to the positive energies around you. Things will get easier and you'll feel luckier! It is important for you to know that not everything will be perfect; there may even be even negative events in your Life in the future! But their number will be less and less, and you will come out of the pits faster than before.

Here's a summary of what you need to do to complete Step Two:

Task: Replace each negative sentence or thought with five positive sentences or thoughts about the same subject. Use selected positive confirmations at least once a day! The best thing to do when doing the gratitude-flow method is to put these at the beginning or at the end of it. This will make your self-improvement ritual even more effective.

Which part of you it affects the most: Mind

How long you need to do this task: Do this task at least until your thinking becomes fundamentally positive. This transformation can take from a few weeks to months. But it's important to hold on and practice! Together with the previous step, they reinforce each other within you.

Some good advice and rules:
1. Your affirmations should contain neither a word expressing negation nor a negative word! Incorrect affirmation: "I'm glad I don't have a jerk for a boss!" Correct affirmation: "I have a fair and respectable boss!"
2. The positive affirmation you read in the previous point may be strange at first reading because it's in the present tense while it has to be about something you desire. That's the second rule. Formulate all your affirmations in the present time and in a declarative manner. Incorrect affirmation: "I want to meet a wonderful man soon who will accept me as I am." This is always pushing this event into the future, so it will never happen. The Universe understands everything literally (you can replace the word Universe with God

or any other word according to your belief system)! Therefore, the correct affirmation is: "I will get acquainted with a with a wonderful man who accepts me for who I am."
3. Never stop! Progress is not continuous. There are always relapses. Most People stop doing affirmations at those times. And you can't stop! The best thing you can do for yourself is to think positively and learn through affirmations.
4. Don't be impatient with yourself. Change is gradual and slow. It is very difficult for us to change our thinking patterns dating back to childhood, copied from our parents. This takes time. Some take years to learn to think positively. I was a very negative-minded and pessimistic Human being. I needed around five years to instinctively become a positive-minded Person. But I had to work at it every day, with a lot of perseverance and practice. However, this process will probably be faster for you, because the previous step accelerates and supports this change.
5. Don't beat yourself up! Do not hurt yourself due to possible difficulties, clumsiness and slowness. Lack of self-acceptance is also a negative reinforcement! Be accepting and indulgent with yourself, it will help you succeed!
6. Don't complain or blame others! Every complaint or blaming of others is a negative affirmation! Quitting complaining and blaming others will already bring a huge qualitative change to your Life, as you will be quitting strong negative affirmations.
7. Finally, the most important advice: Visualize and attach positive feelings to it. The subconscious hardly understands spoken, rational sentences; your subconscious understands images and emotions the

most. Try to visualize your positive affirmations and attach positive feelings to them. Gratitude is ideal. The method still works without these efforts, but it takes much longer and is less effective I needed five years because unfortunately I didn't know this rule. Let's look at an example of how to do the exercise: to affirm "I have enough money", add the feeling you would have if you had a 7-digit balance in your bank account or a stack of 100-dollar bills in your hand.

If you follow these rules and practice persistently, you will gradually have a better Life! However, it's important to know that this method is not omnipotent! The deeper the cause is suppressed in your subconscious that attracts negative things into your Life, the harder it is to override it. If the root of the mental problem is from before the age of three, you should definitely opt for a professional helper. If the root of the problem occurred between the ages of three and fourteen, it depends on how deep and how repressed the problem is. Positive reinforcement also helps in this case, but external help is needed. The subconscious is very strong; its power should not be underestimated! Affirmations are most effective in People who do not have repressed psychological grievances, only bad habits learned from their parents or their environment. In addition, it's also very effective for those whose psychological causes are not exaggerated deep events that occurred after the age of 14.

One of the most renowned representatives of affirmations is Louise L. Hay. I highly recommend all of her books and videos, especially the book titled *You Can Heal Your Life*. **You can find videos with super affirmations on YouTube by searching for "Louise L. Hay, affirmations".** I know this step will help make every Day of Your Life shine even brighter. I support you wholeheartedly!

Now, please stop reading this book until you have completed Step Two of your journey to happiness! Then I'll wait for you back here so we can continue working together!

When you can take Step Three: When negative thoughts and sentences emerge, an instinctive internal brake kicks in and automatically adjusts them. Please remember: you can never think negative things about yourself or your Life! If it happens, you have to automatically correct them to positive!

The Third Step to your happiness (body): Meals and vibration levels

The Buddhist saying that you are what you eat is almost corny, but maybe this chapter will shed some new light on it for you. Every food (like everything else) has vibrations. When we think of food, we usually look at its calorie content or its ingredients. These are important, but so is the vibration level of the food. If you want to stay healthy or regain your health, you should eat foods that have vibrations at least equal to or higher than those of a healthy body. Fresh raw vegetables, fruits, oil seeds, fruits and some essential oils produced from spices and herbs (e.g. lavender) are such. Everything else has a lower vibration value than the vibration value of a healthy body. For example, the meat of a dead animal is around 1 MHz, while cancer cells already begin to form at around 42 MHz.

If you look at food only in terms of calories and protein, it seems like a good thing to eat a lot of meat, but you're also getting low-vibration substances into your body. That's why it's important to eat lots of fresh raw greens with meat if you don't want to be a vegetarian. So here, too, it's about balance. Coffee also has a very low vibration level. Here, we try to keep our energy levels high by consuming caffeine. However, caffeine consumes your body's reserves, so it destroys your body in the long run. A person who switches to a vegetarian diet and a meal with lots of fresh vegetables and fruits will usually be able to quit coffee because they will be more energetic and vigorous than ever before. Unfortunately, alcohol and smoking are even worse for our vibrations. (Author's note: *Tobacco-related spiritual rituals are excluded. Smoking as an everyday activity lowers the level of mental vibration.*) What is bad news for most People is that sweets also represent extremely low levels of vibration. Dairy products are also low-vibration foods. Imagine what state of mind the captive cow is in—with their calf taken away and then put on a milking machine—and what hormones are put into her milk. You consume this low-vibration hormone cocktail when you consume dairy products. Obviously, if that milk is produced from freely grazing animals in a way that respects their motherhood, its consumption is not a problem, but unfortunately this is very rare nowadays. Finally, a few words about carbohydrates. Carbohydrates are less favorable the more concentrated they are. Concentrated carbohydrates are consumed because of their easy digestibility and high calorie content. The most perfect examples are chocolate, sweet pastries, and sugary soft drinks. However, they generate a sudden insulin shot in the body, which causes a significant swing, lowering the vibration level. Often, stomach or abdominal pain also indicates that what we are doing to our bodies is not the right thing to do. This leads to high blood sugar levels, which the body cannot fully use. Thus, part of the blood glucose surge will be deposited as fat. The more concentrated the carbs you eat, the greater the likelihood of migraines and other headache symptoms in your life. This is because this is how the nervous system reacts to the swings in your body.

The things I'm talking about here is based on personal experience, so the solutions definitely work. The goal is for the foods you eat to have the highest possible average vibration level.

To do this, follow these meal rules:
  I. Don't eat meat! If you can't live without meat, minimize the amount of meat you eat! Note that fish is also meat.
  II. Don't drink alcohol (or take other psychotropic drugs)! If you can't live without alcohol, minimize the amount you consume.
  III. Do not smoke! If you can't do without it, minimize the amount!
  IV. Don't drink coffee! If you can't do without it, reduce the amount!
  V. Reduce your sugar and confectionery consumption! Avoid concentrated carbohydrates.
  VI. Do not consume dairy unless it comes from grazing and animal-friendly farming.
  VII. Eat as many fresh vegetables and fruits as possible.

You can't follow so many eating rules overnight. The point is to be gradual and to strive for it. It took me around three years for all of these rules to work instinctively. Although sometimes, when I write these lines regarding sweets and dairy products, I am also a slight "offender". Gradualism sometimes results in relapses. But slowly, our food can be made cleaner and cleaner. Please consider that currently 93% of the animals on Earth are livestock, due to Humankind's excessive consumption of meat and dairy products. This is an unbelievable amount of environmental pollution and a serious cause of climate change. In addition, if all People were vegetarian, up to 20 billion people could live on Earth without starvation. In order to produce 1 calorie of meat, an average of 10 calories of plant foods must be fed to the animal. So, in ecological terms, meat production is a wasteful industry. The other good habits described above similarly protect the Earth's ecosystem and climate. As I wrote in my previous book (*Dittrich, 2021*), what is good for your soul is also good for the Earth's climate. Long ago, meat-eating developed because there were no refrigerators. Thus, People, with the help of the live animal, ensured the availability of fresh food. In today's technologically advanced world, this constraint no longer exists. We only eat meat because of our upbringing and habits.

It's also important to emphasize that the aim of this chapter is not to achieve complete self-deprivation or asceticism. As Buddha experienced before his enlightenment, the other extreme is not good either! Life should be enjoyed, and joys received without guilt and with pure Love! However, today's Western world is built on the excessive pursuit of pleasure, which destroys our happiness, even though we believe the opposite. Moderation brings purification, through which our vibrations improve strongly, making us happier. So gradually remove what you can from the list above without self-torture or self-destruction. Take small steps and you will see that the energy invested is worth it!

Now, please stop reading this book until you have completed Step Three of your journey to success! Then I'll wait for you back here so we can continue working together!

When to undertake Step Four: When the above eating habits are instinctively at the center of your attention. They don't have to be a part of your Life—just have an incentive to pursue them. Give yourself time to gradually change, as it will only be effective if it happens step by step.

The Fourth Step to your happiness (soul): Live your time differently – 'Me' time

My grandmother told me a lot about her youth. In those days, People used to walk, sometimes they used a bus. It took several hours to walk into the city. They didn't have a car, which would have taken only 15 minutes to travel that distance. They washed clothes with a washboard, not with washing machine. Instead of a dishwasher, they washed dishes by hand. Yet the People were not in a hurry and had time for each other. When I was younger, I thought a lot about how it could be possible that so many tools had been developed in order to save time in our lives, even though there had never been a society on Earth that was so busy, with no time for anything—especially for anyone. If you look around, People have the least amount of time. They are constantly rushing, driving, jumping from one thing to the next. And the time pressure and resulting stress is increasing. I lived like this for decades. One of the consequences of my search for happiness is a conscious and instinctive slowdown. I used to be proud to work from Monday to Sunday. I was also proud of the fact that I never had time for anything; I was always swamped. The fact that so many people sought my professional help compensated for my severe lack of self-esteem. It helped make me feel more important, like I was something more. Unfortunately, this was a superficial illusion that would never have filled the emptiness in my soul. Change can only be successful from the inside out! Confirmations from others only make the superficial glaze—the ego—crustier and harder, which helps to suppress internal problems, but only makes them more difficult to solve. This is the trap that most people today fall into. Everyone just follows the crowd. However, society is rushing towards its destruction (*Dittrich, 2021*). The only way out of this terrible future is to individually realize the incorrect functioning of society and to change the direction of our own lives. The key is not to try to save our entire society (although this selfless goal is wonderful), but to find our own happiness in success.

One of the main areas of this is time management. Lack of time is nothing more than a speed dependence, or a deceptive tool of escaping from oneself. If we are always in a hurry, we never have to be silent with ourselves alone. We avoid the strange feeling of emptiness that immediately comes over us and is so unpleasant that we need to quickly dismiss it with some activity. And that feeling of emptiness means that you can never be happy without facing it! In this book, you will be given more and more tasks step by step, which you can accomplish successfully only if you devote enough time to yourself. Without this, you won't be able to move forward in your search for happiness. This is where the concept of Me-time comes in! One of the biggest mistakes Humans make is that they don't have time for themselves! But if you don't have time for yourself, how do you expect to change? If you don't take enough time for yourself, how can you live a happier life? Me-time is incredibly important! And use your me-time to develop yourself or to have quality relaxation. But the most important rule is that you have to have time for yourself every day!

Workaholism, speed mania, time dependence, and constant desire all grow from the same spiritual root. They make you chase a mirage for the rest of your life without realizing that you are actually wasting your Life. Your ego is constantly suggesting that when you achieve this or that, you will be happy. Unfortunately, this is not true! Consciously slowing down means stepping off the treadmill and gradually starting to live slower and slower. This is not running away; it is correcting and consciously simplifying your life, as well as introducing ever-increasing me-time.

I used to have a lot of things to do and I wanted to solve them faster and more efficiently to catch up with myself. However, there is a huge trap in this line of thinking that I didn't realize for years. If I do things faster, I can check off a lot more in a day. However, each task you complete will generate more tasks, creating more to-do items in a given amount of time. In this way, the overwhelmed state is increased, as everything is accelerating. If I consciously slow down, that is: I only do what is really important and only when I really have to, and I use the free time not to do things but to be good to myself, then doing less in a given unit of time will actually manifest the arrival of fewer new things in my future. This is the basis of conscious deceleration. Don't worry—you're still a hard-working Human being! However, the question is whether you can accomplish this change. After all, if you have free time, what will you do with it? Will you choose new ways to escape from yourself? If you're watching a movie or browsing the internet, all it means is that your stress level has slightly decreased. However, this also depends on the media content you watch. But if you spend the liberated time on self-improvement, you will direct your Life—which you will have created for yourself—in a happier direction with each of these periods. In this way, your life will change as you move towards a more qualitative reality. So, the most important rule of conscious slowing down is that you should spend the free time on your own development or quality relaxation!

Here's a summary of what you need to do to complete Step Four:

Task: Classify your tasks as follows:
- ▶ Important and urgent
- ▶ Important, not urgent
- ▶ Not important, urgent
- ▶ Important, not urgent

Do this every day! Always do only the important and urgent tasks! Ignore the rest! Only complete your tasks when the deadline is very close! Spend the resulting free time on self-improvement or quality time leading to happiness or relaxation, and quality time with loved ones. During these periods, focus on experiencing your positive emotions.

Which part of you it affects the most: Soul

How long you need to do this task: You need to do this task until it becomes instinctive and self-protection reflexes are automatically turned on when you are not dealing with important or urgent tasks. The other important aspect is that it should become your inner need to have time for yourself every day. If you miss one day, double it on the next! You can't take from yourself what you've finally won.

Some good advice: If you categorize everything you need to do and there is hardly anything that is both urgent and important, then it means you want to fit into the world too much! In this case, when you do anything, think about how much it relates to your Life commitment and your own happiness. These are the only things that matter. This is not selfishness! Why? Because the happier you are, the more positive impact you will have on your environment. However, until you don't prioritize your tasks according to these principles, you will never be happy.

If you prefer to do the unimportant things first and postpone the important and urgent things, then according to your subconscious program, you need other People to rebuke you, criticize you and make you feel that you are not good enough. You probably took on this faulty code when you were a child. Later tasks will include some which will mitigate this in you. But in the meantime, be disciplined and hard on yourself not to cut yourself off and really deal only with the important and urgent things. If you use the free time for self-improvement, it will start to pull you out of the old trap.

If you don't feel that any of the tasks are important, and that you're only doing them because you need them or you don't have a better idea, then the spiritual vibration level of Apathy is an integral part of your life. You need to learn to select tasks that are important to your Life Tasks and focus your limited energy on them. And for the rest of your time, do the self-improvement steps in this book. This will gradually give you more spiritual strength to manage your Life.

I'll give you another important piece of advice: the difference between successful and unsuccessful People is that successful People focus only on what they can influence. At the same time, unsuccessful People waste most of their energy on things they can't have a significant impact on. For example, unsuccessful People think a lot about politics, while they have no influence on its development, except on the single day of an election. Successful People don't usually deal with politics until they can go and vote. In such cases, they objectively look at which party's program is the most useful and most favorable for them. They make their choice, then they put politics aside and go on with their lives. So, we often mistake something as being important, but if you can't influence it, it can't really be important to you! If you focus on the things you can actually influence, you will be more successful and thus happier.

Now, please stop reading this book until you have completed Step Four of your journey to success! Then I'll wait for you to come back so we can continue working together!

When you can do Step Five: when you automatically instinctively focus on doing only the most important and urgent things. At this point, please begin to continue.

The Fifth Step to your Happiness:
What is good and what is bad?
How to get better? –
The daily scale method

In the field of Human existence and Human relations, there is no such thing as pure good or evil. Both good and evil live inside us. Our Life and the Life around us is also about the constant struggle between good and evil, just as darkness and light are in a constant struggle. Cold and heat, dark and light, good and bad are the drivers of change. These are the opposites that build the Universe and generate its transformation processes. They are therefore a natural part of our lives. That's why above a certain level of enlightenment there is no good and no evil—only the miracle of existence. It already makes sense that these are subsystems that underpin each other's existence.

But let's go back to our "ordinary" life. What is good and what is bad at our level? This is the first thing we need to be aware of! After all, nowadays it is very fashionable to look bad; it is even more fashionable to be a negation of the bad (*John Bradshaw, 2015*). Many people think that doing something bad for a good cause is good. This is also suggested by the famous saying that "the end justifies the means". But let's face it: this is the dominant saying at Pride or lower levels of spiritual vibration, and it's nothing more than the destructive-ego's clever grip on accepting our actions. The series of Harry Potter films has certainly been seen or perhaps even read by most of you. These movies have a beautiful symbolic world as it depicts the struggle between good and evil. The evil and good in Harry Potter are constantly fighting. The protagonist also often questions his own goodness, sometimes feeling that he is no better than evil. But in the movie, the message Harry Potter received from his uncle is clear: the good in us separates us from the bad. Harry Potter was able to detach the evil part of himself by focusing on the good things in his soul, such as the memory of his parents or the wonderful experiences he had with his friends. Harry Potter's inner struggle is no different from ours! Our lives are also permeated by the inner struggle of good and evil. The other symbolic aspect of the movies is that wizards and witches move to the side of good and evil before the final big clash. The movie beautifully shows how negative emotions dominate on the bad side and how positive they are on the good side. Fear, guilt, shame, anger, longing all appear in the movie on the dark side. The motives of love, togetherness, and altruism imbue those on the good side— just as it happens in our own lives, and as I presented the Life Supporting and Life Destroying vibration levels on the Hawkins scale.

At the same time, the "dark side" is very fashionable among young people nowadays, although this is not new. Let's think about the Satanists who were so prevalent in the past, and let's not forget the Emos. It was just that the phenomenon was getting more and more massive. More and more young people think it's good to be bad, although fortunately most of them just want to look bad, though it's actually not. This is a strong symptom of a serious social impairment. It usually stems from the fact that it seems boring to be good. This is a stereotype that is too worn out. Young people see that the world is hypocritical because everyone talks about being good, but all the while evil is spreading very intensely. They are tired of this hypocritical system. However, they are wrong if they think that the right way is to strengthen the bad side, as this will only make the situation worse.

There are always trends in the battle between good and evil that affect where they each reign. Currently, the trend is the strengthening of the bad all over the world. This is shown by the destruction of Nature, the weakening of religions, the strengthening of selfishness. The first step is always to decide if you want to be good at all. After all, I see a lot of Humans who don't really want this path. In Harry Potter, the Death Eaters would rather die than be good, even if they felt that their evil existence was a serious psychological burden for them. It is the spiritual burden itself that fuels their passion. A lot of People are the same way inside. So, please ask yourself: do I want to be good at all? The answer isn't that obvious, is it? I had mixed feelings about this question for many years. I mean, basically, I want to be good, but sometimes it feels good to "misbehave." So sometimes I need to do something that is considered wrong within the system of traditional religious or social ideas. There is a mixed duality in me too. Who experiences themselves as purely good or purely bad is most likely to not have adequate self-knowledge. A purely good Human is one who is fully enlightened, such as Jesus or Buddha. It is the purely bad Person whose soul is completely and permanently imbued with shame and the aggression that feeds on it, such as Hitler's. The largest percentage of People do not live in such incredibly strong extremism.

I don't want to influence the direction you want to go, but it's important to know that an increase in the level of psychic vibration is only possible with the strengthening of the good and the weakening of the bad in you! So, if you want to strengthen the good in yourself, this is your book. If you want to strengthen the bad, you probably wouldn't have gotten this far in the book.

After we have put this in order, I would like to clarify what is good and what is bad, because in this great social turmoil, this question is no longer clear for People. In my opinion, unfortunately, the dogmatism of religions often gives incorrect interpretations and often represents the wrong side by creating a sense of unnecessary guilt. Think, for example, of how much guilt and shame we felt in our adolescence because of our interest in sexuality, yet it is a natural process, and sexuality (if coupled with a proper spirituality) is one of the most wonderful things in the world. So, it depends on our mental attitude whether sexuality is good or bad. It should not be called a sin! Unfortunately, there are several types of guilt arising from such religious dogmatism. Thus, the doctrines of religion can be good or bad, depending on the spiritual attitude they are associated with. The Crusades, the extermination of the South American Indians or the burning of witches were acts carried out with a strong religious attitude, yet they were extremely evil and did not deviate from the horrors of Nazism in any way. They were meant to be a denial of evil, and yet evil grew stronger and flourished. In our history, we have often done the worst for the good. At the same time, many sanctified

People have shown in the past that religion can be a very good thing. As usual, everything depends on spiritual attitude, not on the religion itself.

It's time to sort out what's right and what's wrong. The answer to this question is clear and simple: everything that is Life Destroying is bad, and everything that is Life Supportive is good. Why? Because we are part of Life, that is: this is our camp. We were born in this camp, so we came into the world. **Our main Life task is to support Life itself.** So, we have to be good! I know that for the most part, this is the hard way, but it is still the right way to go (*Dittrich, 2021*).

Let's look **at what this sentence means in more detail: "Everything that is Life-Destroying is bad, and everything that is Life-Supporting is good"**.

Bad actions, thoughts are those that are driven by Life-destroying emotions or that result in Life-destroying emotions in the depths of our souls. These are the following basic emotions or any of their varieties:
- Shame
- Guilt
- Apathy
- Sorrow
- Fear
- Desire
- Anger
- Pride

Good deeds and thoughts are those that are driven by Life-supporting emotions or that result in Life-supporting emotions in the deepest depths of our soul. These are the following basic emotions or any of their varieties:
- Courage
- Impartiality
- Willingness

- Acceptance
- Rationality
- Love
- Joy
- Peace
- Enlightenment

Once we know what's right and what's wrong, we can make a difference. Therefore, it's worth first learning the above definition. It's clear, simple, straightforward, and free of all kinds of dogmatism.

If we understand and accept this definition, then all our actions and all our thoughts can go through this strict filter. Everything we do and every thought we think becomes worthwhile. If we continue this line of thinking, it will turn out that everything bad is actually good if you look at it in the right direction. After all, evil is nothing more than a warning of the need to change direction! Bad things are beacons in our Life that something is not on the right track. For most People, the suffering caused by bad events has brought about the great change that has made them happier, healthier or more successful. So evil is actually good, if you don't look at it from the ego's point of view. The ego always takes what does not happen according to its expectations as a personal attack and thus calls it bad. However, if bad happens to conscious People, then they look within themselves and look for what they need to develop without the blaming of others and the outside world. In this context, there is no good or bad anymore! But to live this magnificent field of view as a lifestyle, you must first teach your ego to see correctly what is right and wrong. Therefore, I ask you to learn the following method. Every night before you go to sleep, think about how much good and how much bad you did that day. This is the essence of the daily balance method. Make a daily spiritual balance every day. And please remember that an action cannot be good if it serves a good purpose but the tool it uses is bad. So don't fool yourself; stay true to yourself! It is important that you do not beat yourself up over the bad deeds of the day. After all, this is again activating bad thoughts and bad energies. Be accepting of your bad deeds that day. Accept that you have done them and think about how you can mitigate them in the future. Be thankful for your good deeds. In this way, you can connect the gratitude flow and the daily balance method.

It is up to us to feed our bad or our good selves. Every thought or action we have strengthens one of our selves, so we can do a lot for our personal development if we strengthen the half of us in the direction that we want to develop. At the same time, remember that resisting evil makes it stronger! After all, the psychological resonance of opposition is anger, so the fight against evil is never the solution! As surprising as it may be, it is the acceptance of evil that mitigates its power. This is also the key to quitting addictions. After all, resistance to the evil in us generates shame, guilt and other negative emotions in our souls. However, accepting the bad in ourselves generates Love and acceptance in the same place. In addition to accepting the bad, strengthening the good further reduces the power of the bad in us. With these, we strengthen our Life-supporting existence, for which we actually received our Life. That's why it matters what you eat, what you drink, how much you sleep, what you think, how you have sex or make love, and what movies or series you watch! Therefore, it makes a difference how you relate to your fellow humans, what you buy and how you do your job! All of these make you who you are, and with all of these you feed your good or bad side every day.

Here's a summary of what you need to do to the fifth step to your happiness:

Task: Perform the daily scale method every night before going to sleep. Accept your daily bad deeds and think about how you want to mitigate them in the future. Feel gratitude in connection with your daily good deeds and connect this with a flow of gratitude. The order is important! Fall asleep every day with a feeling of gratitude for your good deeds.

Which part of you it affects the most: Mind

How long you need to complete this task: This is a lifetime task. It's like a prayer in religions. Be persistent and make this a daily lifetime habit by combining it with a flow of gratitude.

Some good advice: It's important to be gradual! Usually, lasting change doesn't happen overnight! It's important to be patient and accepting with yourself, even when you fall back or when you're not evolving. Self-flagellation wrecks you and pulls you down even further! I know this is very difficult, especially if you have never practiced it before. But consider that toddlers don't hate themselves when they learn to walk and fall; instead, they start practicing optimistically again and again. If a toddler hated themselves every time they stumbled, they would never learn to walk, or would have negative feelings associated with walking all their life. All you need to relearn is what you knew spiritually in your early childhood!

Now, please stop reading this book until you have completed Step Five of your journey to success! Then I'll wait for you back so we can continue working together!

When can you undertake Step 6: once the daily balance method has become an integral part of your Life. You'll notice this because if you accidentally skip a day, you'll miss it already. The other symptom is that an internal alarm will sound more and more during the day if you are about to do something bad or have a bad thought or feeling.

The Sixth Step to your happiness (body): Symmetry and "posture-cure"

The thought process of this method starts from the fact that the existence of individual energy centers has now been verified by measurements. I also have a measuring device operating on the wave genetic principle, with which I usually measure the condition of my energy centers. The basic prerequisite for a healthy body is that all seven energy centers in the body (they are called chakras in the Eastern world) are at the right energy level and their center is located in the body's axis of symmetry. An adequate energy level in an energy center means that it is neither over- or under-energetic. The right side of the body is the father, son and future side, while the left side is the mother, daughter and past side. For example, if someone suppresses their love for their father, their fourth energy center becomes under-energized and shifts to the right side. In the longer term, this causes diseases or distortions in the body, especially in the organs around the fourth energy center. **You can find a very exciting and partial summary of these issues in Annex 3.**

It has also been proven that there is an energy channel along the spinal column (*Dispenza, 2020*). The energy flow between the seven energy centers of the body takes place in this energy channel. The body is healthy when this flow of energy is free. When we release our sexual energies, the energies are temporarily concentrated in the first energy center, but then, if we need our clarity for example, most of the energies flow into the sixth energy center. If the energy flow is limited, energy will be trapped in some energy centers. For example, the energies of sex addicts are trapped in the first energy center and cannot really rise from there. (Author's note: *it is still disputed today whether sexuality belongs to the first or second energy center, but this is irrelevant to the understanding of the process.*)

The free flow of energy requires a naturally straight and symmetrical state of the spinal column. That's also why correct posture is very important! Most People don't really pay attention to this. It belittles the role and importance of correct posture. However simple it may seem, **the first rule of physical health is to have the right posture!**

Proper posture consists of the following 3 criteria:
- Naturally straight spinal column
- Symmetrical hold
- None of our limbs can be crossed

Now, please take a look at your average day. Think about how you sit at the table while eating, how you sleep, how you lie in front of the TV, how you drive your car. Think about the percentage of your daily activity that meets the three criteria above. Mine was terrible before I started incorporating this method into my Life. I couldn't sleep on my back in the first place, because my posture was crooked. I have a slight scoliosis from birth, I ate curved forward at the table, I lay on the couch with my spine bent back and forth, and my legs or hands were regularly crossed or in an asymmetrical position.

Your posture shows your state of mind and the position of each of your energy centers. Or maybe these are just the bad habits of the past. Those with asymmetrical energy centers instinctively feel comfortable in an asymmetrical posture. Lack of self-efficacy, depression or other psychological problems cause curvature of the back. Shame, guilt or lack of Love cause scoliosis in children—not coincidentally, right where the energy center is affected by the given spiritual problem. Crossed hands indicate repressed (or known) anger and rage, crossed feet indicate isolation from the world, fear, or an inadequate level of ancestral trust. You can therefore do a pretty accurate psychological analysis of your posture and the shape of your spine in about two minutes. This can also help deepen your self-awareness. At the same time, this is the reason why it's easier to accept a Person with straight posture, and why we instinctively feel sympathetic when we look at them. This is also why an evil witch is portrayed as having a crooked back in fairy tales.

The good news is that you can do something about it! Symmetry and "posture cure" mean that you consciously start paying attention to your correct posture, which corresponds to the three rules above. The more you are in this position, the more the self-healing processes in your body will be intensified, because the energy flow between the energy centers of your body will be more efficient. Since your body is used to the old state, I warn you that it will be very difficult for you to change! The body always tries to restore its old physio-chemical state until the new balance is established, since the ego is also part of the body. It was very difficult for me, too. But three or four months of mindfulness already led me to instinctively tell myself if I was not sitting or lying correctly. Obviously, since this is not what our body is used to, it will be uncomfortable at first, in addition to requiring a lot of attention. But it's worth investing your awareness and energy in the process.

What did the roughly four-month cure bring? I became generally more energetic, my need for sleep decreased slightly, and my migraines (I had very strong migraines at the time) had lessened. I ate less and it took a few inches from my belly. Of course, I have continued the cure since then, because it has become an integral part of my life. Sleeping on your back and in a symmetrical position maximizes your body's ability to heal itself. This was discovered by doctors at the time of the samurai. The casualties were healed by lying on their backs, lying completely symmetrically and with their heads slightly supported. They knew already in the Middle Ages that this way the body's self-healing ability was at its maximum. And these wounded samurai often went through incredible healing simply because the doctors always forced them back into this lying position. By the way, samurai were required to sleep in this way from the beginning, so they were accustomed to it from an early age. Hence the famous Japanese saying: "the samurai's greatest weapon is good sleep".

Here's a summary of what you need to do the sixth step to your happiness:

Task: Pay attention to your posture in all life situations, even while sleeping. Please note: the correct posture consists of the following three criteria:
- ▶ Naturally straight spinal column
- ▶ Symmetrical hold
- ▶ None of your limbs can be crossed

Which part of you it affects the most: Body

How long it takes to complete this task: This is also a Lifetime task. Poor posture is always caused by the intensification of psychological problems and leads to health damage in the long run.

Some good advice: It's important to be gradual! It's rare for someone to make the switch overnight. So be patient, persistent and have enough self-control! My recommended path isn't easy, but the result is guaranteed! The good news is that with each step, your life gets a little better...

Now, please stop reading this book until you have completed Step 6 of your journey to success! Then I'll wait for you so we can continue working together!

When you can take Step 7: when you already instinctively pay attention to the correct posture and tell yourself if you don't. Then it's time to keep working hard for your happier future!

The Seventh Step to your happiness (soul): Step into the light! (Ventilation)

When you live in a dark tunnel, it's hard to imagine that there's anything better. Being out in the light offers the possibility of more favorable living conditions, but it's not so easy to believe this for someone who has never experienced it before. To exist on the spiritual vibratory levels of Shame, Guilt, Apathy, Sorrow or Fear is comparable to living in a dark cave. It's not easy to get out of there, because according to the reality of the Person living there, the world is a dark place full of selfish, evil, corrupt People. In fact, deep inside themselves these People consider themselves to be bad, worthless, and unlovable. Some people know this about themselves, but others have repressed it so deeply inside themselves that they're no longer aware of it. The beacon that exposes the destructive-ego can be found in your emotions and thoughts. Please observe yourself for a few days and answer the following questions:

- A. On an average day, approximately how long do you feel shame or how long do your thoughts revolve around any aspect of shame? Write the amount here in minutes or hours:
- B. On an average day, approx. how long do you feel guilty or how long do your thoughts revolve around guilt?

Write the amount here in minutes or hours:
C. On an average day, approximately how long do you feel unmotivated or how long do your thoughts revolve around any aspect of apathy? Write the amount here in minutes or hours:
D. On an average day, approximately how long do you feel sorrow or how long do your thoughts revolve around any aspect of sorrow? Write the amount here in minutes or hours:
E. On an average day, approximately how long do you feel fear or how long do your thoughts revolve around any aspect of fear? Write the amount here in minutes or hours:

In terms of answering questions, it doesn't matter whether you experience these thoughts or feelings about others or about yourself. It also doesn't matter whether these feelings and thoughts are legitimate or not. I just ask you to answer each question in minutes: approximately how much time does your mind and soul spend with these emotions and thoughts? In order for you to measure these accurately, I will give you a few more helpful thoughts. Regarding the level of emotions, don't worry about examining how deep the feeling is. A little sorrow is still sorrow; a little fear is still fear. However, shyness is not shame! Don't confuse these two things, please! When we beat ourselves up, blame ourselves, scold ourselves or blacken ourselves, it is all guilt. However, acknowledging our own responsibility or fault for something is not guilt. Lethargy, inaction, and lack of energy all qualify as apathy. Mourning, grieving and sadness are also forms of sorrow. Regret, however, is not sorrow! Worry, dread, fright, and the projection of future negative visions are also fears. However, shyness is not fear.

If you have passed this self-examination, please be aware that the periods you are spending in those states are the biggest causes of unhappiness and bad luck in your life so far. It's also important to know that those who often feel such emotions or thoughts about these emotions usually carry within themselves more secrets that they don't dare to reveal to others. These are secrets that only we ourselves know because we are ashamed of their existence. We are afraid of being judged for them. It doesn't matter what these secrets are. For example, they can be perverse thoughts, unrealistic desires, mistakes made or bad actions done in the past which we experience as sins, or anything else within ourselves that we consider unacceptable, black, bad, wrong or evil.

Now comes the hardest part: bring your secrets into the light! They are kept in the deepest cave of your soul. The first step in the process is to bring out these secrets from there. The method is very simple: you have to tell someone all of your shameful secrets honestly! Proceed one by one, and always tell only one thing. Prepare consciously and be brave enough to do it! I know it's incredibly difficult, but Courage is not by accident the first Life-supporting psychic vibration. But you must. If you tell someone your most shameful secrets, you will bring them into the light and you will be relieved! Why? Because if someone listens without prejudice, their acceptance will soften the urge within you to condemn yourself. If you're unsure about whether something is related to you, ask yourself a simple question: Would you post it on Facebook? If the answer is no, then shame is attached to it! This frank and simple question was once asked to me by Gyöngyi Spitzer (Soma Mamagésa), whom I consider one of my masters and all whose books, courses and social media platforms I recommend to you with great affection.

Here's a summary of what you need to do to achieve Step Seven to your happiness:

Task: Gradually tell all your secrets, even the most shameful ones!

Which part of you it affects the most: Soul

How long you have to do this task: as long as you still have one or more secrets you are ashamed to tell to others, that is, at least one person has listened to it without condemning you!

Some good advice: I know this is incredibly difficult! But as long as you carry these secrets inside you, they will behave in your soul like an incredibly heavy weight! It's important to choose carefully whom you share a secret with. After all, if the person you tell condemns you, it will push you back into the depths. Therefore, it is essential to choose a person who is empathetic, understanding, and skilled in spiritual problems. Before you tell them, ask them if they have the time, strength, and desire to listen to you honestly. Only tell them your secret(s) if they say yes! So, choosing the right person is not enough; you also have to choose the right time. Consciously prepare for "deployment"! Tell it at the right moment and to a good Person! What's even more important is that before you reveal your secret, be aware that you don't expect a solution from them—just that they listen to you. Ask them to keep your secret. Therefore, choose a Person you trust. I know it is difficult to find such a Person, but it is also a sign of stepping out into the light that you dare to trust someone. This Person can be a therapist, a friend, a priest, a soulmate, or a Person with a similar fate. Choose the most suitable Person for each of your secrets. Proceed consciously and systematically for each secret. Once you've told it, you'll be relieved. This is the moment when you've stepped into the light! I congratulate you for it. Make yourself aware of the feeling you experience at that time. Please remember that with most secrets, we are much stricter with ourselves than others would be. We see our secrets as being darker than they are. The destroying-ego does this to us, because as long as these live inside us, it can hold on to them. For the ego, these are anchors fixed with iron chains that it can hold on to. It's time to tear them off, one by one, gradually! One more thing: if you are judged by someone, do not give up! That doesn't mean you did the wrong thing, just that you chose an inappropriate Person to listen to you! Don't give up!

I once had a secret about an unfaithful affair that I carried with me for well over ten years. I felt guilty about it, bad about it, and every time I thought about it, I felt ashamed of myself. After all, I cheated on the partner I had at the time. When I persuaded myself to tell my current partner, it was incredibly difficult for me to tell the whole truth about what happened. To my great surprise, my partner didn't say anything condemning. She replied empathetically that under those circumstances, not many men would have lasted as long in fidelity as I did then. I was surprised by her reaction, but it felt good. The guilt I had carried for well over ten years began to heal that day. What a relief it was to tell it! Even today, I still remember the feeling clearly, but I also remember how many months I had prepared to tell it at the right time. I shared this story of one of my secrets with you to show you that we all have our flaws, and we all have our shadows. One who is snow-white, perfectly pure, and always good, can only be an enlightened Human. But today there are only eight such people on Earth, and these lines were not written for them. This means there are dark parts in more than 7.9 billion People—you and me included. So don't judge yourself! It's time to step out into the light!

Now, please stop reading this book until you have completed Step 7 of your journey to success! Then I'll wait for you back here so we can continue working together!

When you can take Step 8: When you have shared at least one of your secrets with at least one understanding Person and experienced the sense of relief that comes with it, that is, ripped off one of the chains of your destroying-ego, you are welcome to continue!

The Eighth Step to your happiness (mind): Order and System – Avoiding Extremes

"You are what you eat," is the famous Buddhist saying. This saying is absolutely true, but it's also true for all manifestations of our Life. We are characterized by all the motifs of our lives. Our circumference and our behavior reflect our inner state of mind in our object world. The more extreme our lives are, the more serious our spiritual wounds are. The disorder in our lives is caused by our undisciplined mind, which works according to the imprinted programs that have emerged from the experience of our lives so far. So, if there is a mess inside, then the world around us is also a mess. Since the world reacts back to our souls, one of the paths to happiness is to consciously tidy up our environment and lifestyle, and if we persevere in this, it will partially or completely reprogram our minds. This is easy to say, but it takes a lot of willpower to go through it tirelessly. In order for your mind to reprogram itself and thus develop, you need to create persistent and lasting growth in your environment. In this chapter, I would like to give you some examples that can deepen your self-awareness and help you find the right path. It's important to tell you right from the start that your ego will immediately make excuses that none of these things are true for you. But, please, don't fall for it.

   1. **Order:** Look at your room, your apartment, the part of your workplace where you work. Observe your desk, kitchen, bathroom! Look at your garden, your car, your shoes, your clothes. Examine how clean they are, how tidy they are, how often they are kept tidy. Just as these places and objects that are characteristic of your immediate environment, so is the state of your soul. (Of course, if someone else keeps order around you, but you are messy, what I am writing here is irrelevant.) A clean and peaceful soul will only feel good in a clean

and healthy environment! If your environment is not clean, your soul is not peaceful or clean. But I'm sure that something was wrong with it. At the same time, if you fix your environment and maintain it permanently, it can help your soul and mind become more organized. Of course, what I have described here is not true in the world of neat-freaks or cleanliness maniacs; they are going from one extreme to the other. Relaxation can help them move their souls in the direction of healing.

2. **System:** Please take a look at your everyday Life. How much system do you have in your life? Do you wake up at the same time every day and go to bed at the same time? Do you eat at the same time every day? Do you start your work at the same time and finish it at the same time? A peaceful and pure soul feels good only in a system. It's no coincidence that Buddhist monks also live based on a strict time schedule. If your daily time order changes, there is something in your soul that is restless, disordered, or disturbed. It's time to start tidying up. Permanent changes in your lifestyle can help increase your inner peace and harmony. This requires a stable timetable in your lLife, which brings regularity and thus disciplines your mind.

Here's a summary of what you need to do to The Eighth Step to your happiness:

Task: Tidy up around yourself in all areas of your Life! Create a schedule in your Life that you follow as best you can.

Which part of you does it affect the most: Mind

How long you need to do this task: You need to pay attention to this until you are no longer thrown off your normal schedule due to clutter or unexpected reasons.

Some good advice: The more damage you have in your soul, the harder it will be to do this task. After the initial enthusiasm, usually we relapse, and then it's hard to start over again. But changing our self is not easy. It's no coincidence that there are so few happy People wandering the streets. If you want to be one of those few, do it every day. Try reprogramming your mind. This task disciplines your mind, which gradually begins to reduce the extremes in you. Decreasing them will increase your peace and happiness. It's very difficult to change our external world! Because the programs operating in our subconscious affect us too strongly and deceivingly, the ego always wants to return us to our old ways. Do NOT beat yourself up during downturns! Be proactive, build your spirit and get back to work!

Now, please stop reading this book until you have completed Step 8 of your journey to success! Then I'll wait for you here so we can continue working together!

When you can take Step 9: when it becomes automatic for you to warn yourself if there's a mess around you or your schedule is messed up again. You should be so aware of this task that you instinctively pay attention to it. You don't have to be able to always keep everything orderly; it's enough if you remind yourself about it. Then I'll be waiting for you with love for the next challenge!

The Ninth Step to your happiness (body): Boost your melatonin production!

You have already read in detail about the importance of melatonin in your Life in chapter 2.2. From this, you can deduce practical follow-ups that can help you reverse the safe negative symptoms of your life. Obviously, all of these changes are difficult to incorporate into our way of Life, but if you successfully incorporate any of them, it will result in an improvement in your quality of Life.

Here's a summary of what you need to do to the ninth step to your happiness:

Task: Boost your melatonin and reduce your cortisol production by introducing the following ten rules into your life:

1. Set a schedule for your sleep cycle: Always go to bed at about the same time and always get up at the same time.
2. Sleep in the dark—never near a lamp or in front of a TV.
3. For a minimum of one hour before going to sleep, don't watch anything that generates excitement or do anything that causes stress or tension.
4. During the period before going to sleep, do things that turn you off and relax you. For example, reading a quiet book, doing some needlework, listening to pleasant music or watching relaxing videos, etc.
5. Make sure your sleep time is never more than one hour shorter or longer than your ideal sleep requirement.
6. Holidays are important! It's important to choose a stress-free holiday and not just a three-day one, but a longer one. Prolonged stress-free vacations are a good way to "reboot" your body. It is essential that the

holiday is not too active, that is: there should be a lot of rest in it to maximize melatonin production.
7. You are not allowed to work on weekends or deal with any stressors. Your weekend is guaranteed to be stress-free! Do things that cause you to relax! The two days of the weekend are just enough to roughly fix the devastation in your body caused by the five days of running around. But this is only true if your weekend is really stress-free and comes with plenty of sleep. After-lunch naps are really effective.
8. Minimize your consumption of coffee or energy drinks, and don't drink them within eight hours of going to bed.

Which part of you it affects the most: Body

How long you need to complete this task: This is also a lifelong exercise, but there will be suggestions in later chapters that will improve some of the ten rules above.

Some good advice: Anything that spins, exacerbates, irritates, or causes tension and stresses unfortunately produces cortisol. At the same time, any activity that calms you down, creates peace, and brings balance will help your body to produce melatonin permanently during your subsequent rest phase, which can regenerate and heal well. Your way of life is up to you! Since these ten rules mean a lifestyle change, it won't be easy. This is especially true if you live in a family where you have several children. But since my partner and I have both succeeded, we know it's not impossible! The same is true for this step as for the others: it takes perseverance. Few people are truly happy because not many know the recipe, and even fewer can implement it. You already have the perfect recipe, because that's what this book contains! From here, everything depends on your perseverance! If you desire happiness, this will give you strength!

Now, please stop reading this book until you have completed Step 9 of your journey to success! Then I'll wait for you so we can continue working together!

When you can take Step 10: when your average energy level has risen significantly on weekdays. That will be the effect of this tool, but not right away! If you haven't lived like this in years, you've used up your body's reserves. You will therefore feel more tired temporarily, as your body wants to fill those reserves first. Whenever you're low on energy, go back to these ten rules.

The Tenth Step to your happiness (soul): Love languages

A famous university has scientifically studied the secret of a happy life. This was done by making a complete psychological, physical, family and social condition assessment in graduate grades. After 50 years, they then looked at whose Life had developed. The researchers concluded from the results that the most important pillar of a happy life is quality of human relationships. This is no coincidence, as we determine who we really are from other people's reactions to us.

"The right view is formed through the opinions of others and our own reflection." (Buddha's Anguttara Nikaya 2.11.9.)

Furthermore, the basic inner need of every Human is to earn and receive enough appreciation and attention from their fellow human beings. This is true even if we've suppressed these feelings so much that we don't want to acknowledge them.

This means that if you want to live a happy Life, you have to invest a lot of energy in others and build your quality human relationships. The destroyer-ego suggests the opposite to you every day. It says, "Take care of yourself! Other People don't deserve attention and care!" The neutral-ego tells you to invest only your free energies in other People, but to take care of yourself first. Only the creator-ego is capable of infinitely respecting fellow People and, therefore, selflessly giving everything it can to their environment. It's no coincidence that all People living at the spiritual vibratory levels associated with the creator-ego are happy. They have only quality human relationships. At the level of the destructive-ego, we are constantly involved in situations where shame, guilt, fear, sorrow, anger, desire or excessive pride will be our lot. Each of these feelings leads to bad human relationships and drives us to behaviors that further destroy our relationships.

Observe the quality of your relationships and you will quickly realize how much trouble there is in your life. The first step is to qualify your connections with people who are emotionally close to you. In this chapter, I'll give you the tools to move in that direction. The basics of my knowledge and thoughts on this were provided by Gary Chapman's book *The Five Love Languages*. This book is one of the excellent basic works of Human Resources literature, so I wholeheartedly recommend it. The book shows that there are five main love languages, which are:

- ▶ Words of praise
- ▶ Gifting
- ▶ Physical Touch
- ▶ Favors
- ▶ Quality Time

Every Human can express or receive their love through these love languages. It can also be said that all Humans need all five kinds of love languages to some extent. However, everyone has one or two main love languages through which the feeling of love is most evident for us. For example, physical touch and favors are my two main love languages. An important basis for our self-knowledge is to be aware of which one or two of these main love languages our soul likes the most.

It's also characteristic that in our main love language we not only like to receive this wonderful feeling, but we instinctively try to show love in this way too. However, this is not always the right way! I could give you a lot of examples of how the knowledge and proper use of the five love languages improves human relationships. It's known that if all People possessed this knowledge and acquired it to such an extent that they could apply it in their everyday lives, then the average happiness level on the planet Earth would be significantly improved. And why is that? Because People usually start from themselves and therefore tend to express their love as they would be happy to receive it. However, if the other Person's love language is different, they may not appreciate it the way we want them to. Unfortunately, many Human conflicts and relationships going in the wrong direction stem from this. To better understand this, let's look at an example of something that actually happened. Once, a lady came to me who was terribly upset. She'd had another fight with her partner and turned to me for some psychological support. They'd been together for five years and loved each other very much but still fought a lot. She was very distressed. In a freaked-out state, she found herself saying that her partner didn't really love her. This hit me hard because the man had just taken time off and surprised his partner by renovating and modernizing the entire heating system in the lady's family house while she was abroad. The gentleman was not a heating mechanic, so he even took the time to think about it, learn it and do it. I thought that if a man did this for a woman without asking, simply as a surprise, there was no way he didn't love her. About a month after this surprise, he surprised the lady again by pruning the fruit trees in her garden. And the lady, crying on my shoulder, complained that this man did not love her because he never took her to the theater or at least on a pleasant walk alone. It's clear to you what the underlying problem in their relationship was, isn't it? The man's love language was favors, while the woman's was quality time. The man was always doing his partner a favor, which she never took quite as well as he'd hoped. He laid his soul out there, and the lady wasn't as happy as the energy he'd put into his surprises. At the same time, the woman was constantly organizing joint programs for her partner, who was not overly fascinated by these surprises. I asked the lady if she knew about the five love languages; to my surprise, she said yes. Then I asked her what her love language was, to which she said "quality time". So far, we're good, I thought to myself. Then I asked her what her partner's love language was. She thought about it, then said she had no idea. Oops! For five years you were with a man you loved madly and you didn't even know what his language was? Wow! During our short conversation, it became clear to the lady that the man's love language was favors. This brought about a big change in their relationship. When the lady received favors from the man, she began to understand them as a true expression of love, so she was more pleased than ever. And the lady did not bombard the man with quality-time gifts, but had to learn to express her love with favors. Then she tried to make the man understand that her love language was quality time and that it was what she wanted most. The point of the story is that their relationship started to improve significantly.

What important conclusions can we draw from this? First of all, know what your love language is! After that, start observing the People who are important to you from this point of view and determine their love language. This is important everywhere: family, friends, relationships, etc. After that, if you can, give to everyone according to their own love language! If you choose a partner, the best situation is if you have the same love language. However, this is quite rare. If not, show your love in their love language! However, it's also important to lead them to what your love language is.

Here's a summary of what you need to do to complete Step 10 to your happiness:

Task: Make a list of the People who are most important to you. Then observe them and find out what their love language is. When you have that, try to please them in their love language. Don't expect reciprocation—just do it! Those who are important in your life will sooner or later return your kindnesses.

Which part of you it affects the most: Soul

How long you need to do this task: This is also a lifelong task, but do it with at least three people to make this approach instinctive and an integral part of your life!

A few pointers: When you give to someone, don't expect them to reciprocate. Your altruism will be returned by the Universe, but not always from the person to whom you poured it! But the point is, if you approach a Person in their love language, then there's a good chance the quality of your relationship will improve. This is true in most cases. If it doesn't work for someone, then you shouldn't have anything to do with that Person. Accept this and devote your energies to People who will welcome it! The quality of your human relationships can also be improved by removing certain people from your Life and replacing them with more valuable ones. Not all relationships need to be "upgraded" at all costs—only those that have reception from the other side.

Now, please stop reading this book until you have completed Step 10 of your journey to success! Then I'll wait for you back here so we can continue working together!

When you can take Step 11: Once you've done this step with at least three people, you can take the next challenge and do even more for your happiness!

The 11th Step to your happiness (mind): Reduce stress I. – boundaries

The best way to deal with stress is to create strong self-boundaries. What does this mean? We are constantly bombarded with expectations in our lives. Expectations come from the boss, our partner, children, parents, colleagues and so on. People who do not have strong self-boundaries tend to take on all these expectations. This is otherwise called a victim role. I was like that for decades. If I didn't do something that was expected from me, I felt remorseful, worthless or guilty, but most of the time I just had a basic unpleasant inner feeling. For this reason, I always did everything for everyone—even beyond my strength.

When people close to me in my environment become overwhelmed because, for example, there's too much stress on them at work, then I usually mention this old Hungarian saying to them: "every ox draws as much as it allows". Everything is included in this saying. We tend to think that if you don't do something, no one else will. Or we also tend to believe that since only you can do it really well, you won't leave it to anyone else. These are typically erroneous thoughts stuck in the destructive-ego and can easily lead us into the victim role.

The other common misguided strategy is to take the path that seems easier. That is, instead of standing up for our own interests, we prefer to accept the will and needs of others and adapt to them, even if this makes us tense and stressed. In order to establish self-boundaries, it is absolutely necessary to be aware of our self-boundaries and do NOT let them go, no matter how unpleasant it is for others! I know it sounds strange at first, but please believe me, People will adapt to your boundaries if you make them clear!

Setting self-boundaries doesn't mean that we cannot be altruistic. Confirming your boundaries doesn't mean you have to be selfish from now on. Unfortunately, this is a misinterpretation. Strengthening your boundaries means that you do not undertake anything beyond your strength. Famous yogis also help an incredible number of People, but when they can't help, they distance themselves rigidly and firmly. Some yogis retired for years after long work in the Western world to regain their original purity and peace. In our soul-destroying world, even they couldn't perfectly maintain their own boundaries.

Reinforcing your boundaries means learning to say 'no'. You say 'no' to everything beyond your power. This is true even if someone tries to manipulate you into doing what they ask. People have developed a number of manipulation techniques in order to influence others. Examples include emotional manipulations or threats.

Here are some examples: "You'll be fired if it's not done by tomorrow" or "It won't be profitable for the company if you're not done by the deadline" or "Mom loves you only if you do your homework". The number and type of such manipulations is almost endless. Setting self-boundaries is difficult, because they can influence us very effectively. In order not to be susceptible to these manipulations, I would like to share some useful thoughts with you.

One of the most important things is to trust in the power of Life! The ego makes you believe that you can only count on yourself, but that's not true! Life always helps you. When it doesn't, it actually wants to signal something to you, so it actually does help you—just not in the way that you want. From the ego's point of view, it doesn't seem to be helping, but it is. If you trust that Life will provide a solution for everything you want, you won't cringe at things.

Let's take a practical example: As a design engineer, I was stressed out about deadlines for decades. Unfortunately, planning is a very complex job and it's very rare for many tasks to be ready on time. All customers are wired in such a way that they request their plans as soon as possible. Thus, designers live constantly behind deadlines. I was also constantly stressed by the delays. Stress took a lot of my energy, and it drastically decreased my creativity. With reduced energy and a ruined creativity, imagine trying to keep a deadline for a job that requires a lot of creativity! Since stress was a constant part of my life, I naturally didn't realize that the biggest obstacle in my Life was the stress itself. In fact, I was even convinced that stress was good, as it gave me the strength to somehow overcome the difficulties of everyday Life (the psychological vibration level of Fear). Success trainings often teach you that the first step to change is to take a fresh look at your own loser schema. For me, this happened when I suddenly realized that I had been cringing for decades not to be late with work. For decades, customers had been threatening me that if it wasn't ready by the deadline, they will lose EU support or the whole project, etc. (These were the manipulations of yet more People.) Nevertheless, I had been late with the work since the beginning of the year due to unrealistic deadlines, and somehow all the projects were successfully completed. Strangely, the EU support did not evaporate, and strangely, the project did not fail either, etc. Life always somehow found a solution, even if at that moment I didn't see what it was. This recognition brought a new perspective: I cringed about deadlines completely unnecessarily, because nothing really depends on them. There's always a solution for everything! I started to project my trust in Life onto my work and make it my way of being (you can replace the word Life with God or any other belief system). What was the result?

First of all, the stress of deadlines became minimized in my soul. This gave me more energy to work, so I worked more efficiently.

My effectiveness was enhanced by the fact that my horizons, which had been narrowed in the past due to stress, expanded and my creative energies came back. My creativity further increased my efficiency. In the end, the result was that I was much less late with the work than before, even though I spent much less energy on it. What the ego made me believe at the time— that I had to solve everything myself and work hard for the results—resulted in an erroneous and sick way of being. The reality is that Life is a million times wiser than I am, and if I am open to it, it will always help at the right time!

Of course, this doesn't mean that you can sit back and laze around starting today because Life will solve everything. Obviously, we need to work towards our goals. But by working diligently every day and at the same time not cringing or stressing about deadlines and other things that suddenly seem like obstacles, we get rid of a lot of Life-destroying energy and release even more creative Life-supporting energy within ourselves. The result is a more efficient, balanced and happier Life.

Here's a summary of what you need to do for the 11th step to your happiness:

Task: Every time someone wants to overload you, don't take it on! Either wait until you have the strength again, or leave the task to someone else. As of today, be aware of your self-boundaries and don't allow anyone to cross them!

Which part of you it affects the most: Mind

How long you need to do this task: This task should be done until it becomes instinctive and self-protection reflexes automatically turn on when someone is pushing your boundaries .

Some good advice: Finding and enforcing self-boundaries doesn't have to mean rigid resistance! Rigid resistance can cause us guilt or other internal tension. The right strategy consists of the following steps: I. You clearly state your self-boundary, which you cannot let go of. II. You offer to find a mutually beneficial compromise. For example, if someone wants to burden you with an unrealistically short time limit, you make it clear that this is unlikely and that you cannot accept it. Then you offer to agree which subtasks are needed first and which are due later. Then you think together about the schedule until compromises are formed that suit everyone.

My other important advice for you is that when you start to build self-boundaries in your existing relationships, you will experience hard resistance. After all, those People aren't used to your new self standing up for itself. Don't let that deter you! They will constantly want to pull back into their old system. The important thing is to stay purposeful and not let yourself get sidetracked. If this involves cutting out some of your relationships, then do it! Don't be afraid to let go of anyone who has been your partner in the bad patterns of your unhappiness and who isn't willing to accept that you're changing in a better direction!

Now, please stop reading this book until you have completed Step 11 of your journey to success! Then I'll wait for you so we can continue working together!

When you can take Step 12: Once you've automatically triggered an internal warning that you've let someone cross your border again. Then you can move on!

The 12th Step to your happiness (body): Reduce stress II. – two basic breathing exercises

The method of air retention is very effective for local and immediate mitigation of sudden waves of stress. It works by taking a deep breath and holding it for 30 seconds when you're under a lot of stress. During the 30 seconds, focus on counting and don't think about anything. Then slowly exhale. Repeat this several times until the tension in you goes down. This method really works. The physiological explanation is that under stress, the skull bone contracts and puts extra pressure on the brain. This feeling of pressure triggers the internal feeling of tension that switches the body into survival mode under increased stress. Unless you're being chased by a tiger, this mode is unnecessary. The point is that as a result of air retention for 30 seconds, the skull bones will expand back to their natural state. Thus, the tension in the brain is eliminated and the feeling of stress is relieved or completely removed from you. The good thing about this method is that it only takes 2 or 3 minutes and can be done almost anywhere and at any time.

The other useful type of breathing exercise is abdominal breathing. In a stressful state, we usually suppress the tensions in our abdomen. As a result, our abdominal wall tightens, and we often feel a tightening or painful sensation around our stomach. This is because the solar plexus chakra is located around the gastric mouth and this chakra is the headquarters of the ego (*see **Appendix 3** for a diagram and detailed description of the chakras*). But I will write more about this in the next volume. The bottom line is that at the end of every stressful day, sit in a relaxed place in a comfortable position. Keep your hands and feet straight and your spine straight. Keep your posture symmetrical. Inhale slowly and deeply into your abdomen while counting slowly to 7. After that, hold your breath by counting slowly to 7 again. Then slowly exhale as you like. Perform this breathing method approximately 10 to 12 times or until the tension in your abdomen is relieved. This exercise is also good for your lungs and blood circulation. If you do it at least once a day, your general well-being will also improve.

Here's a summary of what you need to do the 12th step to your happiness:

Task: At the end of each working day, perform the abdominal breathing exercise and perform the 30-second breathing exercise during the day whenever you're in a stressful state.

Which part of you it affects the most: Body

How long you should do this task: This task should be done until you instinctively think about it in order to mitigate the harmful effects of stress. The evening breathing exercise is suitable for clearing the mind, after which you can become more attuned to the daily balance method and the gratitude flow. It can be expedient to combine the methods you've learned so far and fit them into your me-time. Thus, you gradually devote more and more time to yourself, which is an effective internal job, as in these practices you only pay attention to yourself and not to any external source of information.

Some good advice: Breathing exercises can improve your quality of life a lot! No matter how much our ego tends to belittle it, there is often a great power in what seems to be the most elementary things. So, please do what I ask and the effect won't go away!

Now, please stop reading this book until you have taken Step 12 towards your happiness! Afterwards, I promise you that we will continue to work together.

When you can take the 13th step: when you automatically turn on an internal warning that you need a thorough breathing exercise now, and this habit has become a daily routine in your life.

The 13th Step to your happiness (soul): Letting go of negative emotions – the balloon and cloud method

Many times, we willingly or unwittingly hurt others or say something out of enthusiasm that we regret afterwards. Of course, there are a thousand other reasons why our souls may develop negative feelings that torment us and cause us to feel sadness, guilt, fear or shame. In our minds, we often relive the "experience" and often regret our actions, which, however, can no longer be changed. Negative feelings are amplified in us countless times, and it happens even more often that they are amplified by our being too strict with ourselves. We often tend to overthink how our actions are judged by others and as a result what they must think of us. These feelings and thoughts are almost constantly buzzing in us and contaminating our day. They may even contaminate things we would otherwise experience with great joy, happiness and gratitude. Not to mention that all of these regrets reduce our overall level of mental vibration, that is: they remove us from our happier Lives. That particular thing has already happened, so you can't change it! It's part of your past. However, you can change your attitude towards the situation. Struggling with it won't solve the consequences of that particular thing, and because it takes a lot of energy from you and destroys your creativity, it even reduces the chances of it being resolved. But this is the purpose of the destroyer-ego. But you can see behind it! It is not obligatory to live your Life like a robot slave to your destructive-ego. So, the first step is to try to psychologically process this situation or at least mitigate its negative psychological impact. For this, I recommend two very simple methods, which I ask you to use regularly in the future. Sit comfortably, try to relax as much as you can with a few deep breaths (you can start with the breathing exercises you already know, for example). Place one hand on your forehead and the other on the back of your neck (alternatively, sit with your open palms and your hands on your thighs). After that, think about the negative feelings about that particular event caused in you. Immerse yourself in the feeling. Don't run away from it! Let it spread through you! Don't resist it! You already know that resistance strengthens the feeling, acceptance weakens it. Then observe where the midpoint of the feeling is. This will be the same as one of the energy centers. You can find exciting details about the energy centers in **Annex 3.** When you can no longer expand, feel the extension. It may be the size of your stomach, or it may be bigger than your whole body. Then imagine a half-empty balloon floating above your head. Realize the fact that the negative feeling you are feeling right now is an energy that can flow. Imagine being able to control this process. Flow this negative energy along your spine through the bulb of your head into the balloon. With this feeling, the balloon fills up and inflates. If it helps with the visualization, you can also do strong exhalations while imagining the balloon expanding and you are blowing negative energy into it. Visualize it as it happens. Then, release this balloon in your imagination and let it fly away. The balloon, as it slowly moves away, floats over a volcano. There, the emission of hot gases burns it and the negative energies cease to exist. (If you have a hard time imagining a balloon, imagine that this feeling has accumulated on your body like dirt and you wash it off yourself while standing in the shower.)

Next, imagine that above your head there is a dark continuous black cloud that is now parting. The sun shines on your head through the gap and you enjoy its warmth. Light is a world of positive feelings. Be grateful that the cloud is slowly dissipating and more and more light is reaching you! Following this, experience a positive feeling that would be caused by the thing you just let go of, the thing that did not happen, or the correction of it making amends in you. Let this positive feeling permeate your whole body. If you can't feel any positive emotion, feel grateful. This is the strongest emotional uplifting feeling. Then take two or three deep breaths and open your eyes.

This exercise takes only one to three minutes and speeds up the processing of the negative feeling. The point is that when it hits you, try to do this exercise as soon as possible. Trust me—it will help!

Here's a summary of what you need to do for the 13th step to your happiness:

Task: In your everyday life, when negative feelings take over, use the balloon and cloud methods. It's important that you focus on your emotions and feelings while performing the method, and that the negative feeling is replaced with a positive one at the end of the process.

Which part of you does it affect the most: Soul

How long you need to do this task: Do this task at least until your average days are dominated by positive feelings. For some People a few weeks is enough, but for some it takes months. If your life goes downhill and you become negatively emotionally overwhelmed again and again, return to this method again and again.

Some good advice: The destructive-ego inside you will do everything in its power to eliminate this method from your Life. This is because it poses a threat to it. It will call it boring, ineffective or stupid. But it may also suggest that it doesn't have any effect on you, or in your case, it simply doesn't work. Don't be fooled by your destroying-ego! Look behind it! The stronger the desire to put it down, the more it works! Please hold on until your ego is transformed and the world of positive emotions is integrated into your life. Also remember what you read about the hormone dependence of your cells. Your body is currently dependent on hormones from the excess of negative emotions. Therefore, getting used to it is time-consuming. If you fall back, don't beat yourself up! Try it again! The relapses get shorter and less deep! I know you can do it!

Another very important piece of good advice for you: Never suppress feelings! Every repressed negative feeling comes back at least 100 times stronger in your future! You've just learned an easy way to let go of feelings. It's very important that instead of repressing your feelings, you turn your habit into processing your feelings. In this way, the negative emotions will be cleared from your future through your efforts today.

Now, please stop reading this book until you've completed Step 13 of your journey to success! Then I'll wait for you here so we can continue working together!

When you can take Step 14: when you automatically turn this method on as soon as your negative emotions become stronger and, as a result, the rate of positive feelings starts to increase in your everyday life.

The 14th Step to your happiness (mind): Neutralizing your fears

The psychological vibration level of Fear is a rather unpleasant "place" where fear is the motive and nourisher of all our actions and thoughts. Some people spend their whole day here, but most of us are often here for short periods of time. To release fear as a negative emotion, you can use the previous method. In this chapter, we set the common goal of changing fear-based thinking.

Fear-based thinking has many disadvantages for our lives and our families. One is that a lot of energy is consumed by the inner spiritual struggle with fears. Thus, these energies cannot be used for more Life-supporting things. Whether it's our own selves or the ones we love, we get less of our true selves. Fear drains our Life force most of the time without us realizing it. It's also very common that fear is so much a part of our thinking that we are unaware of it. That's why it's important to take a few days of your Life and observe yourself. Objectively listen to your own thoughts and see how many times your mind is on things that you fear or that are rooted in fear. Worry is a form of fear, so please consider this as well. Of course, it's even better to observe not only your thoughts but also your feelings from this point of view. Moreover, it is an exciting game of self-knowledge that whenever you catch yourself in fear-based thinking, you observe your body's sensations. Where is the pain and tension in it? Once you clearly see how much time your soul and mind spend a day at this vibration level, you will truly understand how important it is to change that. This level of spiritual vibration is a serious barrier to your true happiness and puts your mind into a strong Beta state.

The ego enters our soul and mind at a very young age by making us believe that it protects us from all evil. Of course this is not true, but most of us still fall for it. Fear is one of the very powerful tools the ego uses to make you believe in its importance. In fact, the ego is not interested in what's good for you, but how it can survive and grow in your soul. The ego is concerned only with its own survival! Observe your thoughts and you will realize that this is how it works in you. The ego is constantly scanning the future and "snooping" for whatever bad things await you in the imagined future. It constantly warns you of a lot of bad things that might happen to you, making you believe that it has actually saved you from these bad things. This is a lie. If you look a little behind the scenes, you'll realize that 99.9% of your fears about the future never happen! Why not? It's not because your ego protected you; it's because 99.9% of your fears about your future are fictional! As you scan for future variants, you're looking at a lot of future alternatives that will never happen. These have been generated by your ego which has even led you to believe that they are the result of rational and logical conclusions. In order to eliminate some or all of the fear-based thinking, you must first become aware of the following:

At least 99.9% of my fears about the future will never come true. If the remaining 0.1% happens, then it happens for a reason. I will experience it because Life wants to warn me that I am not going in the right direction!

So out of one thousand fears, at least 999 are unnecessary! If this is difficult to acknowledge, use the paper method to confirm it, which I will return to in a moment. Imagine how much fear-based thinking is a waste of unnecessary spiritual and mental energy, and please imagine how many wonderful things you could use it for if it were released. And the remaining 0.1% of fears are important to let happen because they are sent to you because Life wants to give you signals! If you walk objectively and with open eyes, you will learn from these, and you will be happier. These causes of fear are therefore the beacons of your Life, not the enemies your ego sets them up to be.

It's important to emphasize that you should not use the bolded sentence above as a mantra (repetitive self-suggestion, reinforcement)! It's for deep understanding. As you have already learned in the affirmations, more elements should not be used in these sentences. For example, we cannot use negative sayings as mantras! If you want to strengthen yourself with a mantra, I recommend repeating the following sentence:

> **"Only good or useful things will happen to me in the future!"**

Affirmations have a powerful effect on your mind, helping you to get fear-based thinking out of your life. In order to make this more efficient and faster, I will also give you the paper method. It is recommended to combine the two methods.

The paper method: We are surrounded by many people who worry more than normal. We are worried about whether we will have a parking spot, or whether we will get somewhere on time, or if we will be ready on time, or if there will be any bread left at the convenience store. Even worse, we worry a lot about what others think of us, and so on. But is this normal? You are right to wonder what is the normal level of worry. The answer is simply provided by Eastern philosophies. **What you won't remember in three years, you probably don't need to worry about!** Do you think you'll remember in three years that you had a hard time finding a parking space on Tuesday morning? This method is also suitable for reducing any fear feelings in addition to anxiety, so if you find it in your self-knowledge, feel free to use it. It's important to know that our fears are very strong anchors that hinder our happiness. The less time your soul spends with such feelings and your mind with such thoughts, the higher your mental vibration level will be and the less your mind will be in the high Beta range!

Worrying unconsciously is built into our ego and becomes part of our Life. We get so used to it that we slowly start to believe that this is normal. However, worries and fears produce a lot of stress hormones in the body; they make us tense. Thus, we become irritable, tired, and inattentive. We don't even realize how much energy and spiritual strength all those tiny little seeds of fear take away from us during the day. We don't understand why we're half dead by evening. And if we do this permanently, our weakened immune system will make us sick more often (or once, but then a lot). So, it's worth quitting worrying and letting go of other fears, because this will make you more energetic, lively, focused and even strengthen your immune system. It's worth it, isn't it?

Many people don't want to give up fear because they feel it gives them extra strength to perform every day! I have some bad news: these are Life-destroying and Self-destroying energies, for which we will pay a heavy price. The good news, however, is that much more effective forces dominate at a higher level of spiritual vibration, so you don't have to fear that you won't have the strength to achieve your goals there! As a reassurance, I would like to clarify that you will have much more power if you will not be afraid and you will have other motivations instead. Desire, anger, pride and courage are motivating forces with a higher spiritual vibration level than fear. If from the level of mental vibration of Fear you will jump to the next level, then one of these will take over the psychological attitude that gives motivation. Since these are less Life-destroying energy levels, you will have more power to develop yourself on the path to happiness. Which level you jump to depends on a lot of things. That's not the point here. The details of this will be included in the next volume. The important thing is to get rid of as much of your fear as possible and your life will improve significantly.

If you think about it, it could be also a type of fear that will give you strength if you are not motivated by fear anymore. You're also afraid of the consequences of losing your fear.

The spiritual reason for worrying is internal insecurity. We do not trust in ourselves, we do not trust in our Lives, we do not trust in our future, we do not trust in the good intentions of Life. You have to discover the reason for this! This method will be most effective for those for whom it is just a bad habit i.e., there is no serious psychological injury in their souls that causes this. For example, this is what they learned from their mother when they were young and therefore they do the same. In this case, almost complete "quitting" will be the result of the method in a few weeks. For those with a deeper spiritual cause, only a reduction in anxiety is expected. But since their Life is difficult as they struggle with their spiritual dragons every day, even this slight improvement can help them to move on. So, it's worth it!

Before presenting the method, I would like to mention that worrying is a healthy feeling. So if we are worried about serious problems, it is a natural reaction and nothing needs to be done about it. The advantage of this method is that you can do it yourself and don't need any help. With a few weeks of practice, you can get yourself out of worrying, fear-based thinking, or at least part of these.

The essence of the method is as follows. Have a piece of paper and a writing tool with you every minute of every day (nowadays your mobile phone is also suitable for this). When you start worrying about something, all you do is write down why you were worried and when. You don't need to rate it—just write it down. Then the day goes on, and if you're worried about something again (whether it's the same thing or another thing), you write down the time and the reason for the concern again. That's how you do it all day. Before you go to bed tonight, take out the paper and think about whether the things you were worried about have been resolved or not. If so, did it make sense to worry about them?

If they haven't been resolved, how much of a problem are they for your life now? In three years, will you remember these problems? It's very likely that reviewing your evening list will lead to the conclusion that you didn't need to worry about 99% or more of the issues. After you have laid down the paper, relax, take a few deep breaths and tell yourself the following affirmation five to ten times with the greatest possible spiritual feeling: **"I trust in myself, I trust in my Life and I trust in my future! I know that Life loves me and helps me! I accept the signs and energies of Life flowing towards me!"** (Instead of the word Life, God, Buddha, Universe, Higher Self, Angels, etc., anything that fits your religion or your views can be used.)

The difference between a successful Person and an unsuccessful one is that when something unfavorable happens to them, they learn from it. They interpret objectively what they need to do differently in the future and incorporate this into their Life. In this case, the unsuccessful People prefer to blame others or look for other ways out, and then they fall into these traps in the same way. In addition, their fears are exacerbated by this. Unfortunately, the cornerstone of change is knowing that you and no one else is responsible for everything that happens to you! As long as you blame others, there will be no positive change in your life. You won't be able to let go of your fears until you really want to! That is, you have to face yourself and first **admit that you are the cause of all your fears.** After all, it's up to you how you feel about the effects of the outside world. After that, you will be able to gradually let go of this feeling if you stop blaming others for it. This is the first step to change!

We must continually catch ourselves gravitating towards the old forms of evil. It's important not to beat yourself up if you fall back! This only deepens fears within you, perhaps even generating feelings of shame and guilt that are even more destructive than fear. Even in such cases, be accepting and devote your energies to future change.

When you realize that 99.9% of your fears are unnecessary and you are the cause of all your fears, you can jump to a another level. This level is based on trust in Life. I know it's strange for you to read this at first. Your ego immediately turns on and suggests that you can't trust in Life since it brought all the bad things that have happened to you. Your ego tells you that if it wasn't there, things would be even worse now. Of course, this is not true, as I have already described above. It's not Life that has brought you evil, but your wrong thinking patterns that are rooted in your ego. Fear-based thinking generates fear. After all, if I send fear-based decisions to my environment, this will create responses in my environment that will attach these fears back to me, and the "self-fulfilling prophecy" becomes operational. Quitting the old thinking pattern is the solution. You can trust in Life, even if it seems strange at first, because the basic rule of Life is as follows:

Life always helps, and if it doesn't, it is warning you that you are going in the wrong direction or doing something the wrong way. (The word Life can be replaced by God or any other word appropriate to your belief system.) Problems actually help, because they act as a beacon to make your life better. This is the next level of the method: to believe that Life is good for you, and to realize that if you don't blame others, but instead purposefully draw conclusions that build your success and your future from all the bad things that happen to you, then you have nothing to fear. After all, your fears and excuses are trying to "protect" you from these beacons and thus make it impossible for you to improve. Once you realize this (it may take months, but it's worth it!), you're on the third level. When a fear-based thought occurs to you, you say to yourself:

If it actually happens, I will do my best to solve it! But in the meantime, I have more important things to do!

That's why you can do it here with your soul believing it, because you've made yourself aware that most of what you fear will never happen. And if it does happen, it's good in the long run because it gives you an opportunity to grow. Here, you've also realized that you can trust Life because it's your real helper—not your ego.

Let's summarize what you need to do to achieve the 14th step to your happiness:

Task: Use the paper method and the above written sentences to gradually reduce the proportion of your fears and concerns in your life. You can relate the paper method to the daily balance sheet method, and please feel grateful that your concerns have not happened.

Which part of you it affects the most: Mind

How long you have to do this task: You have to do this task until you start to think in terms of fear and anxiety only when you have a very good reason to. Remember, a good reason is what you will remember three years from now!

Some good advice: It's very difficult to start on this path. It's going to be weird at first. Your ego will keep inventing reasons why it won't work. In fact, you will feel that you don't have the power to do such a thing, and that this method won't affect you. Think about how hard it was to learn to walk. How many times do toddlers fall and get up again before they finally start to take a few steps? Then, think about how much practice they need before they can walk steadily. By the time they're a big kids, walking and running are instinctive. It works the same way. Overriding a bad thought pattern causes a lot of setbacks. Feeding the seeds of change requires the investment of a lot of energy. At first, you can't do it, then you can barely do it. A little later you can do it a little bit, but only sometimes. Then it gets better and better, and eventually it gets ingrained and becomes an integral part of our lives! This is how any change that is positive happens in our lives! Only changes in the wrong direction are easy. Unfortunately, building is difficult, but destroying is easy.

If you can't change your fears on your own, ask a professional for help! In this case, you probably have very deep psychological wounds that you need help to heal because your thinking is fear-based. You may be afraid to ask for help, but be brave and take this important step when it comes. These kinds of courageous steps made me happier! It's not by chance that Courage is the first level of Life-supporting mental vibration!

Now, please stop reading this book until you have completed Step 14 of your journey to success! Then I'll wait for you back here so we can continue working together!

When you can take the 15th step: When the sentences in bold above are automatically activated as fearful thoughts or feelings arise in you, it's time to take on the next challenge to make your life better!

The 15th Step to your happiness (test): Sports

This chapter will be short, as you have heard enough about it here already. There's a reason for this: daily intuitive movement is incredibly important for our happiness, but most people don't really think about it. Doctors usually recommend regular sports to maintain physical health, which is helpful as far as it goes. But it's important to realize that there is little chance of a truly happy Life in a sick or lazy body. This is what the old Roman saying "a healthy mind in a healthy body" means. We really feel this when we get sick and realize that there is nothing more important in the world than our health. At the same time, there are several levels of health. Just because your body doesn't show the symptoms you would need to see a doctor for doesn't mean you're healthy. As a result of a lack of daily intense movement, the condition of the blood circulation, lungs and vascular system worsens, and these do not cause more serious symptoms for decades. All we feel is that we have less spirit, we are more tired, or we do not have enough zest for life. In a word, our vitality is deteriorating. But since this happens gradually, we don't notice ourselves sliding down a slow, monotonous slope. The bottom of the slope is usually reached after our forties, when, due to decades of inadequate lifestyle, symptoms appear that are difficult or no longer possible to cure. This is no fairy tale: you have to do sports regularly! It's also important to choose a dynamic sport that makes you breathe intensely and sweat. For example, slow, monotonous weightlifting is also a sport, but from the point of view of physical and indirect mental health, intense, dynamic sports are better. Running is one of the best and easiest ways to do this, but of course, it's important to choose something you like to do. In particular, the importance of morning gymnastics or morning running should be emphasized. If you can incorporate it into your lifestyle, your days will start completely differently. They will make you more energetic and successful during the day. If for some reason the morning sessions are out of the question, establish your routine for a different time of day, because regularity is of the utmost importance.

Here's a summary of what you need to do for the 15th step to your happiness:

Exercise: Do dynamic sports (e.g. running) at least three times a week for a minimum of 25 minutes.

Which part of you it affects the most: Body

How long you have to do this task: You have to do this task until sports become your lifestyle. You'll notice this because you miss it when you don't do it.

Some good advice: The basic feature of the ego-dominated body is laziness. At first, it will be very difficult to get yourself into regular sports. Observe how much your ego will object, and you'll find any excuse why you can't do it that day. But you need to develop a schedule in your life in which you have three regular me-time blocks which you spend doing intense sports! Remember that this is quality me-time! When designing it, you can also apply what you've learned in the order and system method.

Now, please stop reading this book until you have completed Step 15 of your journey to success! Then I'll wait for you here so we can continue working together!

When you can do Step 16: When you have set up your weekly schedule with a minimum of 3 intense sports sessions per week and you are actually doing it, let's continue to work together!

The 16th Step to your happiness (soul): Don't color or gray out reality!

When you tell others something that happened to you or just tell them about yourself, how objectively and accurately do you reflect the reality? From this point of view, there are three types of People:
- ▶ Those who embellish, beautify, or "boost" things to make themselves seem better or to make the event seem like more than it really was.

- ▶ Those who tell about and demonstrate the situation realistically.
- ▶ Those who present themselves as being less than the objective reality. In other words, they 'gray out' the narrated event.

Today, most People belong to the first group. After all, we live in a world where we are made to believe that we have to be selfish, so we're "forced" to constantly assert ourselves. It's essential for self-assertion that we always try to present ourselves in the best possible way. One way to do this is to tell past events in a way that seems most favorable from our point of view. One of our most-established methods for this is to tell only those parts of the story that look good on us. In these cases, we don't actually lie, but by omitting certain things from the story, we shape the reality to make it seem more beneficial. The next lower level is while telling the story we color it a bit with the instinctive purpose of appearing better in front of our audience. The third level is when we actually lie in order to make ourselves look better or to avoid certain disadvantages. These three levels are also the three levels of low self-esteem. A liar has the lowest self-esteem and self-acceptance. I once knew a Person who always lied. When she made up a lie, she immediately stored two more in her brain, and if she was caught, she could immediately defend her truth with another logical-sounding lie. She was convinced that only stupid and simple People were sincere. She thought herself incredibly clever and refined. It would seem logical to assume that she was an extremely self-assertive and arrogant lady. At the same time, her lies were only compensations for herself and her world. It's very likely that the root problem is a very deep lack of self-love.

The masters of such story-coloring are the standup comedians who are so fashionable today, but they do it for entertainment purposes, so their distortions are permissible, since their main goal is not to make themselves look better. However, in real life, such "coloring" people are vain, self-advocates, and selfish big-talkers. This is the spiritual vibration level of Pride, but this behavior is characteristic of all the deeper spiritual vibration levels. This is where the greatest masters of self- and external world-deception live. They are the ones who devour external affirmations from the world. In fact, they compensate to the world because, deep down, they have serious self-acceptance problems. You will look at these People very differently if you understand that. The more imaginative someone is and the more arrogant, selfish, and lying they are, the more hurt their soul is and the more help they need. However, the main problem with these People is that they not only compensate in front of the world, but also in front of themselves. The consequence of this is that they never realize that they have such problems and need help because their "system" is all about separation. As you already know, this is one of the strengths of the destructive ego. And sooner or later, the price of this will be serious suffering. Someone who does not awaken by themselves will only do so through suffering.

Those who pretend to be less than they are don't believe that they can be of interest to others, or are afraid of what others think of them. Therefore, they show themselves to the world as being more gray and simpler than they really are. The root of this behavior is also a strong lack of self-confidence, but they are usually aware of their lack of self-confidence. They are most often characterized by psychological vibrations of Shame, Guilt, Apathy, Sorrow, and Fear. Many of them always try to remain almost unnoticed in the world, but they still suffer from people overlooking them or not taking them seriously.

Both groups feed on self-doubt. Those who have a realistic self-image and healthy (but not excessive!) self-esteem do not embellish reality. They evaluate and convey what happened directly and objectively, even if it seems either negative or boastful. They are healthy People in terms of self-esteem and they are also the rare ones—hence the premise that stories heard from other People are only rarely completely true! Among other things, this is why word-of-mouth distorts gossip so quickly. I know it's bad news, but in fact, we should believe almost nothing until we are convinced of the underlying facts. The same is true for this book! First, test it and experience how it affects your life. If you succeed, then you have time to believe.

I used to be in the first group. Although I didn't lie for the sake of beautification, I always sugar-coated and twisted reality to make myself look better and smarter through the stories I told. Today, I am more in the realistic group, but unfortunately, sometimes the old "mode of operation" still turns on. Sometimes, even today, I tend to color things when there are live conversations. The alarm bell in my soul goes off: "Why did you have to do that? If you had shared the completely objective reality, you would have been just as lovable!"

But here's the thing: when you color or grey out something compared to reality and tell it to others in this way, you are compensating in front of yourself. Your soul can't tell the difference between things that come from a lie and things that are real. With this lying, the problem is that this is an obstacle to your change! It will preserve your lack of self-esteem. The coloring type of Person colors the story to get more recognition. But in fact, they don't accept themselves as they are, thus preserving their lack of self-esteem! The graying type of People tell their story more simply because they are afraid and want to avoid their fears. However, this also preserves their lack of self-confidence. In this way, an armor is constructed in the soul, which is a strong bastion of the destroyer ego and makes us believe that everything is fine. In the meantime, we are hindering the recovery of our true self-esteem every day, which is, of course, great news for the destructive ego inside us, but not for you.

So, this bad habit is an obstacle to your change. If you want to find your self-esteem, start passing it on to People in its own reality! This is how to get out into the light because we embellish the things in which there is shame. Believe me, you will be lovable even if you say these things and accept them, and even be more lovable than you are now! Those who embrace themselves with their weaknesses are always far more lovable People than those who don't. Think about it, please! In your environment, do you prefer selfish, pompous colorists, those with a gray background, or those who openly embrace themselves? We like to identify with these latter People, despite their accepted bad qualities, don't we? This shows that it's not so scary to assume ourselves in front of the world, but this is the only way to raise your self-esteem to a healthy level and thus have even more to do with happiness!

Here's a summary of what you need to do for the 16th step to your happiness:

Task: As of today, pledge not to lie to yourself or others! Also, pledge that everything you say to others will be done with complete objectivity without greying or coloring.

Which part of you it affects the most: Soul

How long you have to do this task: Telling the truth is one of the basic virtues, so it has to become your basic habit and you have to live by it all your life if you want to be happy.

A few words of advice: Start small; you don't have to shout out your deepest shame to the world. Take a nice gradual step forward. Be brave and make a difference. If a beautification or a lie comes out of your mouth at any time, don't beat yourself up! In such cases, make yourself aware of the spiritual reason why you did it, and accept that you will take care of it next time. An even more effective solution is to stand in front of the person you lied to or shaded the truth to and tell them the truth.

Now, please stop reading this book until you have completed Step 16 of your journey to success! Then I'll wait for you so we can continue working together!

When you can take Step 17: When every time you embellish the truth, tell a fib or lie a hazard light flashes in your head, you can take a step forward. It's okay that these things are still happening to you, because habits are slowly clearing out of us. The important thing is to realize that you have already done it and to be aware of what would have been better instead.

The 17th Step to your happiness (mind): Reduce stress III. – The method of the door left behind combined with the method of balance

The greatest obstacle to the happiness of today's Western People is stress. This is so true that when I started seeing a kinesiologist and living in the belief that I was already managing stress in my Life, the specialist determined that stress was responsible for 67% of my unhappiness at that time. At first I was convinced it was stupid—even impossible. I felt that I had made a lot of progress in stress management in recent years and that I was only being affected by the extent of my previous stress. My ego was offended that after so much development, a value of 67% still came out. Then the experience settled in me at home. I paid attention to the fact that the more the ego freaks out at something, the more the fact that what it freaked out over is true. It's important that you pay attention to this, too! This is a very serious beacon! That's when I realized that 67% was true in reality, because it's all a matter of perspective.

In the past, the stress destroyed my chances of happiness by over 90%, and as a result of many years of internal work, it was "only" 67% at that time. Although my ego was offended by the fact that the results I thought were great were not so great, the reality was that I still had a lot to improve in this area. Over the next few days, I observed myself and realized how strongly stress was present in my Life. It is true that I could handle it well, that is, it did not pull me back as much as it used to, but it was still present in my Life and negatively affected my soul, thinking and body every day.

The state of being stress-free is also the "privilege" of the enlightened, but reducing stress as much as possible increases our happiness. So, if you reduce the effects of stress in your life by 10%, you will be at least 10% happier. It's clearly worth investing your energy in stress reduction! The closed-door method was developed by me when I was a middle-aged engineer, and since then I have been teaching it to all the colleagues I hire in my companies. Life here is quite hectic. Deadlines are always tight and there's a lot of work to do. This used to cause a lot of fluctuation in my companies. The young people were quickly burnt out. Today there is no fluctuation. Fortunately, this "phenomenon" was reduced to almost zero. Obviously, there are many reasons for this, but one of them is this method. The essence of the method is to explain to young colleagues that it is forbidden to take work home in your head! At first glance, this seems impossible. However, with two or three weeks of practice, you can make it an integral part of your life. Let's see how the method works, and then I'll get to the positive effects. When you walk out the door of your workplace, you're usually full of thoughts about how much more you should have done or solved, but you didn't have time. This generates a lot of tension (stress) in you and this is how you go home. With these thoughts in your mind, you're closing off the workplace part of your day. Of course, you'll take this home with you, so you'll be moody and irritable at home. Stress prevents you from experiencing positive emotions at home, so you can't adequately experience the love coming from your children or your partner. When you're stressed, you can't be grateful, even though this feeling is the basis of all happiness, as you already know. And in such cases, it's more difficult to experience joy, cheerfulness, inspiration, admiration, faith, and many soul-building positive feelings. Obviously, you can't repay them like this either. If you want to relax, you can't really do that either, because stress affects you too. When this is permanently on your mind, you turn to something more "hard" to relax. Many people watch porn, horror, or some kind of fast-paced action movie. In such cases, we may be tempted to reach for alcohol, or we may cuddle up to a computer game that completely shuts the brain off. Anyway, it should only have a concentrated relaxing effect because it's the only thing that makes you forget about repressed emotions and physical and mental tensions. Our tendencies toward addictions are therefore amplified in us at such times. Of course, with this, we continue to destroy our spiritual state. The consequence is that you have bad dreams, sleep restlessly and possibly intermittently. You wake up tired and the morning starts as a nuisance. You have another day of struggle ahead of you, and it's already starting to feel stressful. After all, how are you going to do all the tasks that you left undone at work yesterday in addition to today's tasks?

Now let's see how this method will change that. You step out the door and take a few deep breaths (you've mastered the breathing technique). You are consciously telling yourself:

Today, I did everything I could at work. I have worked diligently to get it right. What hasn't been solved today, I can't do anything about today, so I'll pick it up again tomorrow morning. Until tomorrow's start of work I won't humiliate myself by tormenting myself with work problems. I respect my body, mind and soul so much

that I will devote the rest of my day to family, rest, and recreation—because I deserve it.

After you recite this monologue (or something like it) to yourself, promise not to think about any work-related problems until tomorrow's start. If such thoughts do occur, encourage yourself to return to non-job thoughts. After two or three weeks of practice, you will only be unable to put work problems aside in very difficult work situations.

It's important to know that despite this example, this method is not just for work-related stress. When you leave any Life situation behind, you can use the closed-door method to make sure that you don't carry the problem further in your mind or chew on it unnecessarily.

Now let's see what this will change in your life. You put down your work problems and go home. Since stress doesn't overwhelm your brain and soul, you'll be more open to experiencing positive emotions. You'll be more receptive to the love expressed by your partner and your children, and you can respond to them more sincerely. This is how you will have the strength of spirit. It is incredibly important to experience positive emotions because they invalidate the negative effects of stress. I've told you about one more way, but I'll come back to that later. Because of your positive emotions and increased inner calm, you don't turn to "concentrated" forms of relaxation. You'll have the strength to enjoy an emotional movie, a good book, or a pleasant stream of gratitude. Each one further raises your soul's vibration and heals the devastating effects of stress during the day. After that, you will go to bed with a much more peaceful spirit. Your dreams will be calmer and more balanced. You'll wake up more relaxed and start your day with more energy. Then you will be truly successful in this development, when you will be able to look at the day waiting for you in the morning with gratitude, not like the beginning of the next survival program.

Finally, the balance method previously promised: stress is nothing more than a bundle of negative emotions. In fact, stress is only just the consequence. The root of stress is always some kind of strong negative emotion. Most often it is fear. We are afraid that the work will not be done on time or that my boss will call again. Negative emotions are destroying your body-mind-soul. Persistent and harmful stress will be detrimental unless your stressful periods are balanced with stress-free ones. If you let go of stress at work, when you leave your workplace and can create a peaceful, harmonious atmosphere at home, you will spend 8–10 hours in a stressful state and 14–16 hours in a stress-free state. Thus, you can endure stress for a long time without any health damage or psychological distortion. Balance means having at least as many stress-free hours as you have stressful ones. This is the minimum to keep our physical and mental health stable for a long time. Of course, there are never enough positive emotions, so it's worth increasing this ratio as much as possible. You can use the balance method for other life situations. For example, a friend of mine has a bad family life, so he goes fishing on a regular basis. It is an instinctive realization of the method of balance.

Here's a summary of what you need to do the 17th step to your happiness:

Task: From today, block stressful situations with the closed-door method! From today, create as many stress-free hours in your life as you do stressful ones. A stress-free hour can only be filled with positive emotions and thoughts or relaxation.

Which part of you it affects the most: Mind

How long you have to do this task: After a while, your mind will automatically tell you that you have overdone your stressful hours, or that you are dwelling on a stressful situation again, but you shouldn't. You have to continue this task until it becomes part of your automatic lifestyle.

Some good advice: Like most happiness-seeking methods, this one requires awareness and persistent practice until it becomes an instinctive part of your way of life. There will be setbacks, but don't be discouraged. You have to stand up and do it again. The more effectively you learn these two methods, the higher the level of happiness in your life will be. I wish you a lot of strength, perseverance and growing happiness!

Now, please stop reading this book until you have completed Step 17 of your journey to success! As before, I'll wait for you so we can continue working together!

When you can take Step 18: when the alarm bell rings when there's too much stress or when you're thinking about something you should have left behind. If you've made it this far, it's time to continue working together on your path to a happier future!

The 18th Step to your happiness (body): More smiles

We usually smile when we are happy or when something joyful or humorous happens to us. A smile is the physical consequence of our happiness. However, many studies have shown that this process is not one-way, but the other way around! That is, if we smile, the production of hormones related to happiness starts in our body. So, if you took the edges of your mouth and "tied" them to your ears, forming in your body a forced smile all day, you would have a much calmer, happier, more peaceful day. This is a known fact, so start smiling—even if you have no reason to!

I know it sounds weird, but the more you do it, the more you'll feel like yourself!

Here's a summary of what you need to do the 18th step to your happiness:

Task: Smile more and more, starting today! Pay conscious attention to your mouth, and smile even if you have no reason to.

Which part of you affects the most: Body

How long you have to do this task: Until you instinctively smile in your normal everyday actions!

Some good advice: I know you're going to feel like a total idiot at first when you do this. So did I. I also know that the forced smile looks strange. But at first, do it in a place where they don't pay attention to you or few people do. That way, you don't have to worry about being seen as a fool. Then, when you're doing well alone, bring this practice into the company as well. By the way, if you smile, People will also connect you with more openness and joy. This habit will also improve your Human relationships. You already know that the quality of our Human relationships is the most important parameter for our happiness, so it's doubly worthwhile to use this method!

Now, please stop reading this book until you have completed Step 18 of your journey to success! Then I'll wait for you so we can continue working together!

When you can take the 19th step: when an inner voice turns on that you're not smiling even though there's no reason to look sad, I'll be waiting for you to continue building your happiness!

The 19th Step to your happiness (soul): Best-case method

Now I'm writing about a method the original author said would cure your fears. I was listening about this method in one of Michael B. Beckwith's online courses, whose books and lectures I wholeheartedly recommend to all seekers. I shaped his method for my own life, and if something comes up in me, I still use it today. The effectiveness of the method encouraged me to try to help make your Life better. You can actually apply this method to exit all levels of Life-destroying psychic vibration.

In fact, if we think deeply enough, all levels of Life-destroying spiritual vibration (Shame, Guilt, Apathy, Sorrow, Fear, Desire, Anger, Pride) are nourished by or connected to fear in some way. Thus, successful liberation from our fears brings a significant increase in freedom, peace and harmony. Therefore, it is of utmost importance to face and process our fears. The hormones produced by the feeling of fear also eventually cause physical diseases, so it's also very important to protect or restore our health from the point of view of reducing our fear addiction. I don't use that term lightly; every regularly recurring thought, emotional or action pattern associated with negative mental resonance levels is actually addiction! So, if you can break with your fears or other Life-destroying emotions, addictive habits will automatically disappear from your life.

Fear is our destructive ego's reaction to our future or the future of our loved ones. Our egos are constantly scanning for possible future alternatives by keeping our brains constantly on standby. As a tool for this, our fear clings to the most pessimistic future alternatives that our egos have conceived as thoughts. This also explains why our fears are in most cases ungrounded or exaggerated.

Your ego therefore creates the most pessimistic alternative to the future, where the thoughts flooding your brain immediately generate a sense of fear. This is why those who are fundamentally pessimistic tend to fear more. After all, they are more inclined to create deep, terrifying future alternatives for themselves. This is an inclination that is actually an addiction. The body has become addicted to fear-generated hormones, so even though we know from the brain that this isn't good for us, we regularly fall into the traps of fears coming from our subconscious.

The problem with fear is that it's very hard to shake it off! If we suppress it, it often bursts out even more strongly. So, there are no excuses; you will have to face it sooner or later, otherwise it will ruin your quality of life and, after a while, your health. The solution lies in retraining ourselves! Instead of fear-generated bodily hormones, the cells of our body need to get used to a hormonal system associated with a positive feeling, the details of which you may have already learned. In this chapter, I would like to show how this is done.

When an imaginary terrible future alternative generates fear in you, you must consciously replace it with one that is as positive as possible. For example, if your partner hasn't answered or returned your calls for several hours, many people imagine there's been a terrible accident, or that their partner is making out with someone in a motel and cheating on them. Before I went through a significant spiritual transformation, I remember that I would have gravitated to one of these in such a situation. These thoughts naturally create fear and anxiety in us. It's common for other negative emotions to be associated with the image. We become nervous and tense, and a bad emotional-nervous-hormonal spiral starts, which is a combination of deep self-destructive processes and can be called anything but a happiness generator. In these situations, it's time to connect! If we practice enough, we can detach ourselves from our thinking patterns! So, for example, you should consciously imagine that your partner ran into an old acquaintance on the street, went to a restaurant and had a meaningful and peaceful time chatting there. They probably left their phone in their car, so they'll notice and contact you soon. It's important to add emotion to this mindset! You can replace the most pessimistic future alternative with the most optimistic one if you imagine and get emotionally invested in it. You do the same thing with fear; you add emotion to the picture! If it's going in a negative way, then why not do the same in a positive way?! So, following this example, imagine that your partner is having a very good time and you are enjoying the thought that it's very good for them with sincere joy and love. This unselfish and pure, devoted feeling blows the feeling of fear away from your soul. Whenever you try to return to the old pattern of thinking associated with fear, immediately replace it as described above. It's very important to experience the feelings as deeply as possible, because if you only do it from the brain, it's called repression and it will backfire later! It's like closing the valve on the lid of a pressure cooker. Sooner or later, it erupts more harshly than ever. Replacing it with positive emotions will set off a positive change in your Life, like lowering the stove temperature under the pressure. If you connect gratitude to this process, it will accelerate the healing process a lot, but you already know that, right?

Here's a summary of what you need to do the 19th step to your happiness:

Task: When your mind generates a vision with a negative scenario, replace it with a positive scenario by experiencing the imagined scenario with positive feelings.

Which part of you it affects the most: Soul

How long do you need to do this task: You need to do this task until your Life is dominated by positive emotions.

Some good advice: It will seem strange at first to add positive emotion to a fictitious positive vision, but that's no stranger than attributing fear to fictitious negative visions of the future. The only difference is that one of them will be unusual for you, so it will be difficult to do initially. However, success requires tough perseverance because old thought patterns are hard to dissolve. Imagine how many thousands of times these have appeared in your life so far! You need to replace them with the emotions associated with the best future alternative over several weeks or months for the change to be stable and lasting. Your body's "fear hormone" dependence should be replaced with a hormone dependence related to a positive emotion. I wish you a lot of strength and perseverance on your journey! If you can't do it alone, get help!

Now, please stop reading this book until you have completed Step 19 of your journey to success! Then I'll wait for you so we can continue working together!

When you can take Step 20: When it bothers you that your brain has created a negative scenario unnecessarily and instinctively turns on this method to correct it, please move on!

The 20th Step to your happiness (mind): Affirmations upgrade – Kaleidoscope videos

The inventor of the kaleidoscope videos is Dr. Joe Dispenza, whose books and YouTube videos I highly recommend. In a state of deep meditation, Dr. Joe Dispenza frequently experienced the complex visual appearance of energy waves, which are most similar to those seen in higher-quality kaleidoscopes. Based on this, Dispenza tested the effect of the images created by the kaleidoscopes on the brains of People, and controlled this with measurements. These studies have shown that these images cause our attention to sink from the level of alert Beta brainwaves to the level of Alpha brainwaves. In the Alpha brainwave state, the brain simply receives information and does not evaluate or comment on it. That's what ad makers do with clever tricks. With well-crafted advertisements, we take in the biggest nonsense and build it into our subconscious because the brain is not critical in the Alpha brainwave state, so the mind doesn't analyze anything. Joe Dispenza's position is that what can be used for negative things can also be used for positive things. Therefore, he created kaleidoscope videos that use the tools of affirmation and attraction. However, this method is like installing a turbo engine on a wheelbarrow. The problem with traditional affirmations is that if you use them in a Beta brainwave state, you have to tell yourself a confirmation at least a thousand times before it starts to infiltrate your subconscious. However, if you do the same with a kaleidoscope video, you only have to watch it twice a day for 21 days and the expected effect will start to work. Lots of People have tried it; it really works. It worked for me, too. The advantage of the method is that it is comfortable, doesn't require any professional knowledge and is accepted by everyone, so it will work for you too! All you have to do is look at them. (You can find some handy kaleidoscope videos on YouTube with the search words "Joe Dispenza, kaleidoscope videos.") But if you don't like any of them, you can make a unique, personalized video for yourself, in which you can put your own specific dreams and desires. For this, you can find a service called Mindmovie on the internet, which is paid but not expensive.

Here's a summary of what you need to do the 20th step to your happiness:

Task: Choose an area of your life where you want to make a big difference. Then look for a related video (you can find them on YouTube with the search words "Joe Dispenza, kaleidoscope videos"). Then watch it at least twice a day for 21 days or once a day for 50 days.

Which part of you it affects the most: Mind

How long you need to complete this task: It's advisable to watch the video until the desired goal begins to be realized in your Life.

Some good advice: As a guide, it's important that I provide additional advice for this method. This is the Law of Delay, which you have already read about (see chapter 6.6). Once you've equipped yourself with this, all you have to do is pick a video with your most important goals and watch it at least twice a day. Watching the video is effective if you watch it in a relaxed state, as if you were staring at a boring advertisement. If you can feel heightened emotions (gratitude, love, peace, harmony, etc.) from the music and pictures while watching the video, the method is even more effective. It's important to focus on the video while trying to be a thought-less. If your mind wanders, bring the focus back to the movie over and over again. The more thoughtless you are, the more focused, relaxed, and deeply positive emotions you feel, the more effectively and quickly you will attract the desired goal.

I first tried the free "attraction law" video on the internet in order to test the method. By about the 15th day I had already felt its positive effect several times. Unexpected, illogical events happened in my life that I would not have been able to bring about myself. These are called 'synchronicities' in spiritual literature. The best thing you can do for yourself is to start watching these videos as soon as possible.

Now, please stop reading this book until you have completed Step 20 of your journey to success! Then I'll wait for you back so we can continue working together!

When to take Step 21: when you 've been watching the videos for at least three weeks, and focusing on a new task won't stop you from continuing to watch the videos.

The 21st Step to your happiness (body): Water

In my garden, there's a small ornamental pond with clear water. What does it take to keep the water in this lake clean? The answer is simple: large amounts of water exchange from a clean water source. Insects falling into the lake, tree leaves, dust blown by the wind, substances introduced by the rain and the processes generated by the living creatures in the lake gradually pollute the water of the lake. If the water supply were not exchanged in sufficient quantities, it would soon turn into a green puddle with algae. Therefore, I feed it with clean rainwater from a rainwater reservoir through an artificial small waterfall. The cleaner the water replenishment of the lake and the higher the rate of water exchange, the cleaner the water of the lake will be. Approximately two-thirds of your body is water. Imagine your body's water as a pond like this. I know that the processes in the Human body are more complex, but considering the origin of the processes, the parallel comparison can be made between the lake and the water in your body. So, your body's water should be constantly replaced with water of the highest purity possible. This is how you maintain the purest state in your body. The more contaminated the liquids you add to your organism, the less your body's "pond" is able to cleanse itself. That's why the best thing you can do for your body is to replenish your fluid deficit with clean water whenever you can.

But what is really clean water? I have been dealing with this issue for more than 20 years, as my engineering side is as the designer and expert of many large municipal drinking water treatment plants. I will try to briefly summarize the answer to this complex question. Fortunately, in the western part of the world, we can at least get tap water, so we can choose between roughly healthy and very healthy waters. But let's not forget that there are currently at least 1 billion people on Earth who do not have access to clean drinking water on a daily basis. That's why it's so important to be grateful for every sip of clean water you drink. By doing this alone, you are doing a lot for your spiritual development, as we know the power of gratitude on the soul, not to mention that in the meantime you will brush aside the false suggestion of the destroyer-ego that you are entitled to it.

I'm starting from the assumption that the Reader can at least have access to network water. In this case, the degrees of water purity range from the least clean to the purest:

- ▶ Tap water
- ▶ Tap water treated with domestic water treatment
- ▶ Mineral water in a plastic bottle
- ▶ Mineral water in glass
- ▶ Boiled water (from a verified source)

Unfortunately, tap water is only partially healthy. There are a number of reasons for this, and I'll try to show you some of the more important ones. There are legal requirements in Hungary for the chemical, microbiological and bacteriological purity of water, which comply with average international standards. However, it often happens that the water treatment plant does not meet these expectations temporarily or permanently. In general, however, the water supply does not stop at this time. Even if it meets the expectations, it does not mean complete health safety for the consumer. After all, the water is chlorinated in order to prevent contamination of the water leaving the water plant through the several kilometers of pipeline until it reaches the consumer. In reality, what happens is that chlorine destroys every living organism it encounters during the transport of water, while its amount in water is constantly decreasing. Thus, if your house is close to the waterworks, it's very likely that there is water flowing from your tap that has a low chance of microorganisms but has free chlorine in it. Due to the free chlorine content, the water is not healthy, even if the chlorine level is below the health limit. If your house is far enough away from the water plant, you will run out of free chlorine from the water, so microorganisms and other living things will appear in the water you drink. Of course, these can also be beneficial bacteria, but unfortunately they can also be infectious viruses, bacteria, fungi, eggs, worms and other organisms that are not visible to the naked eye or are barely noticeable. However, it's also important to note that chlorine, when it kills a microorganism in water, will also be a carcinogen among the by-products of the chemical reaction. Thus, with chlorination, although we get rid of infectious risks to some extent (not completely), we also receive a small amount of carcinogenic substances through the tap. In most cases, these are also below the health limit, but it's still not advisable to consume them. But why? This is where the concept of multi-toxicity comes in, surrounding which intensive research is still going on and there are still a lot of scientifically open questions. As you know, if the carcinogenic compounds in the tap water you drink are below the health limit, and then you eat 100g of cold cuts in which the nitrite salt, which is also a carcinogen, is also below the health limit, and then you eat some fruit "blessed" with a little spray agent residue, then the exciting question is how this combination will affect your body. The number of cancers is quite large and increasing. It is quite logical to conclude where the effects of multi-toxicity will lead. After all, many of these carcinogens can never be eliminated from the body. That is, our body collects them all our lives and after a while they accumulate in us to such an extent that they cause serious diseases. Until then, however, they just lurk inside us and our bodies collect them symptom-free from tiny doses of nanograms over many decades.

So, if you can eliminate the contaminant load from tap water from your Life, you have reduced your body's multi-toxicity load. It is important to emphasize that the tap water in our country is not of poor quality, of course; I am not saying that drinking tap water causes a lot of trouble. Rather, I would argue that drinking tap water can slightly harm our health. It's therefore advisable to switch from tap water to another type of water for drinking and cooking.

Our first option is to further purify the tap water. This is not a bad method, and here as well the consumer can choose from a wide range of options. The cheapest solution is the activated charcoal pitcher, which I cannot recommend with a pure heart. As it is known, the active filter in the pitcher filters some of the chlorination by-products (that is, it reduces the carcinogen concentration of the water), but at the same time the bacteria multiply very easily in the filter, and since the water is not contaminated afterwards, unfortunately the risk of infection increases. In many cases the infection is small, so with mild headaches or even asymptomatic symptoms, the result is only the weakening of the immune system, while we don't even know if it's caused by the pitcher we use on a daily basis. Obviously, the regular replacement of filter cartridges mitigates the risks.

In addition to avoiding professional depths, the following system is a good solution for further cleaning the tap water:

microfilter – activated carbon filter – RO equipment – salting cartridge – UV cartridge. If you choose this combination in this order, you will consume high purity water.

Another option is to buy mineral water. This will fix network chlorination and network infection. In this way, you will drink healthier water than mains water in every way. Of course, you should also make sure that there is a "natural mineral water" label on the bottle. Unfortunately, most mineral waters are sold in PE bottles. Small amounts of carcinogenic by-products are released from PE bottles above 30–35 °C. Several tests were carried out where the temperature of the water was measured from the mineral water bottling plant to the shelves of the shops. Unfortunately, in the high heat of summer, the water temperature on trucks and warm storage areas can rise above 35 ° C permanently. So, it's no use taking it off the shelf as cool water in the air-conditioned supermarket if it's been stored in a hot warehouse for weeks beforehand. Consequently, the mineral water you buy is either perfectly healthy or contains a small amount of harmful substances.

The best way to rule out this problem is to buy bottled mineral water in glass bottles. However, there is very little of this on the market and it is also quite expensive. But this solution is great, because nothing from the glass can dissolve in the water!

By the way, I drink spring water from a source whose water collector has no direct human influence. This water is the best because not only is it chemically and microbiologically clean, but also energetically clean. But I will write to you about the energy purity of water in the next volume.

Here's a summary of what you need to do the 21st step to your happiness:

Task: Drink enough clean water every day. Drink as much clean water as possible based on your options. At least 60% of your daily fluid intake should be pure water!

Which part of you it affects the most: Body

How long you need to complete this task: This is a lifetime task.

Some good advice: What does it mean to have enough liquid? The answer was defined very simply by a naturopath friend: 30-40 ml per day of fluid per kilogram of body weight! For example, if you weigh 70 kg, this means 2.1 to 2.8 liters of fluid, including soup and any liquids you drink. Many people neglect the right amount of fluids and destroy their bodies (and indirectly their souls) on a daily basis. We have a wave genetic machine in our family that allows us to examine the condition of our bodies on a daily basis. If I don't drink enough for one day, the machine already shows that the cerebral vessels are in a drastic state. Of course, all I feel from this is that I have a slight headache or I am more tired, but it can permanently cause many serious health problems. And this is just one example of many. Fluid intake should be taken very seriously! I've heard from many People that they don't want to pee so often so they don't drink enough, or they even tell me they don't have time. These are all clever tricks of the ego! I'm asking you nicely: don't believe it!

Now let's turn to the question of water. At least 60% of the daily fluid volume described above should be as clean as possible! Without it, your body's vibration level cannot rise, which has a detrimental effect on your soul! I will discuss the scientific explanation of this in the next volume when discussing the energy purity of water. But in the meantime, accept that your body and therefore your soul need lots of clean water! I often hear excuses for that, too. The most common excuse is that water is tasteless and boring so they prefer to drink other flavored things. This is only an initial perception. It was also very difficult for me to get used to drinking water. But today, if I try the sugar-sweetened beverages I used to love so much, they make me sick. As our consumption habits change, our sense of taste changes. After a while, the water won't be tasteless and boring. Only the transition is difficult, but please hold on, because it's worth it! When I went through the first breakthrough of enlightenment in my life, my body was only able to absorb clean spring water for half a day afterwards. I didn't eat anything and couldn't drink anything else. One of the clear messages of the experience was that the best thing you can do for yourself is to drink clean, fresh water whenever you can!

My heartfelt congratulations!

You've completed the final challenge of this book! If drinking water has also become an integral internal need of your Life and you want to continue your happiness-seeking journey, then I will gladly welcome you among my readers with the next volume of this book or in my courses. At the same time, you can read a very cool collection of self-healing and happiness-seeking methods on my blog, the title of which is found at the beginning of the book. In this regard, I highly recommend Gyöngyi Spitzer's (Soma Mamagésa's) Self-Healing Book, which is very inspiring and useful, in which you will find a collection of serious healing methods!

Afterword

Sudden changes are usually followed by large downturns. Correct change is slow and gradual. We usually don't even notice the change because it happens in such small steps that we get used to it. Therefore, we can track our progress by looking back from time to time and thinking about how we would have behaved in a given situation a year or five years ago. At such times, we can see how much we have developed. Often I am shocked by how far I am from the Ernő Dittrich who, at the age of 26, embarked on the path of spiritual development. Today's Ernő Dittrich is a much more balanced, happier, and more successful Person than he was then. You can experience this change with the help of this book, and much faster than I can, as I will give you everything you need for this. But it takes perseverance and diligence! Please hold on: it's worth it.

When at least 60% of the tasks in this book are already an integral part of your life, answer the following questions again by choosing the most appropriate number between 1 and 10 and circling it. A score of 10 means 'I totally agree' and 1 means 'I totally disagree'.

- ▶ After waking up in the morning, I look forward to the miracles this day will bring me:

    1-2-3-4-5-6-7-8-9-10

- ▶ My relationships are harmonious, peaceful and characterized by spiritual intimacy, honesty and selflessness. I am not critical of myself or others:

    1-2-3-4-5-6-7-8-9-10

- I have as much work as I can do harmoniously with a fast-paced but calm activity. Order and harmony dominate my life:

    1-2-3-4-5-6-7-8-9-10

- I smile a lot, which I do not use as self-defense armor, but is the instinctive appearance of my happiness:

    1-2-3-4-5-6-7-8-9-10

- I rarely feel sad, restless, or impatient, and only for very short periods of time:

    1-2-3-4-5-6-7-8-9-10

- I love my Life and I love myself:

    1-2-3-4-5-6-7-8-9-10

- With pure attention, with an open heart, without thoughts, I am able to live the precious moments:

    1-2-3-4-5-6-7-8-9-10

- I trust in my future and believe that Life will direct my fate in the right direction (You can replace Life with any word according to your belief system, e.g. God, Almighty, etc.):

    1-2-3-4-5-6-7-8-9-10

- I sleep deeply and well every day:

    1-2-3-4-5-6-7-8-9-10

▶ My physical health is in perfect condition:

1-2-3-4-5-6-7-8-9-10

Add the numbers and divide by 10, then write the value with the date here: _____

If this value is higher than what you wrote in chapter 6.7, then the method has worked. If so, please share your joy and success with me at the email address at the beginning of the book so that I can rejoice with you. Even if there is no change, let me know, because in this case I will try to help you find the blockage that makes it difficult for you to develop!

If you have made progress with the methods of this book, I will be happy to see you among the readers of the next volume; it will already provide you with intermediate-level exercises. In return, they can help you succeed more effectively and more seriously on your happiness-seeking journey. All beginnings are difficult. It's like a hard-to-start flywheel. This book was meant to give you a deeper understanding of your Life, to start to see behind your destructive ego and to start to push your stationary or backwards-moving swing in the right direction. If you feel like continuing our work together, the next volume will be about accelerating your flywheel. Until we meet again, I wish you much strength, perseverance and joy in this wonderful journey, both sides of which will be illuminated by lanterns of gratefulness for you.

Acknowledgements

I used to suffer a lot because of how many bad things happened to me in my past. But today I am grateful for every difficult minute of my Life! I can see now that everything happened for a reason. If I had not experienced these spiritual depths and experienced through my own skin how they could be transformed and healed, I would not be able to help others today. Altruism and humility are deep and effective drivers of happiness. I am grateful for every minute of my Life and for the fact that you are now holding this book in your hands as you read through it. My list of thanks is infinitely long, as all People and all living beings, and even all inanimate things with which I have been connected for a longer or shorter time, have brought me to where I am now.

By name, I would like to thank those People who have made a special impact on me through my spiritual development, whether it is our personal acquaintance or just their videos and books that have affected me in an extraordinary way. I consider them my masters and express my sincere gratitude to them: Ildikó Tönkő, Judit Pap, József Murányi, Tamás Miron Varga, János Mátyás, Gyöngyi Spitzer (Soma Mamagésa), Dr. Joe Dispenza, Dr. Gábor Máté, Eckhart Tolle, and Dr. David R. Hawkins.

I offer special thanks to those who contributed to the preparation of this book. By name, I highlight those who are not on the front of the book: Judit Lukáts, Gábor Göndöcs, Eszter Öhlmüller and her team, Krisztina Kreitner, Tamás Puskás, Zoltán Szentgyörgyi, Dr. Zoltán Egerszegi, Ágnes Birkás, Katalin Berényi, Dávid Somfai, and Anett Szekeres. Finally, I would like to thank my family, whose members have always stood behind me and provided a wonderful, loving background to be the person I have always wanted to be: a person who works with selfless love for others.

References
(and suggested readings)

- Barry Michels and Phil Stutz: The Tools. (read in Hungarian translation) Gabo Publishing House, Budapest, 2012.
- Beau Lotto: Deviate: The Science of Seeing Differently (read in Hungarian translation) Libri Publishing House, Budapest, 2017.
- Carl Gustav Jung: Archetypes and the Collective Consciousness - The Collected Works of C. G. Jung 9/1. (read in Hungarian translation) Scolar Publishing House, Budapest, 2022.
- Dr. David R. Hawkins: Power versus force. (read in Hungarian translation) Agykontroll Kft., Budapest, 2004.
- Dr. Ernő Dittrich: The name of the future is Life – A Solution to the Climate Change and World Peace Hungarian Climate Protection Ltd., Pécs, 2021.
- Dr. Joe Dispenza: Becoming supernatural. (read in Hungarian translation) Bioenergetic Publishing House, Budapest, 2020.
- Dr. Gábor Máté: In the Realm of Hungry Ghosts (read in Hungarian translation) Libri Publishing House, Budapest, 2017.
- Eckhart Tolle: A New Earth. (read in Hungarian translation) Freshwater Publisher, Budapest, 2022.
- Eric Berne: Games People Play. (read in Hungarian translation) Háttér Kiadó, Budapest, 2009.
- Gary Chapman: The 5 love languages: tuned in to each other – The secret of love that lasts. (read in Hungarian translation) Harmat Publishing House, Budapest, 2015.

- Gerner-Nagy-Sécsi: Albert Einstein's selected writings. (Hungarian book) Typotex Publishing House, Budapest, 2009.
- James Redfield: The Celestine Prophecy: An Adventure (read

- in Hungarian translation) Alexandra Publishing House, Pécs, 2005.
- John Bradshaw: Healing the Shame that Binds You (read in Hungarian translation) Casparus Publishing House, Budapest, 2015.
- Judyth Reichenberg-Ullman–Robert Ullman: Mystics, Masters, Saints, and Sages: Stories of Enlightenment (read in Hungarian translation) Filosz Publishing House, Budapest, 2016.
- Louise L. Hay: Experience Your Good Now!: Learning to Use Affirmations (read in Hungarian translation) Édesvíz Publisher, 2014.
- Imre Madách: The Tragedy of Man. (Hungarian book) Pantheon Publishing House, Budapest, 1993.
- Muriel James–Dorothy Jongeward: Born to Win: Transactional Analysis with Gestalt Experiments (read in Hungarian translation) Renaissance Publishing House, Budapest, 2010.
- Paul Ekman: Emotions Revealed (read in Hungarian translation) Kelly Publishing House, Budapest, 2011.
- Soma Mamagésa: Self-Healing Book – Methods, ^{2}-, exercises, approaches. (Hungarian book) Jaffa Publishing House, Budapest, 2014.
- Rhonda Byrne: The magic. (read in Hungarian translation) Édesvíz Publisher, Budapest, 2022.
- László Rozsnaki: Software Update 1.0.1, or the Book of Creation. (Hungarian pdf document distributed free of charge)

- Uwe Albrecht: Yes/No: Using the Arm-length Test for Instant Answers and Wellbeing (read in Hungarian translation) Bioenergetic Publishing House, Budapest, 2020.
- Vianna Stibal: ThetaHealing: Introducing an Extraordinary Energy Healing Modality (read in Hungarian translation) Bioenergetic Publishing House, Budapest, 2020.

ANNEXES

Annex 1: Estimation of Spiritual level and self-awareness (with table)

Dear Reader,

In chapter 1.2, I asked you to play an interesting self-awareness game. I hope you will join me in this exciting inner work. First, I'll give you an example of how you can estimate your level of spiritual vibration. Of course, here, too, it's important to be completely honest with yourself. If you get a false image of yourself, it can lead you astray! That's why it's so important to dare to look in the mirror. As an illustrative example, I estimated with emotions typical of my own average day. Through this, I will tell you how you can make the estimation yourself. Below the table you will find the explanation, but please don't be alarmed: it will not be complicated!

Based on the number example above, now complete the blank table below in the 7 steps below:

I. Step 1: In column 4 of row 19, enter how much sleep you got that day. In the example table, there are 7 hours in this cell.
II. Step 2: Go from Shame to Enlightenment and think about how long you've had that feeling on an average day. Enter this as a decimal in column 4 from line 1 to line 17. The completed number example also shows that you should write a 0 there if it's not a typical feeling for you. The other places are the time you spend on an average day.
III. Step 3: Add the values of the period entered in rows 1-17 of column 4 and enter them in column 4 of row 18. In the completed example you will find 17 hours.
IV. Step 4: Add the numbers for columns 18 and 19 in column 4 and enter them in row 20. This is a check line because you should have 24 hours here. If 24 hours have not come out, adjust the duration values of columns 4, lines 1-17 until your total time is 24 hours.
V. Step 5: Then, in rows 1-17, multiply the point value in column 3 by the duration value in column 4, and enter the resulting numbers in the current row in column 5. For example, in the completed table above, the vibration value of 400 in column 3 of row 13 is row 13. Multiplied by the time duration of 2 hours in column 4 gives a multiplication of 800, which is multiplied by the time duration of 2 hours in row 13. Write it in column 5.
VI. Step 5: Then add the numbers in column 5 and enter them in row 18 of column 5 of the table. In the example table, there is an amount of 8444 here.
VII. Step 6: In row 18 of column 5, divide the value in row 18 of the duration value in column 4. So, in the case of the example, 8444 was divided by 17 hours. Enter the resulting value in line 21 of the 5th column.

Congratulations! You have estimated your value of spiritual vibration!

It's important to know that this is an estimate. The extent of the error is as much as your self-awareness is incomplete. Your self-awareness is more incomplete the more powerful an ego you have. If the value obtained is low, do not be discouraged! About nine years ago, I was living at a permanent level of 30 and had genuine suicidal thoughts, so nothing is impossible! Whoever is in the depths has two huge advantages! One is that you can really grow from there, and that's why those who rise from the depths to a happier Life are very happy because they are grateful and can really appreciate the good. The other big advantage is that if you can get out of the great depths, you can help others afterwards. Those who have never experienced depth and try to help others will not be good enough at what they do, as they're talking about something they've never really experienced.

Annex 2: Emotions related to mental vibration levels

In the table below, I've summarized the emotions associated with each psychological vibration level. This will help you orient yourself to what spiritual vibration level you are feeling right now:

Row	Vibration level	Value	Hours/day	Multiplication
1	Shame	20	0	0
2	Guilt	30	0	0
3	Apathy	50	0	0
4	Sorrow	75	0	0
5	Fear	100	0	0
6	Desire	125	0	0
7	Anger	150	0	0
8	Pride	175	0.1	17.5
9	Courage	200	0.1	20
10	Impartiality	250	0.1	25
11	Willingness	315	0.1	31.5
12	Acceptance	350	0.2	70
13	Rationality	400	2	800
14	Love	500	9.3	4650
15	Joy	540	4	2160
16	Peace	600	1	600
17	Enlightenment	700	0.1	70
18	Total		17	8444
19	My sleep time		7	
20	Total hours per day (check)		24	
21	**Estimated value of my mental vibration level**			

Row	Vibration level	Value	Hours/day	Multiplication
1	Shame	20		
2	Guilt	30		
3	Apathy	50		
4	Sorrow	75		
5	Fear	100		
6	Desire	125		
7	Anger	150		
8	Pride	175		
9	Courage	200		
10	Impartiality	250		
11	Willingness	315		
12	Acceptance	350		
13	Rationality	400		
14	Love	500		
15	Joy	540		
16	Peace	600		
17	Enlightenment	700		
18	Total			
19	My sleep time			
20	Total hours per day (check)		24	
21	**Estimated value of my mental vibration level**			

Annex 3:
Energy centers (chakras),
or the body as an energy system

In this appendix, in addition to a lot of new information, you will also find facts you have already read in the main text. This was necessary to give you a new perspective. So, if you come to a part that doesn't feel like it's saying anything new, please read on, because this repetition is only necessary to clarify the whole

Vibration level	Value	Emotions
Shame	20	humiliation, disgrace, wickedness, suicidal desire, contempt, misery, fanaticism
Guilt	30	humiliation, disgrace, wickedness, suicidal desire, contempt, misery, fanaticism
Apathy	50	powerlessness, inactivity, loss, helplessness, emptiness, insensitivity, worthlessness, hopelessness, renunciation, condemnation, feeling condemned, appeasement, rejection, stiffness, unfriendliness, harshness, insensitivity, fatigue, dullness, coldness, exhaustion, boredom, enervation, grumpiness, distance, indifference, sourness
Sorrow	75	grief, despair, self-pity, contempt, feeling hated, sense of tragedy, sadness, mourning, bitterness, loneliness
Fear	100	despair, anxiety, insecurity, withdrawal, pessimism, feeling threatened, frightened, panic, anxiety, alarm, restlessness, worry, dread, alarm, uneasiness
Desire	125	addiction, craving, desire, disappointment, misfortune, failure, craving, passion, yearning, longing
Anger	150	hostility, self-defense, criticism, labeling, judgement, opposition, hatred, debate, quarrel, aggression, violence, revenge, anger, destruction, indignation, nervousness, impatience, being upset, competition, blame, demagogy, struggle, jealousy, nationalism

Vibration level	Value	Emotions
Pride	175	conceit, snobbery, prudence, distinctness, judgment, criticism, belittling, comparison, arrogance, haughtiness, selfishness, egoism, self-interest assertion, possession, exploitation, control, goal orientation, narrowness, condescension, demanding, atheism, self-deception, superiority, adornment, vanity, narcissism, sense of self, pridefulness, complacency, nervousness
Courage	200	problem-facing, solution-oriented, insight, responsibility, empowerment, encouragement, activity, equality, forgiveness, grit, presence of mind, boldness, sincerity
Impartiality	250	experience, real self-image, liberation, trust, neutrality
Willingness	315	enthusiasm, awareness, hopefulness, inspiration, motivation, pure intention, will, aspiration, strength
Acceptance	350	optimism, freedom, balance, self-acceptance, harmony, indulgence, support, help, forgiveness, reparation, transcendence, compassion
Rationality	400	objectivity, reasonableness, idealism, humanism, understanding, significance, being an example, wisdom, justice, chastity, virtue, simplicity, consistency, logic, respect
Love	500	altruism, love of Life, admiration, unity, innocence, patience, humility, devotion, compassion, love, elevation, gratitude, benevolence, service
Joy	550	serenity, fullness, vivacity, overflow, inner joy, cheerfulness, conviviality, cheerfulness, gaiety, happiness, freedom from cares, cloudlessness, pleasure, ecstasy
Peace	600	bliss, silence, order, wholeness, perfect presence, reassurance, tranquility
Enlightenment	700	perfection, miraculousness, luminosity, ego-free state, perfect unity, timelessness

picture. I promise: this appendix will bring you some very exciting conclusions about your Life! Scientific results of this Annex are based on the bibliography of Dr. Joe Dispenza's book, which I wholeheartedly recommend to all happiness seekers. This book is within the top 5 list of my Life so far, and I dare say that my Life has been changed by the perspective it has given me. I hope it will have an equally wonderful effect on you when you read it.

The neuroscience and brain research of the last two decades makes incredibly exciting discoveries every day. What was felt by humanity for thousands of years and then partially forgotten in our over-rationalized world, is now being scientifically proven. Thus, some general statements of spirituality turn into scientifically-founded rational facts.

The latest research results have confirmed with measurements that the functioning of our body is intrinsically related to our thoughts. This is how the process supported at the neuroscience level works: our thoughts either strengthen old neural connections in our brain or create new neural connections. This depends on whether it is a new thought or some old, familiar thought. In the early 2000s, a Nobel Prize was awarded to a researcher who proved that a completely new idea creates 1,300 new connections in the brain. Thus, thoughts have physical consequences almost immediately. (It is important to emphasize here that if the thought is not repeated within three days, these new neural connections will disappear permanently. Therefore, it is important that when a new valuable thought comes into our field of vision, we keep it for at least three days and repeat it until it is completely integrated into our knowledge.) The process continues with the effect of these emotions in the body. Emotions generate the production of hormones and other chemical substances. It is a scientifically proven fact that elevated emotions such as love, compassion, gratitude, joy, inspiration, peace, etc. generate more than 1,400 different chemicals in the body that are responsible for the regeneration and growth of the body. These substances cause these biochemical changes in the body. However, it is also a proven fact that negative emotions such as fear, anger, frustration, competition, envy, etc. generate the production of 1,200 kinds of hormones and other chemicals in the body that take energy from the body in return for short-term self-sufficiency. If these negative feelings and the resulting stress are not short-term but permanent, the presence of these substances generates a deterioration in health. Based on this, it immediately makes sense why it's important that we carry out activities that raise or destroy the level of spiritual vibration which form proportionate thoughts in us in this regard. But now comes the really high-profile scientific discovery! Our thoughts generate emotions, and emotions create a completely unique chemistry in your body. The hormones and other chemicals in your body that act at the neural level still have a completely unique "cocktail" in your body. Nothing else creates exactly the same blend! However, this results in a realization: the chemical imprint of your past emotions is in your body! What's worse is that your body wants you to reproduce these chemicals in your body. This is the physical explanation of how the ego works. It's something like drug addiction, only it's based on the substances your body produces. What your body is currently accustomed to, it wants to produce over and over again. Therefore, it sends stimuli to the brain, which instinctively generates thoughts that produce the same emotions again, which in turn produces the same hormones and other chemicals. Isn't this interesting to think about? I think it's an incredibly exciting collection of scientific discoveries. But there's still an exciting twist to all of this! For me, this was the most shocking result. As a result of these processes, certain genes may be activated in our cells, and certain genes may be turned off or their activity may change. For example, under prolonged stress, the genes responsible for the regeneration of the body are inactivated in the cells of the body. This explains why there are so many cancers.

The above scientifically proven results are in perfect harmony with the intuitions of spiritual leaders and yogis. The only difference is that these have been verified by measurements, so instead of a "spiritual layer" that is difficult for many people to understand, the processes just described have become simple and understandable. From these results, many of the findings can be recorded as scientific facts or logical conclusions. I would like to summarize some of these for you:

1. On this basis, it becomes understandable why almost all diseases are psychosomatic. After all, every disease begins with thoughts that generate negative emotions. Their persistence results first in genetic, then chemical and finally organ changes. Of course, this can also be created by external influences, not just thoughts.
2. Based on these, it becomes understandable why it is important to be good. Because if we do good deeds, it arouses good thoughts in us, as a result of which we experience good feelings that result in good chemistry and the regeneration of the body. So, it's also in one's self-interest to be good, not just in the public interest. This is where one of the basic rules of spirituality comes in: if you do good for the world, it manifests itself in your own Life.
3. It's also clear why soul healing methods that generate positive emotions are so effective, many of which are given to you in Chapter 7 of this book.
4. It's also clear why it's so difficult to change. And why is it so difficult to recover from a deep-seated illness? For this to happen, we need to change our thinking and emotions!
5. But these are very difficult, especially if we have chemically transformed our bodies in this way for decades! But please don't be discouraged, because this is also in the practical part of the book (*Chapter 7*).

6. It also becomes clear why it matters what we think and why it's so important to consciously pay attention to the quality of our thoughts. From this, the law of attraction can be strengthened, to which I will soon return in a little more detail.
7. Furthermore, it's a clear fact why it's worth doing everything to raise and improve your spiritual vibration level.

There are already special measuring devices that can measure the frequency and energy level of the body and individual organs. With their help, it has been scientifically proven that there is a certain frequency of energy flow and energy distribution in the body, which is a part of the communication between cells. Therefore, the body forms a magnetic field in which different organs participate to different degrees. For example, it has been measured that our strongest field-inducing organ is the heart, which generates a field 5,000 times stronger than our brain. From this point of view, our brain is also a strong organ. For example, the magnetic pulses of the heart can be measured at a distance of 2–3 m from the body with a magnetometer detector. In experiments related to this, it has become a fact that when you experience elevated feelings, you not only give important magnetic signals to all your cells, but you radiate them outward to the world. This is also confirmed by the fact mentioned in chapter 1.3 about the group dynamics of mental resonance levels.

Energy levels are fueled by emotions that, when fed back, generate new emotions, as you've already read. The average vibration level of your heart is the energy level resulting from the average of your emotions. And your body does nothing but constantly adjust to it. Imagine that when you start worrying about an event that hasn't happened yet and it becomes more and more ingrained in your brain and you worry more and more about what's going on, you're generating more and more negative emotions that you're making stronger and stronger with your thoughts. Meanwhile, the energy level of your soul is set to this low level. The result will be that whatever you worry about will happen in your Life. After all, your body makes no distinction between feelings caused by external influences and feelings caused by imaginary events. If your soul is already "set" to a level that can be sustained by the events that are the cause of your concern, then your programmed body will provoke you to move your Life towards the fulfillment of this. I think we've all been there. When we're very afraid of something, we typically attract it. Thus, it's nothing more than the physical support of the law of attraction.

When I was in college, I thought I was born under an unlucky star because I was constantly unlucky. I felt like Grouchy in The Smurfs, with a dark cloud flying over his head in sunny weather. I remember I once had a very difficult exam at the university where I had to learn 64 topics. In the oral exam, three topics had to be drawn at random. Despite all the studying, there were six topics I didn't have time to learn. I went into the exam terrified that I would draw at least one of them. Today, it makes sense what I didn't understand then: all three topics I drew were among the six that I didn't know! This has a 0.04% probability, yet it happened! On the same day, a friend sitting the same exam had only learned 10 topics out of the 64. He was a very relaxed and positive-minded guy. I saw him as an "ultra-lucky" man at the time. The point is that two of the topics he drew very from the ten he'd studied, and the third was one he remembered from the lectures. He came out with the second-highest letter grade, and I came out with the lowest, while he had studied about a quarter as much as I did. This illustrates how very strong your subconscious and your programmed body are! Your emotions penetrate your body to the genetic level, making it the perfect magnet for what your emotions are telling you to do.

For example, if you have an intense desire for a good relationship, it will definitely not work out, because the desire itself is what you adapt your body to. Your subconscious mind makes your body a magnet for desire. Thus, it will not shape your future towards achieving the goal, but instead to maintaining your craving. This, by the way, causes the intrusion into the spiritual vibration level of Desire. The same goes for People who are obese. They feel ashamed of their appearance every day and therefore hate themselves. Their emotion is self-loathing and shame. Of course, nothing will change in their lives, as their bodies will be "magnetized" to maintain a sense of self-loathing. Thus, any attempt to lose weight is doomed to failure.

Now I'm going to ask you a simple question: if these situations can work against you, why couldn't positive changes also happen in your Life? All you have to do is to do the same in reverse! It isn't negative feelings that should be associated with an imaginary situation, but positive ones. If you do this with the same intensity and perseverance as you do with worry or self-loathing or shame, it will happen. After all, you raise your spiritual energy level with your emotions, and then your subconscious magnetizes your body in such a way that it will take you towards events that conserve that vibration level. This is how the body and the soul are connected, and for this reason, it is necessary to engage not only with your soul but also with your body when dealing with the methods of raising the level of psychic vibration. Since your mind (the trainer of your thoughts) can help a lot in amplifying these processes, we will not leave it out of the development training.

Once you understand how important the energy level of your soul is and how it affects your soul, body, present and future, it's time to get to know the energy points of your body, because they regulate your present and future, as well as your health. This will give you an even better understanding of how your soul-body relationship works, and will also help you gain deeper self-knowledge.

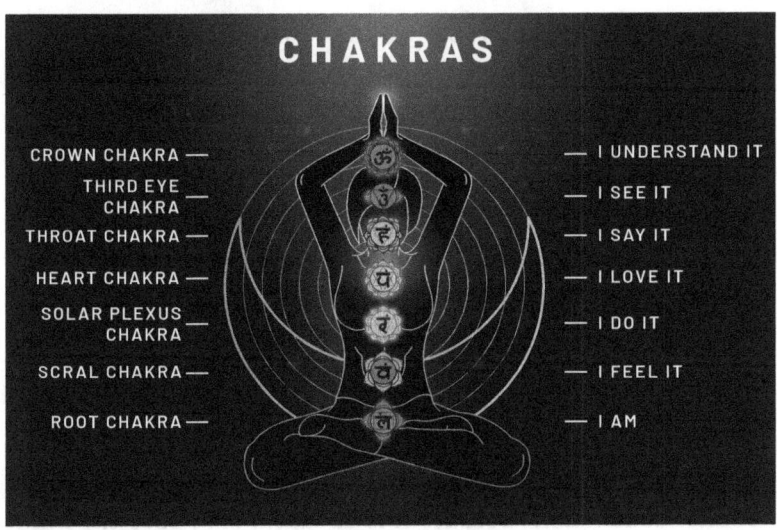

Figure 11: Our Energy Centers

Your body has seven energy centers, as shown in **Figure 11** (*page 330*). These are also called chakras in Eastern cultures. The existence of these energy centers has now been scientifically established. Each energy center has its own nerve center, its own hormone-producing gland, and most surprisingly, its own mind. The body works well when all energy centers are at an optimal energy level and located in the body's axis of symmetry. If there is under-activity or over-activity in an energy center, or shifts to the right or left (asymmetry), it generates certain diseases in the body. These are always rooted in negative emotions and negative thoughts. As a result of this process, the energy center is distorted, which affects the hormonal balance and nerve level function, and if this persists, it causes physical changes.

Let's go through the seven energy centers (you can pair the numbering from the bottom up with the locations shown in **Figure 11**):

- 1st energy center: Sex glands, lower intestine plexus nerve center
- 2nd energy center: Digestive and pancreatic glands, upper intestinal fringe nerve center
- 3rd energy center: Adrenal gland, gastrointestinal nerve center
- 4th energy center: Thymus, Cardiac Nerve Center
- 5th energy center: Thyroid, thyroid nerve center
- 6th energy center: Pineal gland, pineal nerve center
- 7th energy center: Pituitary gland, pituitary nerve center

(There is also an 8th energy center, but it does not have a direct bodily "connection" because it is about 30 cm above the head. This has no direct role in physical health, so I will not discuss it in detail in this volume.)

The distortion of the energy centers is caused by certain types of psychological problems and addictions. As a result, first pain, mild inflammation or allergic reactions indicate the onset of physical change, and then if nothing happens, the body will become ill.

At the same time, it is important to emphasize that the lower three energy centers are responsible for the instinctive and other pleasurable bodily functions and behaviors that can be obtained in the rational world: sexuality, eating, drinking, selection of excess materials, ego, competition, and impatience. The top four energy centers are responsible for higher pleasures, functions and behaviors: love, information transfer, creativity, knowledge, intuition, and faith.

Unfortunately, today's Western world is very strong in "stimulating" the lower three energy centers. The whole world is tempting you to have sex, to eat, to drink, to enjoy, to compete, to possess, to be selfish, and to have all of this immediately (impatience). Thus, most of the People in Western "cultures" are guaranteed to have an under- or over-activation of the bottom three energy centers. Media, commercials, the lure of the internet, and constant stress all have a strong impact on these energy centers. It's no wonder that millions of over-rationalized, emotionally deprived, addicted, and often pleasure-seeking people are everywhere.

The basic key to our happiness is to bring our three lower energy centers to a balanced and optimal energy level. To do this, it's necessary to curb the effects of what the current Western "culture" is constantly tempting. Impatient? Then develop your patience! Do you have a strong ego? Develop your altruism! Are you a competitor? Let others win! Are you gluttonous? Moderate your desire to eat! Are you a drunk? Don't let it dominate you! Do you have a lot of sex? Mitigate the importance of sex in your life! I know that these are the hardest things to do because they are the main sources of joy in your current life! But they are also the reason for your unhappiness. The first step is always recognition, then comes the decision to choose. Once you have that, it's time to do things the right way to make a difference. I have reviewed 21 of these basic exercises for you in Chapter 7 of this book.

It is also important to mention that the under-energy of these energy centers is at least as dangerous as their overheating. After all, the under-energization of individual energy centers can also be the root of serious problems, here are some examples:
- ▶ 1st energy center: sexual anorexia, frigidity
- ▶ 2nd energy center: anorexia
- ▶ 3rd energy center: apathy, depression

The asymmetry of each energy center can also help you understand many exciting things. The right side is usually related to the paternal-male principle-son, as well as the future, while the left side is related to the maternal-female principle-daughter, as well as the spiritual aspects of the past. For example, I lost my father when I was 6 years old. It's no coincidence that my right axillary lymph nodes regularly had problems until I solved this in my soul, as this refers to the right asymmetry of the 4th energy center (heart).

So, if you pay attention to your body's symptoms, you can find out which energy center of yours has problems. From this, you can infer what spiritual reasons may be the cause. With the help of this knowledge, you can regain your physical health, gain a deeper sense of self, and move towards a happier Life and heal the wounds of your soul.

The relationship between the energy centers and your emotions and thoughts can be easily understood by reading the following list:

- 1st Energy Center: I am (primordial trust)
- 2nd Energy Center: I feel (experience)
- 3rd Energy Center: I do (ego-managed)
- 4th Energy Center: I love it (my devotion)
- 5th Energy Center: I say it (my connection)
- 6th Energy Center: I see (my perception)
- 7th Energy Center: I understand (my thinking)
- 8th energy center: I raise awareness (spiritual level knowledge, ego-free state)

The first seven energy centers are connected to the ego. The connection with consciousness (spirit) is the 8th energy center. But with this, I will give you exciting knowledge in more detail in my next book. Regarding the seven lower energy centers, it's still important to understand that the hormonal and neural representations of problems and emotions are always related to a specific energy center. In this respect, it is not possible to automatically link an emotion type to an energy center, because it does not depend on the type of emotion, but on its root cause. To understand this, for example, we can look at the feeling of guilt, from which I had a lot of pressure on my soul for decades until I fully processed it. Even before I was born, I felt a deep sense of guilt because my mother didn't want me, and my growing in her

Number	Its name in Eastern philosophy	Gland (hormones)	Nervous system (mind)	Basic motivation
1	Root chakra	sex glands	intestine-fiber nerve center	I am (primordial trust)
2	Sacral chakra	digestive glands and pancreas	upper intestine-plexus nerve center	I feel it (experiencing)
3	Solar Plexus chakra	adrenal gland	stomach and gastric nerve-center	I do (ego-managed)
4	Hear chakra	thymus gland	cardiac nerve center	"I love" (devotion)
5	Throat chakra	thyroid	thyroid nerve center	I say it (making contact)
6	Third Eye chakra	pineal gland	pineal gland nerve center	I see (perceive)
7	Crown chakra	pituitary gland	pituitary gland nerve center	I understand (thinking)
8	Eastern Philosophers usually discuss the 7th and 8th chakras together	no direct physical contact	no direct physical contact	I raise awareness (spiritual level knowledge, ego-free state)

belly felt like suffering for her (I managed to extract this knowledge from my emotional memory using a special method, but this is an advanced-level exercise not yet discussed in this volume). This guilt is related to primordial trust, so it was deposited in my 1st energy center and caused its extreme overactivity and slight left asymmetry. My father committed suicide when I was six years old. At that time, I felt guilty because my childish soul and mind thought that he left me because my first semester school certificate was not good enough. My deep guilt about this affected my 2nd and 4th energy centers. The result was the under-functioning and right asymmetry of the 4th energy center and the strong over-functioning of my 2nd energy center. My guilt about the birth of my son was deposited in these same chakras 33 years later. This wasn't accidental, because what we do not process perfectly reproduces itself in our future. I hope this personal example helps you to see and understand more clearly the relationship system of our body-soul-mind. By observing your body's symptoms, you can get closer to knowing yourself. I wish you every success on this incredibly exciting and inspiring journey! Finally, in the table below, I summarize what has been written so far so that you can take it out and quickly review it at any time during your own work:

Annex 4: Curiosities about vibrations

The advances of modern physics—particularly quantum physics and string theory—have proven that everything, even matter, is energy. Matter is nothing more than a condensed version of energy. Since we know this, we can say that everything has a vibration. If this is true, then it's clear that there are vibrations of the soul, mind and body, and even consciousness, but they are at different rates of vibration. We can already measure the vibration range of the mind and body with specific physical measurements, but we can only confirm the vibrations of the soul using the so-called body response method of kinesiology. Consciousness is an even more special thing, but I will explain this in later volumes because this book does not yet convey enough knowledge to deal with consciousness in more depth. The purpose of this annex is to understand that even if we cannot measure something with a physical measuring device, it still exists. So, if everything has a vibration (this is already a fact), it's only a matter of time before we can measure the vibration level of the soul with a physical measuring device. Why am I so optimistic about this? To understand this, see where our scientific knowledge has evolved with vibrations over the past two centuries! The next table shows the vibrational ranges that we can actually measure (László Rozsnaki):

The table on the page 302 shows the wavelength and frequency values of the vibrations known by science. This table has grown big in the last two centuries. Before, we knew little about vibrations and could only experience or measure a few smaller ranges. With the dynamic development of science, new frequency ranges have become measurable almost every year. Today we are here, as shown in this table, but if the development of human technology does not break, this table will continue to expand in the future. So, if we can't yet measure the vibration levels of the soul and consciousness with a physical device, it only means that they

Name	Wavelength	Frequency
extrem low frequency	100.000 km - 10.000 km	3 Hz - 30 Hz
super low frequeny	10.000 km - 1.000 km	30 Hz - 300 Hz
ultra-low frequency	1.000 km - 100 km	300 Hz - 30 kHz
very low frequency	100 km - 10 km	3 kHz - 30 kHz
longwave	10 km - 1 km	30 kHz - 300 kHz
medium wave	1 km - 100 m	300 kHz - 3 MHz
short wave	100 m - 10 m	3 MHz - 30 MHz
ultra short wave (or very high frequency)	10 m - 1 m	30 MHz - 300 MHz
decimeter wave	1 m - 10 cm	300 MHz - 3 GHz
centimeter wavw	10 cm - 1 cm	3 GHz - 30 GHz
milimeter wave	1 cm - 1 mm	30 GHz - 300 GHz
microwave	30 cm - 300 µm	1 GHz - 1THz
terahertz radiation	3 mm - 30 µm	0.1 THz - 10 THz
far infrared radiation	< 1,0 mm	> 300 GHz
medium infrared radiation	< 50 µm	> 6 THz
near infrared radiation	< 2,5 µm	> 120 THz
red light	780 nm - 640 nm	384 THz - 468 THz
orange light	640 nm - 600 nm	468 THz - 500 THz
yellow light	600 nm - 570 nm	500 THz - 526 THz
green light	570 nm - 490 nm	526 THz - 612 THz
blue light	490 nm - 430 nm	612 THz - 697 THz
violet light	430 nm - 380 nm	697 THz - 789 THz
soft ultraviolet radiation	< 380 nm	> 789 THz
hard ultraviolet radiation	< 200 nm	> 1.5 PHz
X rays	10 nm - 0.1 nm	30 PHz - 30 EHz
gamma	10 pm - 10 fm	30 EHz - 30 ZHz
cosmic ray	30 fm - 0.3 fm	10 Zhz - 10 YHz

have a frequency of more than 10 YHz, which corresponds to 10 quadrillion hertz. This is quite logical, as lower energy cannot create itself, but higher energy can create lower energy. During the process of creation, the intuition (highest level of energy) released by consciousness appears in our emotions (one lower level of energy), from which thoughts are activated in our mind, then our creation is manifested in matter (lowest level of energy), and finally, the matter is further degraded by the law of entropy. Therefore, intuition is the most powerful force that People can use. When our intuition guides us, everything happens smoothly—almost on its own.

However, it is important to know that all frequencies can only be formed if they have a source. If consciousness is the source of our emotions, emotions are the source of our thoughts, and thoughts are the source of matter, then what is the source of consciousness? Religions provide answers to this. The source is an all-pervading infinite intelligence that most religions call God, but you can replace that word with any from your belief systems. I think the most exciting level of understanding is when we realize that all frequencies are actually information, that is, they can be defined by information. The whole Universe is therefore one huge set of information. Thus, we understand the message of the movie The Matrix, which is a testament to the same thing in a way, hidden in the sci-fi visual world. However, if everything is information, then the Universe could only have been formed by an incredibly intelligent source of information. However, I will write more about this in a later book, where I can introduce you to more basic concepts in the interest of deeper understanding.

Returning to the thought process of creation, when the ego tries to create, consciousness is not present, so in this state, the emotion is the highest creative energy. That's why it's important that when we apply affirmations, we associate them with emotions. This makes this activity much more efficient. At the same time, this is why the creative capacity of the ego is much more limited than that of the consciousness, which I will teach you to know in my next book. That is why, living in the ego, Life becomes a struggle.

www.ingramcontent.com/pod-product-compliance
Lightning Source LLC
Chambersburg PA
CBHW060338170426
43202CB00014B/2809